A STOWAWAY UKULELE REVEALED

A STOWAWAY UKULELE REVEALED

Richard Konter and
the Byrd Polar Expeditions

LARRY BARTRAM
with DICK BOAK

Hal Leonard Books
An Imprint of Hal Leonard LLC

Published in 2018 by Hal Leonard Books
An Imprint of Hal Leonard LLC
7777 West Bluemound Road
Milwaukee, WI 53213

Trade Book Division Editorial Offices
33 Plymouth St., Montclair, NJ 07042

Printed in the United States of America
Book design by Kristina Rolander

Library of Congress Cataloging-in-Publication Data
is available upon request.

ISBN 978-1-4950-9948-9

www.halleonardbooks.com

To the good America,
with love.

CONTENTS

PREFACE by LARRY BARTRAM

Stringed musical instruments manufactured by the renowned craftspeople of C. F. Martin & Co. in Nazareth, Pennsylvania, have helped chart the course of American music since 1833. Although best known today for exquisite guitars, the company produced other instruments during its long history—notably mandolins and ukuleles—to satisfy the musical tastes of changing times. This book presents the story of one special Martin ukulele and its colorful owner.

My part of the story begins in November 2010, which is when (after decades of trying) I finally convinced myself that my best chance to cure a nagging ailment (lack of guitar playing ability) would be to own a genuine Martin. I clenched my teeth and went to visit (the late, great) Stan Jay at Mandolin Brothers on Staten Island. A few hours later, feeling pretty badass, I left carrying my brand-new Martin OMC-28M Laurence Juber guitar.

My playing definitely improved, but by late 2013, the finish on my guitar needed some attention. I decided to bring it—under its lifetime warranty—back home to the factory for inspection. I dropped off my guitar with Martin's Jimmie Kleintop. He told me that the necessary work would be covered, but it would take some time. On my way out, I visited the Martin museum. What an unexpected treat. The museum was filled with historically significant artifacts. I learned much from the fascinating narrative it presented about the company's role in the history of music.

Among the instruments I saw during my museum visit was one that stood out to me, despite its diminutive size. It was a ukulele literally covered with autographs. According to the display placard, the instrument had once belonged to a Richard W. Konter and it had been to the North Pole, along for the ride on Richard Byrd's famous 1926 flight. Incredibly, the first signature I noticed was not particularly conspicuous, and I could have missed it easily. Maybe something in my subconcious had me looking for it. It belonged—unbelievably—to someone out of my own past. Right there, big as

Laurence McKinley Gould, geologist and second-in-command on Byrd's first Antarctic expedition, March 18, 1929. *Public domain. Photo by Wide World Studio Photographer, March 18, 1929.*

life, on the top of the ukulele near the bridge, I saw the signature of my glacial geology professor, Dr. Laurence Gould.

Gould had been chief scientist and second-in-command on Byrd's first Antarctic expedition, which took place during 1928–1930. He was eighty-one years old when he taught me about nunataks, drumlins, and firn while I was an undergraduate at the University of Arizona in the spring semester of 1978. Despite his age, this tough old bird had still been making trips to Antarctica as recently as the year before I enrolled in his course.

Despite his signature on the ukulele, Professor Gould wasn't actually part of the Byrd Arctic Expedition—his own achievements in Antarctica with Byrd had come a couple of years after the ukulele's trip to the North Pole. But I drove home that day feeling somehow connected to this little instrument.

I decided that when I returned to pick up my guitar, I would bring with me a copy of my professor's 1931 book *Cold.* Gould's account of his Antarctic experiences is thrilling reading. It is nearly impossible for the modern reader in a comfortable chair to comprehend what he and his "geological party" accomplished. To me, what he did in Antarctica makes Byrd's flight seem, by comparison, a stroll in the park. Gould led his men over 1,500 miles *by dogsled* across the Ross Ice Shelf to the Queen Maud Mountains to describe their geology and collect samples—the first geological work in Antarctica. This trip, across a virtually unexplored continent, took nearly three months—an average of almost seventeen miles per day. I remember when Gould choked up in class as he showed us slides of the canine friends to whom he'd entrusted his and his companions' lives. His affection was undiminished by the years; he still knew each dog by name.

Some months later, I got the call that my guitar was ready to be picked up. Dave Doll of Martin's repair department met me to return it. Dave opened its case and handed it to me. It looked brand new and sounded sublime.

I told Dave about the ukulele I'd seen in the museum and of my personal interest in it, and showed him Gould's book. Dave listened for a while and then told me to hold on—there was someone with whom I needed to speak. Dave called Martin's director of museum and archives, Dick Boak, and asked him if he would join us. A few minutes later Dick came downstairs. I filled him in on my interest in the ukulele, and he told me to follow him.

Dick took me into the museum, and we walked to the case where the ukulele hung. He unlocked it and instructed me to bring the ukulele and follow him upstairs for a closer inspection. For the next few hours, we pored over the autographs on the ukulele with the index of Gould's book open nearby. We soon discovered several of the signatures on the ukulele were by men connected with Byrd's later Antarctic expedition, too. All told, we identified nearly twenty forgotten signatures that day. We both knew then that our collaboration had begun.

Since that day, we've become good friends as we've pored over the ukulele and the autographs it carries—researching signatures, photographs, geographic locations, and biographies, reckoning timelines, conducting interviews, tracking down hunches, but mostly trying to make sense of a vast quantity of information.

We began simply, tackling the task of trying to read accurately the autographs and inscriptions on the instrument. We realized quickly that our efforts would not result in one hundred percent identification of the signatures. Some had been strummed out of existence. Others may not have been all that legible or durable in the first place.

Next, we attempted to learn as much as possible about the identity of the signers whom we could (or thought we could) identify. Online sources gave us convenient access to information that would otherwise have required prohibitive research trips to distant libraries and archives. Where online resources did not suffice, we did visit archives and people who knew Richard Konter. There were many wonderful surprises along the way. Published here for the first time are Konter's accounts of many events, to date known only from other sources and perspectives.

Except in outline form to provide needed context, we've tried to avoid retelling the story of the Byrd Arctic Expedition and the first Byrd Antarctic Expedition. Many other books written by participants in Byrd's expeditions, and later historians, have covered that part of the story better than we could. One book we have enjoyed particularly is Sheldon Bart's *Race to the Top of the World: Richard Byrd and the First Flight to the North Pole*, published in 2013. Instead, our book focuses on the remarkable life of Richard Konter, his Martin ukulele that went to the North Pole, the men and women who autographed this incredible instrument, and our own journey of discovery to reveal the true tale behind it all.

We started this project with a simple goal, to write something about "the ukulele in the museum that went to the North Pole." Over time, as we uncovered more of the ukulele's secrets, our project turned into something much larger and more satisfying. A book about a musical instrument is, in itself, a dry thing. It is the music it made and the people who played and signed it that give it life and historical meaning. This ukulele is dripping with both.

Konter's autographed ukulele continues to hang quietly in the C. F. Martin & Co. museum. Our visit with this special little instrument is now complete. We feel privileged to have spent some time with this globe-trotting, jumping flea and its remarkable owner. He has taught us how it is possible to appreciate history in the making, record it, and preserve it in unique and meaningful ways. It's amazing how many lives this little instrument draws together, how many threads, how many stories. They're all here—history, biography, adventure, polar exploration, music, romance, and more. We sincerely hope you enjoy this book as much as we have enjoyed uncovering this amazing tale and the secrets of Konter's North Pole ukulele.

ACKNOWLEDGMENTS

A number of generous individuals and organizations have helped us in the preparation of this book. Each taught us much about the story of this ukulele, its owner, and the fragility of history. We acknowledge gratefully their assistance and enthusiasm, for they have made our book a pleasure to write. We hope our efforts live up to their expectations, but we bear all responsibility for the flaws that remain.

Foremost, we wish to thank C. F. Martin & Co., Inc., of Nazareth, Pennsylvania, in whose museum Richard Konter's North Pole ukulele resides. Martin has encouraged and supported our work, encouraging us to study it in detail and write about what we discovered.

At the Smithsonian Institution, we'd like to thank Dennis Stanford, Bill Fitzhugh, Bruno Frohlich, David Hunt, Adrienne Kaeppler, Randall Kremer, Ken Slowik, Janet Douglas, Paula DePriest, Robert Koestler, and E. Keats Webb and her interns, Emma Tucker and Alicia Hoffman. Kay Peterson of the Archives Center at the National Museum of American History helpfully scanned for us two glass-plate images of Konter and his North Pole ukulele.

At the National Archives and Records Administration in College Park, Maryland, Netisha Currie offered us cheerful professionalism, kindness, pro tips for our research, and lots of help via email.

At the Library of Congress, Bruce Kirby of the Manuscript Division kindly provided us with a copy of Konter's *Wreck of the U. S. S. Charleston, Camiguin Island, Nov. 2nd, '99.*

At The Ohio State University, polar curator Laura Kissel and her staff in the Byrd Polar and Climate Research Center Archival Program welcomed us warmly, provided us with a comfortable work space, assisted with our research, gave us permission to publish a number of photographs in their collections, and helped us solve several mysteries.

Jean Neptune of Springfield, Illinois, graciously welcomed us into her home and allowed us to interview her. Jean shared with us artifacts, documents, photographs, stories, and laughs, and provided invaluable information unavailable previously to researchers. From Jean, we learned much about her mother, Johanna Cohen, and her stepfather, Richard Konter.

Finally, a host of other family and friends have helped us in a variety of ways. For their help and encouragement, we'd like to thank Kevin Almeida, Lane and Jill Bartram, Laura Bartram, Laurence Bartram Sr. and Leona Bartram, Lisanne Bartram, Logan Bartram, Jim Beloff, Dan Brown, Dave Doll, Lee

Feist, Stanton and Claudia Green, Michael Gurian, Eric Hillemann, Greig Hutton, Bill Jones, Heidi Katz, Kerry Keane, Sandy Kling, David Lowenherz, Chris Martin, Susan Ellison Reed McQueen, Emily Meixell, Fred Oster, Terry Polt, Steven Raab, Kilin Reece, William Stewart, James and Gabrielle Traxler, Thomas Walsh, Marianne Wurlitzer, and Ann Gwinn Zawistoski.

INTRODUCTION by DICK BOAK

I started working for C. F. Martin & Co. in late October of 1976. When I arrived, there was a rather impressive circular museum area with a small concentric array of cylindrical Plexiglas display cases that each contained a historic guitar or two. But within a few years, that space was claimed by Martin's gift shop, the 1833 Shop, and the museum was relegated to a less than desirable tiny room to the right of the receptionist. The museum collection was meager—perhaps ten or fifteen instruments with minimal descriptions, plus one seemingly ancient soprano ukulele with some signatures on it.

I didn't really pay too much attention to that ukulele. Martin's historian Mike Longworth had mentioned it to me a few times and had actually given it its own page in his book *Martin Guitars, A History*. There, Mike explained that Konter's ukulele "is distinguished not by its construction but by its historical value."

Longworth went on to tell the basic story of Konter's participation in Byrd's 1926 expedition, and how pilot Floyd Bennett had smuggled the ukulele aboard the *Josephine Ford* trimotor craft, making it the first ukulele to cross the North Pole.

During the expedition, Konter had solicited the members of the crew (and others) to autograph the instrument. Lastly, Mike indicates that the ukulele was gifted to the Martin Museum, where it resides "with a photograph of it being shown to members of the expedition beside the aircraft."

Mike had told me that the large signature on the headstock was believed to be that of the expedition ship's cook, "Marie." That proved to be a myth. We discovered that Marie was, in fact, the much loved queen of Romania, and the granddaughter of her highness Queen Victoria!

The ukulele received a bit of attention when Chris Martin updated the visitor center in 2006, but the incredible chain reaction that ultimately unraveled this amazing story began when Larry Bartram, visiting the factory to have his guitar repaired, innocently meandered into the museum and zoomed immediately onto the signature of his former glacial geology professor, Laurence Gould.

Through Larry's wide-reaching contacts, he managed to get permission for us to spend a concentrated day in Washington, D. C., with digital imaging specialist Keats Webb of the Smithsonian Institution's remarkable Museum Conservation Institute. There we hoped to see into and under the instrument's finish to better visualize the more faded and abraded signatures. This was a fascinating and fruitful effort. We spent the next day at the National Archives, inspecting more than two dozen boxes of photographs and papers of Richard Konter and R. E. Byrd. We were able to make high-resolution scans of images and documents. We came home with renewed energy, and every week that passed seemed to reveal more interesting and endless tangents to the story.

Larry and I agreed that this incredible story needed to be told. As we created outlines, databases, and a tentative table of contents for this book, Larry pushed forward with plans to visit Jean Neptune, the daughter of Johanna Cohen. Cohen had married Richard Konter later in life, after the passing of her first husband, "Battleship" Bill Pool. And so we flew to Springfield, Illinois, for an amazing visit and interview with Jean. She possessed many crucial albums of photos, which we scanned, and the personal recollections of her mother's later years with Richard Konter added tremendous detail and soul to our ever-expanding story.

From Illinois, we rented a car and drove to Columbus, Ohio, for two days of research at The Ohio State University's Byrd Polar and Climate Research Center. There we met OSU archivist Laura Kissel, who provided great assistance in searching their vast holdings. Perhaps the most important documents we found were letters and official crew lists that included authentic signatures of virtually everyone affiliated with the North Pole expedition. These documents and autographs proved invaluable in further identifying or confirming the signatures on the ukulele.

Back in Nazareth, I invested in a Wacom graphics tablet. With this device, I could mirror the screen of my iMac computer and zoom in on John Sterling Ruth's high-resolution images of the ukulele. By creating layers in Photoshop, I could render the signatures directly onto the tablet with a digital pen. Albeit time-consuming, this task proved incredibly beneficial on a number of counts. The process of "inking" allowed me to examine the signatures in detail. I was able to focus on how individuals put their letters together to make a signature and also what pairs of letters typically do or do not combine to form common names. Once a partial signature was inked in, the comparison to existing signatures made identification much easier. One great example of this is the signature of Adolph Ochs, founder of *The New York Times*. His swirly signature was completely unreadable, but after inking it and then seeing his actual signature on a letter found at OSU, we were able to immediately confirm its origin.

The digital tablet also enabled us to color-code our confidence attributions, delineate our confidence in the identifications, and focus on the signatures that remained elusive. As inking neared completion, it occurred to me that the rendered signature layers could be isolated from each photograph to produce artwork for the laser machines used in Martin production to etch serial numbers onto the wood of the front block. Such technology would allow for replicas of the ukulele to be produced either for historic or limited-edition purposes. Three prototype replicas were conceived and created with great help from my friends Michael Gurian and Kevin Almeida at Gurian Instruments in Seattle, Washington.

In February of 2017, after three years of hard work, Larry and I took our findings and drove to Montclair, New Jersey, for a meeting with John Cerullo, publisher at Hal Leonard Performing Arts Publishing Group. John agreed that the story needed to be told, and thanks to the efforts of many friends and colleagues, you hold in your hands the results of our own expedition. We hope you enjoy it.

AUTHOR'S NOTE

For the sake of accuracy, we have reproduced the grammar, spelling, and punctuation of quoted materials exactly as they appear in the source documents, leaving any typos or other errors uncorrected.

Additionally, we spent many hours working to identify the subjects of photographs—in particular, Richard Konter's shipmates on the S. S. *Chantier*—closely comparing scores of captioned photographs published in newspapers, magazines, and elsewhere. Despite our strong confidence in them, we do not present the results of our photographic identifications here as definitive, but rather as "working hypotheses" as to the identities of the individuals pictured.

PART ONE

RICHARD
"UKULELE DICK"
KONTER,
A SAILOR'S LIFE

1

A Ukulele
Goes North—
Way North

IN THE EARLY YEARS OF the twentieth century, a diverse collection of seriously audacious people took some extraordinary chances and made history. Some were highbrow scions of old American families, while others lived as far from privilege as can be imagined. Whether rich or poor, mighty or mean, already famous or utterly unknown, they all had moxie. Their story is a quintessentially American cocktail of adventure, romance, hard work, exploration, politics, and competition, shaken by ocean voyages and airplane engines—and served on ice. Almost incredibly, a tangible testament to their intermingled lives survives today in the form of a little ukulele that carries talismanic traces: the signatures of those who made it happen. Telling its story is our task in this book.

This musical autograph album exists thanks to the vision of an historically minded salty dog named Richard W. Konter. Konter was a Navy veteran who had been, literally, all around this world. He had witnessed, firsthand, the emergence of the United States as a global superpower, the tragic folly of World War I, and an unprecedented stream of discoveries about the world and its people.

Although his formal education was limited (he left school at fifteen for the Navy), he was intelligent, sensitive, perceptive, and industrious. Luckily for us, he was also one of those rare individuals who both recognized history as it unfolded before him *and* also made the extra effort required to document it. And magically, his is no mute testament. Konter's testament makes music.

In early 1926, when he asked Konter to volunteer to be a member of the Byrd Arctic Expedition, Commander Richard Evelyn Byrd Jr. was soon to become the world's most famous polar explorer. Byrd was a dashing Naval commander, eager to make his mark in polar exploration. His expedition's goal was nothing less than to make the first flight over the geographic North Pole. Despite enormous organizational, financial, technological, and personnel challenges, he achieved that goal. Byrd recognized Konter's abilities as a mariner and an entertainer, and his decision to invite Konter was rewarded. Konter's contributions to the Byrd Arctic Expedition as an able-bodied seaman, musician, and a surprisingly steady-handed helmsman earned him a second invitation, to participate in Byrd's first Antarctic Expedition of 1928–1930.

Yet for Konter, personally, the Antarctic expedition was far from a replay of the feelings of self-esteem and accomplishment he enjoyed after the Byrd Arctic Expedition. Things went wrong for Konter both during and after the Antarctic expedition. Following a desperate psychological breakdown in the summer of 1930, soon after the expedition's return from Antarctica, his association with Byrd came to an unnecessarily screeching halt. Despite this self-inflicted severance and the Great Depression, which prevented him from finding employment once he left the Navy for good, his life was far from over—Konter became a well-known musician and bandleader who entertained widely. Significantly, he would marry for the first time at the age of eighty; the bride was a woman he'd known since her teens and to whom he'd already proposed decades earlier. His tenacity paid off, and they remained married until his death at the age of ninety-seven.

Few survive today who remember the first quarter of the twentieth century. This era, one of tremendous change, can be roughly but reasonably divided into three episodes: First was a pre–World War I interval, beginning with the Spanish-American War and the Philippine-American War, during which nineteenth-century Victorian cultural norms and sensibilities continued to pervade American culture. Yet the output of explorers and scientists during this time was extraordinary—events such as the 1904 Louisiana Purchase Exposition (the St. Louis World's Fair) displayed their discoveries and achievements. Americans were confronted with vast amounts of new information about their world, and they tried to make sense of their place in it. David Bailey and David Halsted wrote:

> At the start of the twentieth century, questions about the nature of American identity haunted the people of the United States. Suddenly an imperial power, overwhelmed by waves of immigrants across the

Atlantic and the Pacific, stunned by the effects of urbanization and industrialization, the nation needed an identity (Bailey and Halsted 1998).

The next era, World War I, known then as "the Great War," lasted from mid-1914 through the end of 1919. "The war to end all wars" has been called "a tragic and unnecessary conflict" by John Keegan in his well-regarded one-volume history (Keegan 1999).

For the most part, Americans wished to avoid involvement in the war. However, Germany's initiation of nearly unrestricted submarine warfare, including the sinking of the world's largest passenger ship, the RMS *Lusitania,* on May 7, 1915, eventually swayed popular and official opinion enough that the United States entered the war on April 6, 1917. Despite patriotic support for the troops, Americans had few illusions about the senseless slaughter in Europe, which would eventually cost nine million lives.

At home, a demographic shift was under way. Between 1910 and 1920, many Americans moved from rural areas to rapidly growing cities. Dependence on the agricultural economy declined as burgeoning employment opportunities, mainly manufacturing jobs in factories, promised a higher standard of living in the urban areas. Many African-Americans migrated from the rural south to the more industrial north, fleeing both poverty and racism. Such displacements, combined with a continuing influx of immigrants from overseas, had a profound effect on the cultural life of the country, infusing even more diversity into the growing cities of the north.

A postwar episode of exuberant American isolationism followed World War I. It would last until Black Tuesday, October 29, 1929—the beginning of the Great Depression. During this third phase, sometimes called the "Roaring Twenties," many Americans wanted to put the carnage of World War I behind them and make a clean break with Europe's problems and the horrors of the war. During this postwar interval, America enjoyed a booming economy based on a large, increasingly urban workforce that included many women who had entered America's factories during the war. After the war, many women continued to work, and with the passage of the Nineteenth Amendment in 1920, women had won the right to vote.

The economy boomed for many middle- and upper-income Americans. Opportunity came knocking, and rags-to-riches stories proliferated. Despite some real hardship and economic disadvantage for many Americans, overall there was a positive mood about the possibilities of scientific and industrial progress, reinforced among average working people by the appearance of new and affordable luxuries such as automobiles and radios, as well as by the excitement of aviation, exploration, and scientific achievement. Optimism abounded.

Although life was far from ideal for many New Yorkers in the 1920s, there was a "can-do" feeling on the streets of Richard Konter's city. The collective psyche swung to an upbeat tempo that would be hard to recognize today. If this kind of optimism seems naive now, it didn't then. Young people, especially, were anxious to shed residual Victorian stuffiness and enjoy the excitement of "Jazz Age" America. And, despite Prohibition's dry years from 1920 to 1933, America still managed to grab a drink. Recorded music, radio, and film, relatively new media, spread like crazy. Popular music was composed and played at home on pianos, ukuleles, banjos, mandolins, and guitars, and recorded for the popular new media. Dick Konter's identity as a musician, arranger, and bandleader was profoundly shaped by this popular culture milieu.

The first quarter of the twentieth century was the era of silent films—movies captivated the American imagination. The early heart of the film industry was in and around New York City. Later, films made by the dominant Hollywood studios—such as Warner Brothers, Paramount, RKO, Loew's (later MGM), and Fox Films—would compete with pictures from studios of lesser but growing importance, like Universal Pictures, United Artists, and Columbia Pictures. Movie theaters, also known as "movie palaces," became wonderfully elaborate.

> The America of the 1920s can be characterized in many ways, but the artifact which best summarizes the social conditions and bourgeois artistic tastes of that decade is the Movie Palace. Through opulence and a taste for the unusual and exotic, theater architects of the 1920s tried to create a world of their own through the use of rich materials and works of art where any individual with the nominal price of admission could rub elbows with the rich and live like a king for an evening (Soren 1975).

After 1911, when Charles Pathé created the first newsreels, a trip to the "movies" offered an eager public, both urban and rural, an inexpensive source of entertainment and current events. Newsreels were usually shown before the main feature, but they were also well liked on their own. Events like the Byrd Arctic Expedition were tailor-made for newsreels, and the public devoured them.

The largest urban theaters were fortunate to have world-class musicians in their orchestra pits, but nearly everywhere, silent-era films were accompanied by live musicians playing program music during the film, and their own interpretations of the hits at intermissions and between features. Of course, this required sheet music. Producing it fueled another major industry of popular culture—music publishing. "Talkies" began to appear in 1926 with advancements in sound-on-film technology, and in 1927, Warner Brothers' film *The Jazz Singer* changed motion pictures forever with synchronized music and dialogue, connecting Americans from coast to coast with stories of compelling immediacy, often shown in opulent venues, truly an escape from the ordinary that books and magazines could not match.

A radio set was another affordable luxury, one that quickly found its way into many American homes. Radios were available at many different price points, from inexpensive, do-it-yourself crystal sets to more elaborate status symbols that targeted the well-heeled listener. Between 1923 and 1930, radios were purchased by sixty percent of American families. In their masterful book *The 'Ukulele: A History*, Jim Tranquada and John King write, " . . . radio's explosive growth after World War I left contemporary observers struggling for adjectives . . . KDKA of Pittsburgh, the country's first commercial radio station, went on the air in November 1920; by the Fall of 1922, there were almost 500 stations nationwide" (Tranquada and King 2012).

Thanks to the combined popularity of inexpensive theater entertainment in growing cities, affordable radio sets, and the generally upbeat mood of the times, the American appetite for popular songs was prodigious during the 1920s. That appetite was fed largely by New York City's "Tin Pan Alley," a concentration of music composing and publishing powerhouses whose rate of creative output was like nothing the world had never seen.

Although the origins of the name "Tin Pan Alley" are a subject of some debate, it began as a real place in Manhattan, on West 28th Street between Fifth and Sixth Avenues, where the so-called "Great American Songbook" was largely composed by musical luminaries such as Harold Arlen, Irving Berlin, Sammy Cahn, Hoagy Carmichael, George M. Cohan, George and Ira Gershwin, James P. Johnson, Scott Joplin, Jerome Kern, Cole Porter, and Fats Waller.

Composers of the American Songbook. Left to right: Gene Buck, Victor Herbert, John Philip Sousa, Harry B. Smith, Jerome Kern, Irving Berlin, George W. Meyer, Irving Bibo, and Otto Harbach. *Public domain. World Telegram & Sun photo by Al Aumuller.*

Tin Pan Alley composers cranked out the hits for music publishers like M. Witmark & Sons, Irving Berlin Inc., Shapiro, Bernstein & Co., Harms Inc., Remick Music Co., Robbins Music Corp., and E. B. Marks Music Company. As David Jasen writes:

> The 1920s saw the biggest outpouring of songs of all the decades in Tin Pan Alley's history. The good times were reflected in the popularity of jazz bands and in the number of dance bands that were being recorded around the country. The entertainment industry was going full-blast, with the sale of player pianos and piano rolls peaking in 1926. (Jasen 2003)

Tin Pan Alley's output was made accessible to the masses in the form of the sheet music created by these publishers, who made a killing delivering these songs to an adoring public, eager to obtain the music to a popular new song from a hit show or movie. The sheet music usually included a snazzy graphic or photographic cover, often featuring a picture of a famous performer. The music included a melody line for voice, a piano arrangement, and perhaps guitar or ukulele tablature, as well. And the sheet music itself was used as advertising space for other songs available from the same publisher. For example, no fewer than four ads (two of them full-page) appear in the six pages of Shapiro & Bernstein Music Publishers' sheet music for Al Jolson's hit "If You Knew Susie (Like I Know Susie)," arranged for ukulele by Dick Konter.

Of particular interest to our story is the immense popularity enjoyed by the ukulele (or "jumping flea," in Hawaiian) that swept the mainland United States and abroad after 1915. Although the instrument was introduced to Americans at the 1893 Columbian Exposition in Chicago, its presence at the 1915 Panama-Pacific International Exposition in San Francisco is what really stoked its popularity. The Hawai'i

Sheet music cover published by Shapiro, Bernstein & Co., Music Publishers. *Public domain.*

pavilion at the exposition was visited by some thirty-four thousand people per day. Many visitors came to enjoy the exhibits of indigenous Hawaiian fishes and the pineapple juice, but what they brought home were pleasant memories of Hawaiian melodies. Whatever the draw, the "exotic" sound of the ukulele presented a happy alternative to the darkness of the "war to end all wars." The little instrument and the tropical connotations it conjured made a deep impact on the eighteen million fair-goers, and soon ukuleles spread like wildfire (Tranquada & King 2012:92-113).

Nearly overnight, ukuleles turned up everywhere in the United States. Writing of the early 1920s some years later, Dick Konter remarked, "At that time the little Ukulele, was not a fad, but a mania . . ." (R. W. Konter, *Adventure Ahoy! Part II*, Konter Files, National Archives and Records Administration, College Park, Maryland). Stringed instrument manufacturers struggled to keep up with demand for the little instrument that had created a welcome windfall. Walsh and King note that "[i]n just its seventh full year of ukulele production, Martin had built more ukuleles than it had produced guitars in its celebrated ninety-year history" (Walsh and King 2013:51).

As popular culture expanded in new directions, so did science, engineering, and geographic understanding. Exploration of the more "remote" corners of the earth, wondrous new scientific discoveries, and the promise of technological achievements in aviation had fully captured public attention in the early years of the twentieth century. "Discoveries" such as Hiram Bingham III's in 1911 at Machu Picchu, Peru, as well as the unprecedented pace of achievement in science and engineering, whetted the public's appetite. From Howard Carter's 1922 archaeological finds in Egypt's Valley of the Kings to Edwin Hubble's 1924 demonstration that galaxies exist beyond the Milky Way, discovery in science and exploration during the 1920s was firing the imagination of people the world over. The public was riveted by such exciting stories, now easily disseminated on radio and film as well as through newspaper accounts. People were coming to expect a steady dose of discovery.

Sheldon Bart wrote, "The quest for the transpolar flight was itself part of a larger context. From roughly the end of World War I to the beginning of World War II, Americans became obsessed with expeditions to the ends of the earth" (Bart 2013). Surprisingly large areas of the globe remained unknown in the early years of the twentieth century. Incomplete geographic knowledge encouraged speculation about what might be discovered at the top of the earth or the bottom of the oceans. Today, in an age of pinpoint satellite imagery, the Global Positioning System, and high-speed communications, it can be difficult for us to remember that, even relatively recently, there was significantly less ink on maps of many areas of the globe.

If geographic speculations of the first third or so of the twentieth century seem quaintly naive today, we would do well to consider, for example, how current medical therapies for cancers and mental illnesses will look to physicians a century from now. Before remote sensing or robotic technology, filling the gaps on maps required real people to travel to these places, often at risk to their lives, lending a romantic quality to the quest that captured the public imagination. Those daring enough to explore (and survive) these inaccessible regions were assured of fame and riches.

Despite previous attempts to fill in the blanks on polar maps by reaching the northernmost latitudes on earth, by the mid-1920s, large gaps still remained. For example, Donald Baxter MacMillan was convinced, based on Peary's observations, that there was land to be found in what we now know to be the Arctic Ocean:

> In June 1906, Commander Peary, from the summit of Cape Thomas Hubbard, at about latitude 83 degrees N, longitude 100 degrees W, reported seeing land glimmering in the northwest, approximately 130 miles (210 km) away across the Polar Sea. He did not go there, but he gave it a name in honor of the late George Crocker of the Peary Arctic Club. That is Crocker Land. Its boundaries and extent can only be guessed at, but I am certain that strange animals will be found there, and I hope to discover a new race of men.

The prospect of a huge, undiscovered landmass exerted its own attraction—too much for some to resist. MacMillan, among others, was set on finding it, and in 1913 he set out to do just that. With sponsorship from the American Museum of Natural History, the American Geographical Society, and the University of Illinois, MacMillan launched the ill-fated Crocker Land Expedition (Freed 2012). "Crocker Land"—also known as "Harris Land," as well as by other names (Bart 2013)—turned out to be nothing more than a *fata morgana* mirage, as Peary's Inuit guides knew full well at the time. In the end, because of the immense difficulty of land- and sea-based exploration in the far north, MacMillan's expedition failed to provide the necessary cartographic information to fill in the maps (MacMillan and Ekblaw 1918).

Imaginary lands of the north, fancifully rendered. As published in *The San Francisco Call*, July 27, 1913. *Public domain.*

Ignorance of what, precisely, *was* to be found around the north geographic pole would drive MacMillan (repeatedly), Richard Byrd, Roald Amundsen, and others, to attempt aerial reconnaissance of the same regions for the same basic reason—inking the map and claiming new territories for their respective nations, not to mention fame and potential riches for themselves.

In contrast to earlier land and sea expeditions, these polar explorers took advantage of the enormous efficiencies offered by aerial reconnaissance. In doing so, they also employed and helped develop new technological advances in aviation.

The 1920s marked a golden age in American aviation. Lighter-than-air craft, mainly airships, were generally reliable after World War I and were still used, albeit less frequently, for a variety of tasks. However, the real excitement was with the speedier, maneuverable airplanes, which since 1903 had captured the imagination of aeronautic designers and pilots after the successes of the Wright brothers. The daring "flying aces" of World War I, like the German "Red Baron," Manfred von Richthofen, and American Eddie Rickenbacker, only added to the swashbuckling quality of the early days of aviation. "Barnstormers" cashed in on this and took to the skies at increasingly popular air shows. Contests offered substantial monetary prizes and notoriety to pilots and their acrobatic sidekicks who showed off aerial daredevilry to the amazement of the crowds below (Corn 1983).

Increasingly, the goal of many farsighted aviators was to make air travel safe and reliable enough that it would be the preferred mode of future transportation. The commercial success of the enterprise would demand demonstrations of the feasibility and safety of long-distance travel. Prizes like the one offered by Raymond Orteig for a transatlantic flight (claimed by Charles A. Lindbergh) accelerated technical advances in aviation while captivating the public imagination for the future of flying.

It was during this exciting time that Richard Konter came of age. He was able to experience the era from the multiple perspectives afforded him by extensive international travel with the U. S. Navy, as well from his home in the cosmopolitan melting pot of New York City. We now turn to what we've learned of his background.

2

Richard Wesley Konter

RICHARD WESLEY KONTER WAS a Brooklyn, New York, native who became an accomplished ukulele player, arranger, and bandleader. He worked with Tin Pan Alley composers and publishers, arranging and creating the ukulele tablature for many popular songs.

Konter was a veteran of the Navy, with thirty years before the mast, including service in both the Spanish-American War and World War I. When Richard Byrd asked him to volunteer for his Arctic Expedition, it was Konter's Naval record and abilities that secured him a place on the crew. Although his jovial personality and musicianship were of secondary importance, they sure didn't hurt his chances. He was also a strict teetotaler, a man of temperate habits whose military service record is full of "record clear" notations.

Yet Konter was a character. Just hours before takeoff on the polar flight, Byrd's plane, the *Josephine Ford,* had to be unloaded and repacked to save weight after a false start. That task revealed many souvenirs hidden by expedition members. All were removed, along with some extra fuel, to save weight. Despite these measures, Konter, unbeknownst to Byrd, was in cahoots with pilot Floyd Bennett, who hid Konter's ukulele between some furs onboard the plane. When the *Josephine Ford* returned safely after the polar flight on May 9, 1926, the ukulele, itself bearing cargo, was still on the plane, unscathed.

According to *The New York Times* of March 16, 1926, "the greatest news story of the year" was that of the first aviators to reach the North Pole. During the expedition, Konter was able to get his ukulele signed by nearly all the members of the Byrd Arctic Expedition, as well as those of the members of another, rival expedition led by the Norwegian explorer Roald Amundsen and American financier and explorer Lincoln Ellsworth, and their Norwegian and Italian crew. As unlikely as it seems, Konter's ukulele had become the ultimate souvenir of an important era of Arctic exploration.

In the weeks following the expedition's return to the United States, Byrd and his crew were honored at many events, including a ticker-tape parade and a White House reception. Richard Konter, ukulele in hand, attended several of them and managed to obtain more autographs for the ukulele. Many were from many celebrities, politicians, athletes, musicians, military men, scientists, and other personalities of the time.

Konter continued to play the autographed ukulele after the expedition, using it for years as his main instrument. It was a focal point of his many concerts and lectures in later years.

The year after the North Pole flight, Konter corresponded with C. F. Martin III, asking to meet him in New York City. Although Konter never realized his stated wish to become a dealer of Martin instruments, a relationship was established between the men. On October 24, 1952, twenty-five years and two weeks after he first wrote to Martin, the seventy-year-old Konter typed, "Please accept this ukulele in exchange for one of your very famous guitars for which I thank you for this was a life's ambition to own one of your instruments." This small-for-large instrument exchange put Konter's Martin Style 1K soprano ukulele, plus a few facts recorded in his letter, back into the hands of C. F. Martin & Co.

3

Background
and
Early Life

RICHARD KONTER'S FATHER, Eibertus ("Ibert") Antonius Konter, was born in Germany in 1838. He emigrated to England and was already a widower at about the age of twenty-six. He married again in 1864, and took a third wife in 1870, at the age of thirty-two. His bride, Amelia Pritchard, was just seventeen or eighteen. Amelia and Eibertus emigrated to the United States after their wedding in April 1871. On June 19, 1871, the couple suffered the tragedy of a stillborn baby girl. Whether because of this or something else, the marriage foundered and the couple had no more children. Five years later, Amelia was back in England, where she remarried.

Eibertus stayed in New York and became a dealer in real estate. There, he and Marie Conradine Kuck, also a German immigrant from Pomerania, gave birth to Richard's eldest surviving sister, Antoinette ("Nettie") Konter, on April 18, 1876, in Brooklyn. Marie was twenty-one. About a year later, on April 23, 1877, the couple was married. Their first son, Charles G. Konter, was born in 1879, and another daughter, Bertha, was born a year later. Richard was born on January 8, 1882, followed by Henry J. Konter in March 1884 and finally Eibertus Konter Jr., about a year later. For a number of years, the couple lived with their six children at 68 Snydam Street, Brooklyn. Marie died on March 30, 1897, just before her twentieth wedding anniversary, from causes unknown to us. She was only fifty-two, and Eibertus was distraught.

Two years later, after visiting her grave at Evergreen Cemetery on the afternoon of April 30, 1899, Ibert returned home to an empty house. He went to the dining room at about 8 p.m. and attempted suicide by inhaling gas through a tube. His son Henry came home around 9 p.m. to find his father unconscious in a chair. The elder Konter was rushed to St. Catherine's hospital, where he was revived during the night. Ibert Konter told the

Manhattan Avenue Police Court that he had suffered from melancholia ever since the death of his wife. He pleaded not guilty to an unspecified charge and was held for three days in lieu of $500 bail. The elder Konter's children dispersed quickly thereafter.

We know little else about Eibertus Konter, but apparently, like his son Richard, he was a Mason, was ambitious, and had an inquiring mind. Eibertus was granted United States Patent 133864 for his original invention: an improved cigar perforator (E. Konter 1872).

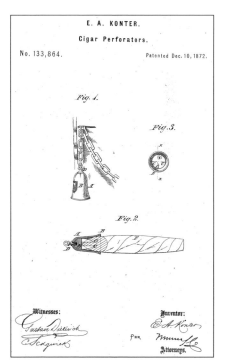

His son Richard Wesley Konter was born into the heart of New York City's *fin de siècle* cultural milieu, making his debut in Bushwick, Brooklyn. Richard lived and grew up with his family on Snydam Street in Bushwick and attended Kosciusko School on Bushwick Avenue.

When Richard was six years old, on March 12, 1888, a monstrous blizzard made quite an impression on him. The storm paralyzed the East Coast and was responsible for four hundred deaths. Konter would later recall the storm at regular meetings of "The Blizzard Men and Ladies of 1888." Konter's participation in this group went on for years, and often made the paper. His accounts from their thirty-fourth annual luncheon in 1963, when he was eighty-one years old, recalled eighteen-foot snowdrifts on Boerum Street in Brooklyn. Temperatures dropped so low that,

Illustration of E. A. Konter's patent for an improved cigar perforator. *Public domain, U. S. Patent Office.*

he said, "[t]he East River was frozen over sufficiently to allow wagon crossings." (*Asheville Citizen-Times* [Asheville, North Carolina], Monday, March 11, 1963, page 2). It seems that Konter's eye for the historical moment sharpened early.

Richard joined the United States Navy on March 30, 1897, the day his mother died. He was only fifteen. That a son would join the Navy on the very day of his mother's passing cries out for an explanation. We speculate that Marie Konter's family likely knew that her death was imminent, and so they devised a plan to distract Richard from his grief over the loss of his mother. This would explain why young Konter's grieving father gave his consent, as was required by law, to allow his son to enlist in the Navy at such a tender age.

Richard left his Snydam Street home and enlisted as an apprentice in the Navy. He would cruise the world as a Navy man for the next thirty years.

During 1897–1898, Konter served in the Navy as an apprentice, a rank which became defunct during his lifetime. That he had served at this rank was later a point of pride for him and his fellow "boys"—who between the ages of fifteen and seventeen were enlisted at the rank of Apprentice, 3rd Class. Requirements included the

Spanish-American War Military and Naval Service Summary, 1898–1902, for Richard Wesley Konter (obverse). *New York State Archives.*

ability to read and write, plus the aforementioned parental consent, given by signing the apprentice's enlistment application. (Konter 1968, *Trade Winds*, NARA Konter Files).

Upon entering the Navy, Konter learned the ropes of ships by starting at the beginning—literally. He entered the Navy aboard the storied wooden frigate U. S. S. *Constitution*. The *Constitution* was the first ship in the Navy, named by George Washington himself. She was, by the time of Konter's enlistment, a "receiving ship," a usually obsolete or unseaworthy ship moored at a navy yard and used for new recruits or men in transit between stations. From the *Constitution*, Konter was assigned to the U. S. S. *Vermont* and the U. S. S. *Constellation*.

UNITED STATES NAVY VESSELS
ON WHICH RICHARD KONTER SERVED.

VESSEL	DATE OF TRANSFER	RANK
U. S. S. *Vermont*	30 March 1897	Apprentice, 3rd Class
U. S. S. *Constellation*	August 1897	Apprentice, 3rd Class
U. S. S. *Essex*	1898	Apprentice, 2nd Class
U. S. S. *Vermont*	1898	Apprentice, 2nd Class
U. S. S. *Richmond*	1898	Apprentice, 2nd Class
U. S. S. *Minneapolis*	1898	Apprentice, 2nd Class
U. S. S. *Yosemite*	1898	Apprentice, 2nd Class

U. S. S. *Buffalo*	5 February 1899	Apprentice, 2nd Class
U. S. S. *Charleston*	21 November 1899	Apprentice, 1st Class
U. S. S. *Glacier*	31 December 1899	Apprentice, 1st Class
U. S. S. *Solace*	29 January 1900	Apprentice, 1st Class
U. S. S. *Bennington*	31 March 1900	Apprentice, 1st Class
U. S. S. *Yosemite*	30 June 1900	Apprentice, 1st Class
U. S. S. *Oregon*	31 March 1901	Apprentice, 1st Class
U. S. S. *Kentucky*	28 May 1901	Apprentice, 1st Class
U. S. S. *Culgoa*	18 July 1901	Apprentice, 1st Class
U. S. S. *Vicksburg*	30 September 1901	Apprentice, 1st Class
U. S. S. *Solace*	8 August 1902	Apprentice, 1st Class
U. S. S. *Monterey*	18 August 1902	Apprentice, 1st Class
U. S. S. *Buffalo*	30 September 1902	Apprentice, 1st Class
U. S. S. *Columbia*	31 December 1902	Apprentice, 1st Class
DISCHARGED	7 January 1903	Seaman
U. S. S. *Columbia*	31 March 1903	Seaman
U. S. S. *Hancock*	30 September 1903	Electrician, 2nd Class
U. S. S. *Cleveland*	31 December 1903	Electrician, 2nd Class
U. S. S. *Olympia*	30 June 1904	Electrician, 2nd Class
U. S. S. *Minneapolis*	31 March 1906	Electrician 1st Class
U. S. S. *Washington*	31 December 1906	Electrician 1st Class
U. S. S. *Hancock*	14 February 1907	Electrician 1st Class
DISCHARGED	27 March 1907	Electrician 1st Class
U. S. S. *Hancock*	31 August 1907	Electrician, 1st Class
U. S. S. *New Jersey*	30 September 1907	Electrician, 1st Class
U. S. S. *Wabash*	30 September 1909	Electrician, 1st Class
DISCHARGED	1 July 1911	Electrician, 1st Class

U. S. S. *Sylph*	30 September 1915	Chief Electrician (Radio)
U. S. S. *Birmingham*	6 November 1915	Chief Electrician (Radio)
U. S. S. *Vestal*	31 March 1916	Chief Electrician (Radio)
U. S. S. *Colhoun*	30 June 1918	Chief Electrician (Radio)
DISCHARGED	14 September 1918	Chief Electrician (Radio)

Konter had photographic "Season's Greetings" cards made of himself in uniform, the photo taken, according to Konter (Konter 1968, *Trade Winds*, NARA Konter Files), "One week in the Navy, 15 years old, March, 1897."

Apprentice 3rd Class Richard W. Konter, age fifteen. *Collection of Jean Neptune,*

Konter's sailing education on the *Vermont* and the *Constellation* prepared him and 165 other sailors to man the square-rigger *Essex,* a two-mast, wooden-hulled, sail/steamer built at Boston and commissioned in 1876 (John 1999). Konter sailed on the *Essex* on a goodwill voyage from Newport, Rhode Island, to Plymouth, England, in twenty-two days. It was on this voyage and his subsequent liberty in England that Konter enjoyed his first taste of the world beyond Brooklyn.

With the destruction of the battleship U. S. S. *Maine* on February 15, 1898, in Havana Harbor, Cuba, the United States entered the Spanish-American War. Konter was transferred to the U. S. S. *Minneapolis*. At the time, the *Minneapolis* was the fastest ship in the world, making twenty-three knots. The *Minneapolis* was assigned to seek out the Spanish fleet in the Caribbean. While searching for the fleet, the *Minneapolis* captured a Spanish merchant brig, the *Maria Dolores*. Konter wrote, "Years later, I decided to apply for my share of prize money because I was almost broke" (NARA Konter Archive, Box 1, Biographical Materials, US Navy service, 1902–1954). During a time when sailors received bounty money, usually from $1 to $100 for such a capture, Konter received a check for his part of the prize—in the amount of thirty cents.

Konter was to have one of his most memorable voyages after being ordered to ship out on the cruiser U. S. S. *Charleston*. She left San Francisco on May 21, 1898, for Honolulu, Hawai'i, where she was joined by three chartered steamers transporting troops to the other theater, the Philippines. He served on the *Charleston* during the Philippine Insurrection engagement at Subic Bay, September 24, 1899, and by October the *Charleston* was patrolling the waters around the northern Philippines alone, without the benefit of radio or modern navigational aids. The *Charleston* was about to become the first steel-hulled ship ever lost by the U. S. Navy.

The U. S. S. *Charleston* (C-2). *Courtesy of the Naval History & Heritage Command.*

Just before daybreak on November 2, 1899, the *Charleston* ran aground on an uncharted reef north of the island of Luzon (R. W. Konter 1920). Despite reversing her engines immediately, she began to take on water, and all hands were ordered to abandon ship. The lifeboats were launched. By early that evening, the entire crew in their lifeboats had drifted some thirty miles from where the *Charleston* sank to a small, uninhabited, and waterless island, most likely northeast of the larger Camiguin island. The next morning, after a scouting party turned up nothing to eat or drink on the island, the captain asked for ten men to volunteer to make the trip to Camiguin. Konter and a seventeen-year-old shipmate were first in the boat and made the thirty-minute trip.

At Camiguin they were met by some islanders who showed them where to find water. The landing party filled their barrels with water and returned to their grateful shipmates on the uninhabited island. The following day, the entire crew moved to Camiguin Island. A deal was struck with the islanders to trade needles, fishhooks, hammers, and nails for enough rice that each man could have two small meals per day.

On the fifth day after running aground, the crew of the *Charleston* prepared the largest lifeboat for an open-sea voyage to seek help at Manila, three hundred miles to the south. Eight men were chosen as its crew, while

The U. S. S. *Helena*, photographed between 1897 and 1901. *Public domain. From Detroit Publishing Co. collection, Library of Congress.*

the remaining sailors waited on Camiguin. Beach bonfires were kindled and tended day and night to attract the attention of passing vessels. On the fifteenth night, a ship was finally sighted.

The huge bonfire attracted the attention of the passing gunboat *Helena,* whose crew had already seen and rescued the eight men in the lifeboat. A launch from the *Helena* was sent to investigate at Camiguin, and on November 12, 1899, all 228 men from the *Charleston* were rescued and taken aboard the *Helena,* bound for Manila.

Despite their rescue, Konter and the sailors of the *Charleston* weren't quite out of trouble—they had to endure a seventy-two-hour long typhoon on the voyage to Manila (R. W. Konter 1920). They made it, though. Once in Manila, the sailors were reassigned to other ships in the fleet.

After brief stints on the U. S. S. *Glacier,* the U. S. S. *Solace,* and the U. S. S. *Bennington,* Konter's next assignment was on the U. S. S. *Yosemite.* The *Yosemite* had seen duty in Cuba, Jamaica, and Puerto Rico during the Spanish-American war. After a refit, the *Yosemite* left New York on May 10, 1899, bound for the Mediterranean Sea, the Suez Canal, and the Indian Ocean. She arrived in the Mariana Islands, at San Luis d'Apra on Guam, on August 7, 1899, where she resumed duty as a station ship. On April 17, 1900, she departed to Japan, where she underwent repairs at Yokohama and Uraga and subsequently made calls in Nagasaki and the Philippines, before returning to Guam in July 1900, where she served as station ship.

On November 13, 1900, a tremendous typhoon hit Guam island, and the *Yosemite* was blown off her moorings, first on to shore and then out to

sea. Although the crew was able to make it ashore with the aid of the Navy collier *Justin,* the *Yosemite* took on water and her screw was damaged. Shortly after the storm passed, the Navy made a decision that the *Yosemite* was not worth repairing, and she was towed out to sea and scuttled. For Dick Konter, that made two typhoons in one year.

The U. S. S. *Vicksburg* (PG-11), photographed in 1898.
Public domain. U. S. Naval Historical Center.

Richard W. Konter in Niu Zhuang (now Yingkou), Liaoning Province, China, in 1901. *National Archives and Records Administration, Richard W. Konter papers.*

Telegram from Richard Konter to Byrd Arctic Expedition, 14 March 1926. Courtesy of Expeditions: North Pole Flight, Admiral Richard E. Byrd Papers, *The Ohio State University, Byrd Polar and Climate Research Center Archival Program. Used with permission.*

Konter left Manila and was assigned duty on the gunboat U. S. S. *Vicksburg* (PG-11), to patrol the southern Philippine islands. The U. S. S. *Vicksburg* was also one of two American warships stationed in China at the end of the so-called Boxer Rebellion. Konter was photographed in modern Yingkou (known then as Niu Zhuang, or "Newchwang" on the picture postcard—literally "cow town," 牛庄), a city in Liaoning Province, China. He and his shipmates on the *Vicksburg* were frozen in on the Liao River for four months during the winter of 1901–1902, as he wrote in a telegram to the Byrd

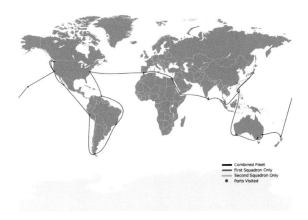

A map of the route taken by the Great White Fleet from December 1907 to February 1909. Created using this blank map by João Felipe C. S. as a template. Note that the countries are drawn with their modern boundaries (not as they were in 1907–1909) and are there for reference. *Created by TastyCakes, Wikimedia Commons.*

Arctic Expedition via the Navy Department.

While serving in China, Dick Konter did what any good sailor would: he got tattooed. *Contra* Bart (2013), who writes "Around his arms coiled a pair of dragons," Konter wrote (in his own hand) that he had a cockfight inked on his left forearm, while on his right forearm he had a dragon and a butterfly (Konter, questionnaire for

The Great White Fleet under way from Hampton Roads, Virginia, 1908. *Public domain. U. S. Navy photograph.*

Permanent Records of the Byrd Arctic Expedition, Byrd Polar Archives).

Konter's first tour of duty in the Navy ended on January 7, 1903. He took a ten-week break from active service in the Navy, but soon had the itch to travel again. On March 28, he reenlisted and got his wish.

Towards the end of his presidency, Theodore Roosevelt ordered two squadrons of American battleships, sixteen in all, to make a circumnavigation of the earth. The aim of the so-called "Great White Fleet" was to call in ports of friendly countries, display American naval power (especially directed at Japan), and provide practical blue-water experience for the expanded Navy in the aftermath of the Spanish-American war. The hull of each ship in the fleet had been painted in the United States Navy's peacetime color scheme—white—with gilded scrollwork and a red, white, and blue banner on each ship's bow.

U. S. S. *New Jersey* (BB-16) in Sydney Harbor, Australia, in late August 1908. Stereophotograph on card by Underwood & Underwood, photographers. *Public domain.*

Konter served as a radioman on one of the fleet's battleships, the U. S. S. *New Jersey* (BB-16). Konter wrote, "It was a good-will trip. We brought the greetings of the United States to many foreign lands" (R. W. Konter 1967). His duty on the *New Jersey* lasted sixteen months.

The Great White Fleet's voyage was broken into four separate legs. The first got under way on December

16, 1907 from Hampton Roads, Virginia, to San Francisco, California, a distance of 14,556 nautical miles. There was no Panama Canal at the time, so

the fleet had to travel around the tip of South America via the Strait of Magellan and then up the western coasts of South and North America. The second leg was from San Francisco to Seattle and back, with stops in six Washington State ports. The third leg was from San Francisco to Manila, some 16,335 nautical miles. The fleet departed San Francisco on July 7, 1908, arriving in Honolulu on July 16. All but the U. S. S. *Minnesota* set sail at 6 p.m. on July 23 for Auckland, New Zealand, arriving there at 8:40 a.m. on August 9, 1908. Both squadrons arrived in Manila by November 7, 1908. The final leg of the voyage took the fleet back

Kodak Brownie Camera. Likely the camera used by Konter while with the Great White Fleet. *Public domain.*

to Hampton Roads, departing Manila on December 1, 1908, and arriving after stops in Colombo, Ceylon; Suez, Egypt, and Gibraltar, on February 22, 1909.

Once again Konter recognized history in the making, and he documented the Great White Fleet voyages with many photographs. We don't know precisely when Konter began making his own photographs, but it began at least as early at the voyage of the Great White Fleet in 1908, and he pursued it seriously. Introduced in 1900, the Kodak Brownie camera made photographic technology available to the masses, and it is likely this inexpensive camera was Konter's first.

The Monday, July 12, 1909 *Courier-Journal* of Louisville, Kentucky, includes an article about the accidental death of a shipmate of Konter's, Arthur Decker, and his mother's eerie premonition of her son being killed by a train (which is precisely how Decker died) in Melbourne, Australia:

"The letter from Richard W. Konter, electrician, U. S. N., reads: "U. S. S. New Jersey, Manila Bay, P. I.—Dear Madam: It is with much respect that I forward herewith a set of pictures taken by me at the funeral services of your son, Arthur J. Decker, which I beg you to accept, and will enlighten you of the Christian and military burial which he received while in Melbourne, Victoria.

"It pains every one of us for the loss of our late shipmate who was so unfortunate to have passed away in this manner. Trusting this token of sympathy might help you bear your great and sad loss, I remain, most sincerely, Richard W. Konter."

Konter's photography and kind letter brought solace to a grieving mother who could not attend the funeral services held for her son held half a world away in Australia.

On October 12, 2007, an album of photographs taken by Konter on the voyages was sold for $190 (the estimate was $200–$300) at an auction of Space Memorabilia & Collectibles held by Regency-Superior Ltd., of St. Louis, Missouri, as lot number 1137. The album contains some two hundred black-and-white photographs, described as follows:

Never before seen group of about 200 different black & white photographs in varying sizes taken by a crew member during the famous cruise by 16 new battleships sent by then President Theodore Roosevelt around the world. These photos are excellent for an amateur, taken by Richard Wesley Konter (who later sailed with Admiral Byrd on his first expedition to the North Pole and as assistant steward on the Byrd Antarctic expedition). We note photos taken at sea, in Egypt, England, Australia, etc. Daily life, formations, militaria, all are shown in these shots from a century ago. Rarely do we see such history available. (https://new.liveauctioneers.com/item/4207636_1137-1908-original-photos-great-white-fleet-cruise)

Interestingly, lot 1200 at the same auction was an album of black-and-white or sepia photographs taken by Konter on the first Byrd Antarctic Expedition and sold for $500 (the pre-auction estimate was $600-$800). The description reads:

Almost 200 different black & white or sepia photographs from a personal photo album belonging to Dick Konter, Assistant Steward on the First Byrd Antarctic Expedition. Konter, an expert amateur photographer, took these photos of various events, scenes & people related to the expedition. Most amazing is a group of 36 different photographs of members of the expedition. All have been identified by writing to surviving members of the expedition with photocopies of these individuals. (https://new.liveauctioneers.com/item/4207699_1200-byrd-south-pole-expedition-photo-collection)

Name: KONTER- RICHARD WESLEY			Service Number 103-01-54		
Enlisted at NAVAL RENDEZVOUS WASHINGTON D.C.			Date 7-9-15		
Age at Entrance 33 YRS.6 MO.	Rate ELECTRICIAN		1ST CLASS RADIO		U.S.N. U.S.N.R.F.
Home Address 375 MCDONOUGH STREET			Town BROOKLYN		
M County --			State N.Y.		
Served at	From	To	Served as		No. Days
USS VESTAL	4-6-17	4-28-17	CHIEF ELECTRICIAN		
RECEIVING SHIP NEW YORK	4-28-17	7-25-17	RADIO		584
RECEIVING SHIP BOSTON MASS.	7-25-17	8-9-17			
HARVARD RADIO SCHOOL					
CAMBRIDGE MASS.	8-9-17	2-25-18			
TRANSFERRED TO FLEET NAVAL RESERVE CLASS-1-D- 2-25-18					
HARVARD RADIO SCHOOL CAMBRIDGE MASS.	2-25-18	6-6-18			
USS COLHOUN	6-6-18	11-8-18			
XXXXXX RECEIVING SHIP NEW YORK N.Y.	11-8-18	11-11-18			

Date Discharge 7-26-20		CHIEF ELECTRICIAN
Place Inactive Duty RECRUITING BUREAU NEW YORK N.Y.	Rating at Discharge RADIO	

Richard Konter Naval Service record, April 1917 to November 11, 1918. *New York State Archives.*

The fact that both albums had been owned by Konter suggests to us that they had been auctioned by a relative who had inherited them, but our attempts to identify either the seller or buyer have gone (appropriately, unfortunately—a reputable auction house would never reveal the name of a lot's buyer) unanswered.

With the entry of the United States into World War I on April 6, 1917 (until November 11, 1918), Konter was serving in the Navy as Electrician 1st Class (Radio), on the U. S. S. *Sylph,* the U. S. S. *Birmingham,* and the U. S. S. *Vestal,* then in both New York and Boston, and at the Harvard Radio School in Cambridge, Massachusetts, starting September 30, 1917, through February 25, 1918. *The Brooklyn Daily Eagle* of Sunday, December 2, 1917, lists Konter as a member of the "Honor Roll" of Anthon Lodge of the 2nd Masonic District in Brooklyn.

Konter, getting restless, joined the crew of the U. S. S. *Colhoun* (DD-85), and between June 30 and September 14, 1918, the U. S. S. *Colhoun* traversed the North Atlantic as a convoy escort to ships carrying troops and supplies between New York and European ports. "He saw London, Rome, Paris, and Berlin, a couple of submarines and some explosive mines 'but no action.'"

After almost twenty years in the Navy, Konter was transferred to shore duty, and on Christmas Day 1918, he was transferred to the Naval Reserve. He arrived at the receiving ship in New York on December 3, 1918, and was working in communications for the 3rd Naval District headquarters in New York City on December 31, 1918. He remained in New York and was assigned recruiting duty on June 30, 1920. By July 26, 1920, he was listed as "inactive" and was back in New York City. Thus, from the end of 1918 to the time of the Byrd Expedition in 1926, Dick Konter was mainly living in Brooklyn.

Konter finished up his last year in the Navy as an enlistment officer in New York City. In fact, because of this assignment, there was some concern that he might not be able to join the expedition. However, in a March 24, 1926 memo, Byrd asked Captain L. B. Porterfield (a ukulele signer) for help in postponing Konter's enlistment duty until after the expedition. Byrd wrote, "I must admit that I am anxious to have him with us."

4

Konter
the
Musician

AN UNDATED FEATURE ABOUT Konter appeared in the New York *World-Telegram* with what may be the best information available on when he started playing instruments. In the article, Konter is identified as being eighty years old. The author, Herbert Kurz, does not mention Konter's marriage, so the piece is probably from early 1962. Kurz interviewed Konter for the article, and reported that Konter

> spent the winter of 1901 in Manchuria, enduring 35-below-zero cold, and that's where he learned to play the guitar for lack of anything else to do. His guitar playing soon became the only entertainment for the British, America, and Russian sailors and troops along the river, he said. "When we left, the Russians sent a tug from Mukden with a 100-piece band to escort us the 20 miles down the river," he said. "I like to think that's the way they paid us back for my guitar playing."

A June 23, 1964 article in the New York *Daily News* (Brooklyn section) states that Konter, ". . . has played a guitar since 1901. He learned to play it from shipmates while serving in the Navy."

The earliest known photograph of Konter playing an instrument was published on a website, now defunct, about the Great White Fleet. (Parts of the website can still be viewed at: http://web.archive.org/web/20080410171623/ http://www.greatwhitefleet.info:80/GWF_Sailor_Richard_Konter.html.) Featured on the page is a tiny image, presumably from 1908, of Dick Konter in sailor's garb and playing an acoustic guitar. Nothing is known of the exact date or location of the photo, but it was apparently removed from an album, judging from the material adhering to the back of the photos. In fact, this owner of this website may have been the successful bidder on the album of Konter's photos from the Great White Fleet mentioned above.

The next-earliest-known photograph of Konter with an instrument is from 1920, some twenty-three years after he joined the Navy. In it, Konter and another man stand on the deck of a ship. The thirty-eight-year-old Konter holds a Gibson harp guitar, and a shipmate holds a six-string Martin guitar. The relative complexity of Konter's instrument suggests that he was already a skilled player.

When did Konter first learn the ukulele? A wire service feature on him appeared in the *Neosho Times* (Neosho, Missouri) on Thursday,

Richard Konter playing guitar on Great White Fleet voyage. *Public domain.*

November 6, 1930, headlined, "Ukulele Played at Both Poles by Explorer." The unnamed author concludes the article, tantalizingly, by stating that "He is an ex-Navy man and between polar jaunts teaches the ukulele which he learned first-hand in the Hawaiian Islands." In fact, Konter visited Hawai'i as a sailor aboard the U. S. S. *Charleston* in 1898. He likely heard and may have even purchased his first ukulele during this trip. If it was not on that voyage, we can place Konter in Hawai'i again a decade later, during a six-day period between July 16 and 22, 1908, when the U. S. S. *New Jersey* visited Honolulu with the Great White Fleet.

Richard Konter *(left)* playing a Gibson harp guitar with unknown sailor *(right)* playing a Martin guitar, 1920. *National Archives and Records Administration, Richard W. Konter Papers, XRWK - A1 131 (2 boxes).*

In either case, Konter was already a grown man when the ukulele fad began sweeping the country in 1915. He was likely an accomplished ukulele player by that time, as well. Moreover, Konter would have already had the musical credibility needed to publish his own ukulele method, which is exactly what he did, and he was recognized as an obvious choice as a go-to ukulele arranger for the big New York City music publishing houses. Back in New York, but before his discharge from the Navy, Konter developed a reputation as a reliable arranger for some of the most important popular music

   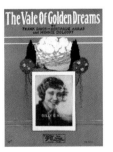

Sheet music covers of songs arranged by Richard W. Konter. *Public domain.*

publishers of the era. Notable among them were Shapiro, Bernstein & Co. and Clarence Williams Music Publishing.

The earliest example of Konter's published ukulele arranging is the venerable "Down on the Farm (They All Ask for You)." The sheet music was published by Skidmore Music Co. Inc. and distributed by Shapiro, Bernstein & Co. The 1923 song was extremely popular at the time, and a copyright was issued June 1, 1923. Some fifty-six years later, it would inspire Paul Barrère's track for the 1979 album of the same name by Little Feat.

Less than seven weeks later on July 19, 1923, Skidmore Music Co. copyrighted the iconic tune "Yes, We Have No Bananas," with ukulele arrangement by Dick Konter. It was sung by the famous Eddie Cantor in the 1922 Broadway revue *Make It Snappy,* and the tune stayed at number one for five weeks in 1923.

There are many more examples of Konter's arrangements, including the already mentioned "If You Knew Susie (Like I Know Susie)," but to put it simply, Richard Konter the Navy man was the ukulele arranger of choice for some of the biggest publishing houses in New York during the instrument's heyday.

Once he had been assigned to "shore duty" on the East Coast, Konter had the idea to form a musical group for kids. It's hard to tell exactly when this occurred, but Konter wrote:

When I had served almost twenty years in the navy, I was transferred to shore duty, and during that assignment I happened to get acquainted with families who had children, I was very fond of children. At that time the little Ukulele, was not a fad, but a mania, and one night when I was visiting a family, they had a number of neighborhood children in their home. The boys, and girls ranged in age, from 8 to 12, whom I taught to play the ukulele, and that same week-end they were singing the latest songs, while accompanying themselves on their ukes.

I then took them to various hospitals, home for the blind, they even played for the Sing Sing inmates, they always made a big hit, they were among the first children to sing and play on the radio . . .

Eventually I was unable to fill all the requests for their appearances (Konter, R. W. Adventure Ahoy! Part II).

The earliest documented performance we have found of Konter leading such a group was published in *The Brooklyn Daily Eagle* on Sunday, June 11, 1922. It lists a radio performance to be broadcast the following Saturday,

June 17, 1922, at 9 p.m. on Station WVP, Amateur Radio Reserve. WVP was a longwave station (1,450 meters) operated by the U. S. Army Signal Corps on Bedloe's Island (now called Liberty Island) in New York Harbor. The program that evening was entitled, "Mother Davidson's [sic] Army and Navy Night." Selections were to be performed by "Banjo and Ukulele Club, under the direction of Richard Konter," along with Ada Tully, humorist, Miss Lou Stow and Miss Pauline Jennings, and Fay Foster playing the piano. The show was repeated two weeks later with different performers.

Some of Dick's Ukulele Club members. Halftone from first (1923) edition of *Dick's Ukulele Method. Courtesy of Tom Walsh.*

Konter wrote that, in addition to radio performances, the children's group "made appearances all around New York City, Brooklyn, Staten Island, and Connecticut." Dick's Ukulele Club (it went by various names over the years) was, in fact, a big hit around New York City. The club put on at least five radio performances, and the club's individual performers put on even more. Additionally, there were performances in other venues, such as at the Brooklyn Naval Yard the day the expedition left New York City (a picture of this concert appears on page 45), during the ticker-tape parade on the Byrd Arctic Expedition's return to the United States, and at a dinner held in Konter's honor after the expedition, among others.

Konter enjoyed teaching the ukulele to kids. He published a popular ukulele method (R. W. Konter 1923) that was sold by music stores that also carried ukuleles. He clearly held a special place in his heart for these kids. They feature in a photograph on page two of *Dick's Improved Ukulele Method* over the caption "A few admirers of Dick's Ukulele Method." He adopted a simple, if idiosyncratic and non-standard, chord nomenclature in his methods, using Arabic numerals (for

Ukulele, With Cover and Pick

$2.65 For the Outfit

A UKE is of little account unless its tone is clear and well bodied. In these instruments, despite the low price, this much sought quality is distinctly refined. They are of well seasoned wood, colored a good mahogany brown, and strung with Hawaiian strings and fitted with good tuning pegs.

The cover js of green felt with taped edges and the pick is of the professional type.

$2.65 Buys the Outfit Complete. Regularly $3.35

Song Books for Ukulele Players

May Singhi Breen's Collection of Songs ....33¢	Witmark's Collection, Black and White Series ....48¢
Mills' Comic Song Collection.23¢	Popular Songs with Ukulele Accompaniment ....48¢
Comic Song Folio, Nos. 1 and 2, at ....23¢	Dick's Ukulele Method.....59¢
Eukadidles ....23¢	E-Z Method for Ukulele.....23¢
Foolish Songs ....33¢	

Loeser's—Fourth Floor.

Advertisement appearing in *The Brooklyn Daily Eagle* (April 2, 1925) for Loeser's Department Store for a ukulele, cover, and pick. *Dick's Ukulele Method* is available for 59 cents. Konter's friend and fellow ukulele player and signer Bill Rider was the manager of Loeser's musical merchandise department.

example: 1, 2, and 3 for tonic, subdominant, and dominant triads). He did this to keep things simple for the beginning student, but also to allow a single book to be useful to players of differently tuned tiples and baritone ukuleles, as well as for ukuleles and taropatches.

One of the older female members of the club also captured Konter's special attention. Johanna Cohen was the love of his life.

Johanna was a talented musician and a multi-instrumentalist. She was born to Isaac "Arthur" Cohen and Regina "Rickie" Sonneborn on January 20, 1907, in Brooklyn. Johanna was their only child. According to her daughter, Jean Neptune, Johanna could play everything—ukulele, piano, mandolin, guitar, banjo, even the saw. She also sang. Jean also told us, "She played the ukulele fantastically. She could play anything on that uke, even classical." During our interview, Jean told us that her mother had her own fifteen-minute broadcast on a station in

Photograph of Richard Konter inscribed "Fondest wishes to Johanna from Dick." Ex-apprentice insignia patch (knot) visible on right uniform sleeve. *Courtesy of Jean Neptune.*

34

Brooklyn when "there were very few people on the radio at the time." It is easy to see why Konter would have been interested in young Johanna Cohen.

Jean Neptune also told us that her mother first met Konter through a mutual acquaintance who was a member of Dick's Ukulele Club (Jean Neptune, personal communication, 2016). We think this person was likely to have been Betty Moore, a ukulele club member and a close friend of Johanna's, according to her daughter. Betty probably appreciated what a fine addition to the club Johanna would be.

Johanna Cohen as a child. Courtesy of Lee Feist.

The date of Konter and Johanna's formal introduction is hard to establish—the earliest we can place them together is December 15, 1923, when Konter and Johanna appeared on the same program on station WHN (Manhattan, 360) between 3:45 and 5:30 p.m. Their performances were not as members of "Dick's Ukulele Club" or some variant of that name, but rather as soloists. On that date, Johanna would have been sixteen years old, almost seventeen. After that date, a number of other radio performances that included Konter and Cohen were mentioned in various newspapers between 1924 and 1926.

Some of Dick's Ukulele Club members (including Johanna Cohen, fourth from left, playing a tiple) being photographed with Mother Davison (third from left). Date and location unknown. *Courtesy of Jean Neptune.*

DATE	TIME	STATION	PERFORMER	LOCATION
6/17/22	9:00 PM	WVP 1450	Mother Davison's Army and Navy Night. Selections by Banjo and Ukulele Club, under the direction of Richard Konter.	Bedloe's Island, New York (Libety Island)
9/29/23	2:15 PM	WHN 360	Dick Konter's Kiddie Ukulele club, Mother Davison's Hospital Entertainers, and others listed separately.	Manhattan, New York
9/29/23	4:15 PM	WHN 360	Dick Konter's Kiddie Ukulele Club and Mother Davison's Hospital Entertainers.	Manhattan, New York
12/15/23	3:45 PM	WHN 360	Various performances including Johanna Cohen and Elizabeth Werfelman, and Richard Konter.	Manhattan, New York
12/21/24	7:30 PM	WAHG 316	Dick's Childrens Ukulele Chorus.	Brooklyn, New York
2/4/25	9:00 PM	WAHG 316	Hawaiian Ensemble, R.W. Konter, Ed Howard, Charles Howard, and Arthur Butler.	Brooklyn, New York
10/26/25	4:00 PM	WGCP 252	Johanna Cohen, trio.	Manhattan, New York
11/7/25	4:00 PM	WGCP 252	Johanna Cohen, ukulele, songs.	Manhattan, New York
12/5/25	4:00 PM	WGCP 252	Johanna Cohen, ukulele; Sylvia Miller, soprano.	Manhattan, New York
12/22/25	7:30 PM	WGCP 252	Dick's Ukulele Club.	Manhattan, New York
2/14/26	4:00 PM	WGCP	Cohen, Konter and Moore, entertainers.	Manhattan, New York
12/17/26	9:00 PM	WBBC	Ukulele Bill Rider (with Anna and Margaret Fabrizio).	New York City
10/19/28	1:00 PM	WGBS	Konter's Ukulele Club.	New York City

36

| 3/22/29 | 11:00 PM | WNJ | Ukulele Dick, songs. | Newark, New Jersey |
| 10/19/28 | 4:00 PM | WGCP | Johanna Cohen, trio. | New York City |

In fact, at 4 p.m. on February 14, 1926, St. Valentine's Day, "Cohen, Konter, and Moore, entertainers" played on WGCP 252 in Manhattan, according to *The Brooklyn Daily Eagle* of that date. First names are not provided in the short listing, but it seems likely that the paper refers to Johanna Cohen, Richard Konter, and Betty Moore. Each was already a seasoned radio entertainer, and they had all already performed previously as soloists and with the ukulele club on WGCP.

Sometime before leaving for Antarctica in 1928 (or perhaps before leaving for the Arctic in 1926), Konter proposed marriage to Johanna. Jean Neptune explained to us, "In those days, you went to the woman's father to ask for permission to ask for her hand . . . and my grandfather said, 'No way.' He said to Dick, 'You're the same age as me! You're too old.'"

Memories have faded and no documents now exist, if any ever did, to reveal the date of Konter's proposal to Johanna and her father's refusal to give Konter her hand. If his proposal was offered before he voyaged north on the *Chantier* in 1926, Johanna would have been nineteen. If Konter waited until he was about to leave for Antarctica on August 25, 1928, the oldest Johanna could have been would be twenty-one years and eight months. But whenever the proposal was made, according to Jean, "Dick was evidently quite smitten."

William G. "Battleship Bill" Pool. *Courtesy of Jean Neptune.*

After his 1926 trip to the Arctic, Konter spent a year and a half in New York before he joined Byrd's first Antarctic expedition in 1928. Jean doesn't know if her mom had known her dad, William Pool, before she met Konter, but Konter certainly knew his old shipmate and may have introduced them. It's easy to imagine that, after hearing that Konter had struck out with Johanna, Bill proposed and Johanna said yes. And this time, so did her father. Thus, it seems that a twenty-five-year age difference was just a gulf too large for her father to accept, but a fifteen-year difference was apparently fine—Bill Pool was nine years and five months younger than his old shipmate. We know Konter's proposal was offered and rejected sometime before the Antarctic departure, because Johanna married William Pool on June 16, 1930, just two days after Konter returned to New York. Konter may have needed an adventure after his rejection, but we simply do not know in which direction that adventure took him, north or south.

To Bill Pool, Johanna was always known as "Josie." Together they had two kids, William III and Jean. They would remain married until Bill's death twenty-three years later.

Photograph of Richard Konter, twice inscribed. "To Johanna from Dick (Byrd Arctic & Antarctic Expeditions)" and "To Johanna Cohen from R. W. Konter." *Courtesy of Jean Neptune.*

5

The 1926 Arctic Expeditions

IT IS HARD TO OVERSTATE the national and international excitement that accompanied the expedition organized by Commander Richard E. Byrd Jr. to attempt the first flight over the geographic North Pole. The expedition was a featured story in every major newspaper in the country, and, via the wire services, most of the minor ones, too.

The expedition was the brainchild of Richard "Dick" Evelyn Byrd Jr. Byrd was a child of privilege. He came from one of Virginia's oldest and most prestigious families, a clan of early and sustained political influence. Well before the existence of the United States, Dick Byrd's ancestor William Byrd was politically active in the seventeenth century. But despite his advantages, Dick Byrd worked hard to achieve his fame.

He spent his childhood in Winchester, Virginia, in the Northern Shenandoah Valley. He had already been around the world at the ripe old age of thirteen, traveling from the Philippines to South Asia, Egypt, and Europe. After stints at Virginia Military Institute and the University of Virginia, Byrd enrolled as a midshipman at the U. S. Naval Academy in Annapolis in 1908 as a prelude to a career in the Navy.

While in Annapolis, Byrd became a member of several Naval Academy athletic teams. In a football game against Princeton University, he broke his foot quite badly. Later, as a senior and captain of the gymnastics team, Byrd specialized in the rings. While attempting a dangerous maneuver, he missed a ring and re-fractured the same foot and ankle he'd injured against Princeton in football. Despite his injury, he managed to graduate with the class of 1912.

After graduating, Byrd served on several vessels, as ensign on the *Missouri*, the *Washington*, and the *Birmingham*, as well as the *Mississippi*, which had an aviation unit. He took his first flight in an airplane with that unit.

His leg continued to bother him, but he was promoted rapidly, partly thanks to his determined performance and partly due to his familial connections. By 1915, Byrd had been assigned to the presidential yacht, the *Mayflower*, on which he served for a year. There he impressed not only President Woodrow Wilson, but also other government officials who met him on board.

Dick Byrd married Marie Ames on January 15, 1915, and by 1916, his career seemed ended because of his injuries. He applied for and was granted a disability retirement. However, he was back in uniform in the Navy Reserve by June, preparing a militia unit for possible service in the Great War. In 1917, he appealed to the medical board for flight training for eventual duty in military aviation. He was especially interested in, and talented at, designing navigational instruments for aviators. His inventions found their way into naval seaplanes. By 1923, Byrd had helped create the Bureau of Aeronautics in the Department of the Navy, from whence he was well placed to learn about the use of aircraft for long-range exploration. Of particular interest to many was the potential of an undiscovered land mass in the Arctic. The idea captured Byrd's imagination, as well. Because of a series of unfortunate setbacks to several of the better-known Arctic explorers of the day, Byrd found himself in a position to consider seriously the notion of accompanying such an expedition, or maybe leading his own.

Byrd was assigned to duty in Washington, D. C., in January 1924 to help prepare an airship, the *Shenandoah*, for a flight across the Polar Sea. However, the expedition was canceled for political reasons. Byrd was reassigned to other duties in Washington, and later in Boston, New York, and Chicago. However, he'd impressed his superiors in the capital, and by the end of the year, he was working at various jobs on Capitol Hill representing the interests of the Navy Department in Congress.

While there, Byrd dreamed of organizing his own expedition north to search out new lands in the Polar Sea. Initially, his interests led him to be teamed with Donald MacMillan on an expedition to northwest Greenland. Under MacMillan, Byrd flew thousands of miles on reconnaissance missions in amphibious biplanes. Much new land was discovered, especially on Ellesmere Island. On this expedition Byrd became the first flyer to cross the Greenland ice sheet, a feat he accomplished on August 22, 1925.

In his memoir *Skyward: Man's Mastery of the Air*, Byrd identified two reasons for his desire to fly to the North Pole. The first was the same desire held by earlier expeditions: "we might discover some new land or unexpected scientific phenomena." The second reason was equally compelling: "a successful flight would, like the first crossing of the Atlantic, be sure to accelerate public interest in aviation" (Byrd 1928).

After his Greenland experiences, it became clear to Byrd that the best way to explore the far north was to launch his own expedition with private sponsorship. Thus, Byrd's first order of business was financing the expedition. With the help of his connections in the Navy and Washington, he began the search for funding. Before long, he had secured the interest and investment of a score of prominent Americans, including Edsel Ford, John D. Rockefeller Jr., and Vincent Astor. A large number of companies also provided supplies and equipment. Yet by the time the expedition was under way, Byrd had spent over $100,000 but had raised just over $74,000, despite their backing and that of others. He was personally liable for the balance, and this fact weighed upon him heavily.

Byrd and his expedition staff, including Floyd Bennett, Robb Oertel, and "Rex" Noville, worked tirelessly in the months leading up to their departure. A crew needed to be hired and fed for the length of the long voyage; equipment and supplies had to be obtained, transported, warehoused, and stowed. An airplane had to be acquired for the polar flight. Byrd obtained for $25,000 the prototype of a Fokker trimotor plane. He named her the *Josephine Ford*, in honor of Edsel Ford's youngest.

Besides the airplane, a suitable vessel had to be found to transport the expedition to its aerial departure point. Byrd knew that surplus vessels retired by the United States Shipping Board (U. S. S. B.) after the war represented excellent value. He requested that a steamer be leased to the expedition for one dollar per year. The U. S. S. B. came back with the war-surplus S. S. *Chantier*. Without Byrd's offer she would have ended up as scrap, so no protests were heard about the low rate. However, the *Chantier* needed a lot of repairs to bring her up to standard after floating idle for five years. Byrd put Rex Noville in charge of refurbishing her.

The *Josephine Ford*, May 9, 1926. Byrd Arctic Expedition's North Polar plane. *Courtesy of Jean Neptune.*

Insurance proved difficult to obtain for the *Chantier*, but Byrd eventually prevailed. He had to accept a provision that nothing would be paid unless it was a total loss and claims exceeded $150,000. In the end, "Byrd paid $3,876 down, one dollar for the ship and three thousand eight hundred and seventy-five dollars for insurance coverage for the first four months" (Bart 2013).

It was decided that the jumping-off point for the polar flight would be Spitsbergen, about seven hundred miles north of Norway and the largest and only permanently populated island of Norway's Svalbard archipelago. The tiny community of King's Bay or Kongsfjorden (today called Ny-Ålesund, 78°56' N 11° 56' E) was chosen as the launching site for both Byrd's and Roald Amundsen's attempts to reach the pole. The village is adjacent to a fine harbor on the western side of Spitsbergen. It is only about 770 miles to the pole from King's Bay.

Byrd scholar and former OSU archivist Raimond Goerler notes that Spitsbergen was an excellent choice as a jumping-off point for aerial exploration of the North Pole. One of the principal reasons for choosing Spitsbergen as a departure point was because in addition to its northerly location, its harbor was ice-free relatively early in the year. The same warm Gulf Stream currents that helped break up the ice also made reaching the northern Svalbard archipelago relatively safe from the eastern United States.

The crew of the expedition was hand-picked by Byrd and his top assistants. It included a variety of men, some of who would perform specific technical expeditionary roles in Spitsbergen. However, during the voyage to Norway, all were expected to serve as members of the crew of the S. S. *Chantier*.

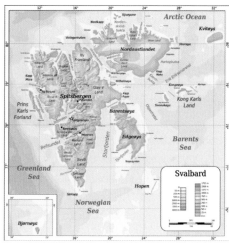

Byrd hired Michael J. Brennan to serve as captain. Brennan wrote:

Of the 52 men on board when we sailed only nine had seagoing experience: Pilot Floyd Bennett, U. S. Navy, myself, Chief Engineer Thomas B. Mulroy (now Commander, U. S. Navy, serving in the Pacific); 1st Mate Frank deLucca *[sic]*, a former Navy 'bluejacket'; 2nd Mate James B. Slaughter; 3rd Mate Edward J. Nolan; Boatswain James V. Madison (an old navy shipmate of the Admiral); Aviation Machinist's Mate Leo M. Paterson *[sic]*, U. S. Navy, and G. O. Noville, Flight Engineer (Brennan 1945).

Brennan's recollection was not strictly accurate. Konter, among several other Navy veterans, had sailed the seven seas. However, most of them were just sailors, not officers.

On February 8, 1926, Byrd wrote to ask Konter if he would volunteer for the expedition:

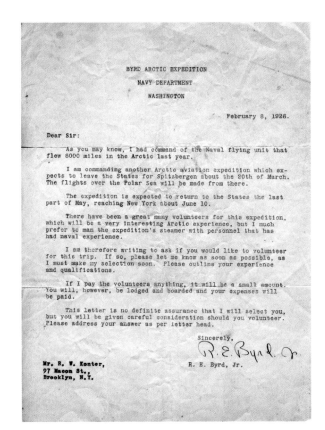

Letter from Richard E. Byrd to Richard Konter dated February 8, 1926. Byrd asks that Konter apply as a volunteer on his upcoming Arctic expedition. *National Archives and Records Administration, Richard W. Konter Papers.*

There have been a great many volunteers for this expedition, which will be a very interesting Arctic experience, but I much prefer to man the expedition's steamer with personnel that has had naval experience.

At the time of Byrd's letter, Konter was working at the Guaranty Trust Co. of New York (Telegram, Konter to Byrd, March 14, 1926), but the musical sailor had other priorities:

. . . since my 30 Years naval service was over, and just as I was about to retire, my captain got me a swell job with a fine bank. Several times a week I had to carry small or large sums of money, between the bank, and other financial institutions, where I was always highly received, for the children's Ukuelel [sic] Club, unknowingly was giving me a lot of fame, I became known as Ukulele Dick, all of which I gave up, because of a coming world adventure.

Commander Richard E. Byrd, was organizing an expedition in which he hoped to be the first to fly over the north pole, and I was thrilled when I received a letter from him, in which he invited me as a member to help him. When I put in my resignation to the bank, the officers almost begged me to remain with my job, because they

Group photograph of some of the crew on board the *Chantier*. *Photo courtesy of* Expeditions: North Pole Flight, *Admiral Richard E. Byrd Papers, The Ohio State University, Byrd Polar and Climate Research Center Archival Program. PA.2012.12_56. Courtesy of Laura Kissel, polar curator.*

said, they considered me a very good worker. I politely refused to stay, because of the thought of putting Old Glory over the North Pole, first (R. W. Konter, *Adventure Ahoy! Part II*, Konter Files, National Archives and Records Administration, College Park, Maryland).

Years later Brennan recalled, "And what a crew we had! Never did a more happy-go-lucky crew go down to the sea in a ship!" (Brannan 1945). Konter saw things a little differently. He writes of an event of April 4, 1926, the day before the expedition left Brooklyn:

Richard Konter with members of Dick's Ukulele Club on board the *Chantier*, Brooklyn Navy Yard, 1926. *Courtesy of Jean Neptune.*

Others had volunteered, and our first job was to be members of the crew of Byrd's expedition steamer, *Chantier*, and one would think that on an adventure such as this that there would have been a certain amount of comradeship between the volunteers, and the officers, but after it was too late, I found that it was everything but.

The *Chantier* was tied up to a dock in the navy yard, in Brooklyn N.Y. without notice my kids appeared on the dock, broke out the ukes, and began to sing popular songs, in no time the dock was jammed with yard workmen, who were fascinated, with the children, I invited them aboard where they put on a show. They made a big hit with the crew, and Byrd, who couldn't sing their praises enough and added that what the children had done was a big morale builder. A few of the crew told me confidentially they were going to quit, but the children gave them such inspiration they decided to stick it out (R. W. Konter, *Adventure Ahoy! Part II*, Konter Files, National Archives and Records Administration, College Park, Maryland).

Also among the crew was Byrd's much-loved dog, Igloo (Walden 1931), (Seiple 2013). He had been given to Byrd before the expedition by Dr. Anita Maris Boggs of Washington, D. C., to whom he was known as "Dynamite." However, the fox terrier's name soon morphed permanently into Igloo. He became Byrd's trusted companion and close to many of the crew, including Konter.

Igloo, Richard Byrd's dog.
NARA, Epaminondas J.
Demas Papers, 1923–1979.
National Archives and
Records Administration,
College Park, Maryland.

Not his master's voice: Richard Konter serenades
Igloo, Byrd's dog. National Archives and Records
Administration, Richard W. Konter Papers,
XRWK - A1 131 (2 boxes).

The hard work of loading the expedition's equipment fell to the largely inexperienced crew of the *Chantier*, as well as a detachment of sailors released by the Navy Department to assist in moving, loading, and stowing gear. In all, "The *Chantier* carried two airplanes and their fuel, food to sustain the expedition for six months, and enough coal for fifteen thousand miles, or half again as much as Byrd expected to need . . ." (Byrd and Goerler 1998):147. The Fokker plane and its spare parts dominated the forward hold of the *Chantier*. Special care was taken to avoid damaging the fragile wing.

A huge throng was on hand when the hour finally arrived for the *Chantier* to weigh anchor. Amid a flurry of dignitaries and personal farewells, the *Chantier* cast off from Berth 10 at Clinton Avenue in the Brooklyn Navy Yard on April 5, 1926, at 3:15 p.m.

Konter somehow managed to take (or have taken) a photo of the *Chantier* steaming down the Hudson River just beneath the Brooklyn Bridge with the Manhattan skyline in the background. If, as it appears, Konter took this photo himself, he would have been able to rejoin the *Chantier* later that day off Fort Hamilton, Brooklyn, which was the first overnight anchorage. Fort Hamilton wasn't far from their embarkation point. This unplanned stop was made after Captain Brennan realized that, in the craziness of their departure from Brooklyn, many crates of the expedition's cargo remained unsecured on deck, loaded on board but not stowed properly. These crates could become lethal projectiles or lost overboard in high seas, so the crew set about making the cargo seaworthy. Byrd wrote,

The ship is in an entirely disorganized condition and there are a lot of green men in the crew. But they are a high type all around and I predict that it won't take long to get fairly well organized. (Byrd 1928)

Despite their work ethic, the crew of the *Chantier* overall could reasonably be described as half-assed sailors. Few had prior seagoing experience, and few took to it well. In his diary entry for April 13, 1926, Byrd observed:

Loading expedition cargo onto the *Chantier* for the voyage to Spitsbergen. *Photo courtesy of* Expeditions: North Pole Flight, *Admiral Richard E. Byrd Papers, The Ohio State University, Byrd Polar and Climate Research Center Archival Program. PA.2012.12_408. Courtesy of Laura Kissel, polar curator.*

Loading the smaller expedition plane onto the *Chantier*, Brooklyn Navy Yard, 1926. *Public domain.* Original Acme News photo in *C. F. Martin & Co. archives.*

[W. W] Ehrgott, one of the West Pointers, has been in the mess room. Hates it and has broken over twenty dishes. Put him on deck and tried him out at the wheel. He did very well until the captain came on the bridge when he was 80 degrees off the course. I bet his bawling out beat anything he ever got at West Point.

Several memorable stories have been told regarding Captain Brennan's less-than-charitable words for some on his crew when, for example, the captain and Byrd were awakened one night by a warning from the watch about a "light, dead ahead!" An imminent collision was narrowly averted when someone observed that the light turned out to be Venus, the evening star. For an electrician's mate, Konter was quite impressive at the helm and proved to be one of the crew's most linear thinkers.

On the way to Norway, the *Chantier* was moving extremely slowly because of the large, poorly distributed weight of the coal in the ship's holds. Byrd wrote in his diary entry for April 15, 1926:

We are still so low by the stern that we have decided to move the coal from no. 3 hold, one of the after holds, to the starboard and midship bunker. We filled this hold with 900 tons of coal in order to have enough of coal to get to Spitzbergen and back to New York without coaling. Everyone on board including the Pathe news men, except the doctor, have turned to at the important job. The spirit of the men is great (Byrd 1928).

The *Chantier*, the Byrd Arctic Expedition steamer, leaving New York Harbor en route to Kings Bay, Spitsbergen. Photo by Richard Konter, *Courtesy of Jean Neptune.*

Konter, again writing from the perspective of the crew, saw things a little differently:

Because of the long voyage to Kings Bay, things proved that had the *Chantier* been manned by regular seamen, even if they had been paid they would have been within their rights to refuse to do what we volunteers did, without a murmer. The *Chantier*, was unevenly loaded, the forward hole held only the Fokker plane, and its spare parts, while in the after hole there was 900 extra tons of coal.

On our way to Spitsbergen, the ship's bunkers were getting emptier, and had to be refilled by the coal in the after hole. For this reason about six volunteers want down the after hole, and filled a barrel with 100 pounds of coal, that was then hoisted to the top deck. Here it was dumped on the deck where six other volunteers shovelled it into the nearest empty bunker, which work was done five days a week. before signing on we were not told that th.is was part of the program, but which we volunteers did without complaining (R. W. Konter, *Adventure Ahoy! Part II*, Konter Files, National Archives and Records Administration, College Park, Maryland).

Byrd boarding the *Chantier. Public domain. Bain News Service photo, Library of Congress Prints and Photographs Division.*

On April 24, 1926, the *Chantier* anchored near Trondheim, Norway, to send a stowaway home and take on three new expedition members. The stowaway passenger, Malcolm P. Hanson, was a radio engineer entrusted by Byrd to get the radio operational on the *Chantier* before they embarked for Spitsbergen. However, the radio was not ready in time, and Hanson stowed away without leave from the Navy. Byrd, using his connections, explained the situation to his superiors, who surprisingly looked upon it favorably. No disciplinary action would be taken as long as Hanson was put on a ship home as soon as possible. Hanson was put onto a tugboat and exchanged for three new crew members: William Bird of *The New York Times*; Isak Isaksen, an ice pilot; and Leslie Wyand of Pathé Gazette. Bird brought along a Primus stove, an item neglected by the outfitters of the emergency gear Byrd and Bennett would need in case they had to ditch the plane during the polar flight.

Twenty-two days out from New York Harbor, the *Chantier* began sailing past floating ice. The twenty-four-day outbound voyage of the *Chantier* ended on April 29, 1926, as she entered King's Bay after radioing ahead, requesting a berth alongside the dock.

Aside from his job as an able-bodied seaman, Konter relished his role as an entertainer on board the *Chantier*, and a March 15, 1926 letter from the expedition's fourth-in-command, Robb C. Oertel, to Konter (NARA, Konter Archive), confirms Konter's appointment to the expedition as a seaman. Oertel concludes his letter with the sentence, "Thank you for your suggestion about musical instruments. We will do our best."

Konter writes:

Since I played simple tunes on several musical instruments, I took along a mandolin, and two ukuleles. In less than a week I had two of the volunteers playing the ukes, and they were doing so well that we decided to serenade Byrd, up in his cabin.

While standing in front of his cabin door, I was playing the mandolin, while the other two, strummed on the ukuleles, Byrd came out to see what the music was. He was surprised to see the three of us playing our instruments, and invited us into the cabin, where we continued to entertain him. During our stay here he told us about his coming flight to the pole, then thanked us for the concert, after which we returned to our quarters (Konter, R. W. Adventure Ahoy! Part I.)

Richard Konter at the helm of the *Chantier*, Byrd Arctic Expedition. *Photo courtesy of* Expeditions: North Pole Flight, *Admiral Richard E. Byrd Papers, The Ohio State University, Byrd Polar and Climate Research Center Archival Program. PA.2012.12_43. Courtesy of Laura Kissel, polarcurator.*

There is documentary and photographic evidence of both of these ukuleles aboard the *Chantier*. Two ukuleles can be seen together in the same crew photo on the *Chantier*, one being played by Robb Oertel and the other by Dick Konter.

We can also document at least one chromatic Hohner harmonica in a photograph of Konter and Bennett, and again in two photographs of Konter and Igloo. Additionally, an inscription on the ukulele (now gone) refers to a harmonica, as well (see below). *The North Adams Transcript* (North Adams, Massachusetts) newspaper of Saturday, June 26, 1926 (page 8), published a wire photo also seen in *The Decatur Herald* (Decatur, Illinois) of Monday, June 28, 1926 (page 10), of Konter playing for Igloo, who is posed hanging out of a porthole. Konter is strumming a ukulele and has a harmonica in his mouth. The caption states, "They're first uke and first mouth organ to fly over the pole, for both were in Byrd's plane."

Also at Spitsbergen at the same time as the Byrd Arctic Expedition was another expedition, co-organized by explorer Roald Amundsen, at the time the most famous polar explorer in the world. His 1911 dogsled conquest of the South Pole had secured his place in history when he beat the ill-fated British expedition led by Robert Falcon Scott (Solomon 2001). Along with Amundsen was American polar explorer and co-sponsor Lincoln Ellsworth.

Their goal was to fly, with a sixteen-man crew, a dirigible called the *Norge* from Spitsbergen over the North Pole,

Group photograph of some of the crew on board the *Chantier*. Provisional identifications made by Larry Bartram by cross-referencing other photos from many sources. *Courtesy of Jean Neptune.*

and then continue on to explore the roughly one million square miles of unknown area between the North Pole and their ultimate destination, Point Barrow, Alaska (Amundsen and Ellsworth 1927; Bown 2012).

Amundsen chose an airship over a heavier-than-air craft for several reasons. Dirigibles had greater range, were better platforms for making navigational measurements, and were safer and more reliable (". . . an airship floats in the air even if all the motors should fail" [Amundsen and Ellsworth 1927]).

Amundsen had not forgotten the twenty-six days he and Ellsworth had spent trapped on the ice the previous year, when one of their two Dornier Wal seaplanes failed mechanically. The Norwegian contingent of the expedition's crew included helmsman Oscar Wisting, navigator Hjalmar Riiser-Larsen, elevatorman Emil Horgen, radio expert Birger Gottwaldt,

The Hohner "Chromonica" chromatic harmonica. Ti to the neck of Konter's signed ukulele, this model of harmonica was the first of two musical instruments tc fly to the North Pole. *Photo by author.*

meteorologist Finn Malmgren, journalist Fredrik Ramm, radioman Fridtjof Storm-Johnsen, and flight engineer Oscar Omdal. Amundsen knew and trusted these men, and they admired him greatly.

Amundsen's expedition had purchased the *Norge* at a discount from the Italian government of Benito Mussolini. The airship's designer was Umberto Nobile, who had designed airships previously for the Italian air force. Nobile's dirigibles were somewhat smaller than the norm, but their range was nearly as great. Amundsen selected Nobile to be a member of the expedition because of his expertise and familiarity with the craft. In turn, Nobile selected a group of his own countrymen to help fly the airship. The Italian contingent rounded out the *Norge* crew and included chief mechanic Natale Cecioni, rigger Renato Alessandrini, and mechanics Ettore Arduino, Attilio Caratti, and Vincenzo Pomella.

Norway's greatest polar explorer: Roald Engelbregt Gravning Amundsen (1872–1928).

The airship *Norge* in flight after leaving its hangar in 1926. *Public domain.* Library of Congress, George Grantham Bain collection.

On April 21, 1926, Amundsen and Ellsworth arrived in King's Bay to await the arrival of their airship. To assist in Amundsen's attempt to reach the pole, the Norwegian government sent a gunboat, the *Heimdahl*.

Amundsen and Byrd knew one another's plans, and the two explorers had maintained a cordial personal relationship. Byrd, Amundsen, and Ellsworth had met in Washington, D. C., on October 21, 1925. At that meeting, Byrd had told the other men of his hopes for the following spring, and Amundsen and Ellsworth assured Byrd of their help.

Despite this, a huge disappointment awaited Byrd upon their arrival at King's Bay on April 29, 1926—despite radioing ahead to the Norwegians to announce their arrival the following day. Konter described the scene:

After about 30 days at sea, the ship finally reached Kings Bay, Spitsbergen, and we were now 700 miles or so from the north pole, we immediately saw that Byrd had a rival here, for half way up on a distant hill, we could see a large hanger. This told us that it would eventually be a world race between Byrd, and Amundsen, to see who would be the first to get to the north pole.

Norge crew aboard *Victoria*, the vessel brought them from Nome to Seattle after their successful crossing of the Polar Sea. In back row, Navigator Riiser-Larsen; journalist Ramm; Gottwaldt, who provided radio communications; Wisting as a elevation rudder operator; mechanic Omdal; meteorologist Malmgren; ranger Alessandrini; Storm-Johnsen, who provided radio communications; chief mechanic Cecioni; mechanic Arduino; mechanic Caratti; and mechanic Pomella. In the front row are expedition leader Amundsen, Ellsworth, and pilot Nobile. The picture was probably taken by Emil Horgen, who was an assistant in the navigation and took pictures along the way. *Public domain. The National Library of Norway.*

Some of the Norwegian and Italian crew members of the *Norge* on board the *Victoria*. From the left are Arduino, Cecioni, Wisting, Ramm, Storm-Johnsen, Gottwaldt, Pomella, Caratti, Alessandrini, and Horgen. The Italian members pictured are Arduino, Cecioni, Pomella, Caratti, and Alessandrini. *Public domain.* The National Library of Norway.

Amundsen, and his American financial backer, and his ground crew of 200 young Italians, and Norweigans, were living in a nearby mining town, where they were waiting for the dirigable, *Norge*, to arrive from Italy. In the meantime we saw that Byrd wasn't any too welcome here for there were two big signs on the dock that read: "No cameras, or pictures to be taken ashore", and "No landing without permission" signed Amundsen, and from what came later we knew he meant business.

The Norwegian gunboat *Heimdahl* was tied up at the only pier at which the *Chantier* could have docked and unloaded. Byrd was furious, but there was little to be done. Despite assurances from Amundsen himself, the *Chantier's* crew had to come up with an effective plan B. Byrd, a normally cautious man, overruled the objections of his officers. Konter describes what happened next:

Tied up to the only dock in the bay, was the Norweigan gun-boat Heimdal, taking on a load of coal, and that same evening she was fully loaded and her crew were now idling about the decks. Byrd, asked Amundsen permission to use the dock to land his plane, but was told that the gun-boat had to use the dock to take on coal. We knew this answer was a ruse to keep Byrd from using the dock, so the captain Brannan of the *Chantier* tried to use the dock anyway.

The captain ran the *Chantier* alongside of the Heimdahl, where he tried to tie up to the dock, but unfortunately the much larger steamer was unable to remain alongside of the small gunboat, so he had to return to the bay and anchor there again, now we ran into more headaches.

Unfortunately there were no tugs, or barges, to hire in this isolated part of the world, so we did the next best thing, by using the *Chantier's* four life-boats. After lowering them we lashed them together in twos, than tied each pair, one behind the other, and thus made a sort of improvised pontoon, after which the acting carpenter, a volunteer seaman, built a platform on it, and used it as a home-made barge.

We ran the pontoon up against the port, forward side of the *Chantier*, where it was held in place by suitable ropes and the plane's spare parts placed aboard after which, with the help of the steam which. the fusalege was hoisted up out of the fore hold, and placed aboard the -toon, after which came the ticklish job, of putting on the Fokker's big wings. (Fokker was the name of Byrd's plane.)

The wing was made of ply-wood, and regardless of its size it was very light, and for this reason it had to be handled with the utmost care. With the help of the steam winch, the huge wing was hoisted out of the fore hole, then swung towards the port side, and lowered carefully to the fusalage, and now came another ticklish job, or alining the fusalege's four holes, with the four on the wing, to which steel bolts, were placed through, the steel nuts, screwed on, and what a big releif it was when this was safely done. (R. W. Konter, *Adventure Ahoy! Part II*, Konter Files, National Archives and Records Administration, College Park, Maryland)

Konter continues, describing the perilous voyage of the pontoon to the shoreline of King's Bay:

Now that was over, the next one was to get the pontoon ashore to the beach through the ice of the frozen over bay. Fortunately, luck and the Almighty was with us, for the bay water was salty, and the ice was soft and mushy, which made it rather easy to work through it, and we finally got it to the beach, where there was an ice wall about eight feet high, which we would have to lift the plane.

Previously we had landed a small plane that was used for local flying, and I had been detailed to remain ashore to watch it, and other expedition gear that might be landed. While on duty here I used an ax to chop a small improvised runway from the ice wall, to a spot about twenty feet back of it. Since I had chopped about four feet off the ice wall, this spot was used to land the plane, after which Byrd, congratulated me for my forethought.

With the planes and gear safely on shore and the *Chantier* anchored safely in King's Bay, getting the *Josephine Ford* off the ground proved a challenge. On one nearly catastrophic attempt, the weight of the plane and the soft, patchy condition of the "runway" caused a landing ski to sink into the snow and break. It had to be replaced. Sometime later, Konter wrote:

. . . we were horrified to see it headed for the frozen over bay, at great speed, strangely what would have caused a disaster really prevented it. Since the plane had no brakes to stop it, the left ski sunk into a soft spot, which eased the plane's headway somewhat, but its momentum caused its tail to shoot skyward, and looked as if it surely would topple into the bay on its back. Fortunately the sunken ski held, and the plane dropped back safely, much to the relief of everybody . . .

Ferrying the *Josephine Ford* from the *Chantier* ashore in Kings Bay. The ship's lifeboats were lashed together to make a barge on which the plane could be ferried. Photo by Richard W. Konter, 1926. *Courtesy of Jean Neptune.*

Byrd needed to repair the plane if there was to be a flight to the North Pole. It has been said that a member of the *Norge*'s ground crew, Norwegian aviator Bernt Balchen, provided critical help to the Byrd Arctic Expedition when they needed it most, but this has been disputed (e.g., Bart 2013). The *Chantier*'s carpenter "Chips" Gould and others repaired the damaged aircraft skis with wooden supports from the *Chantier*'s lifeboat oars. The repaired skis worked perfectly. The idea for the repair and its supervision have been said to have been Balchen's. Bart (2013) reminds us there is no contemporary account of this and, strictly speaking, that seems true. Yet, some years after the expedition, Konter wrote:

> Instead of remaining in the mining village with Amundsen's ground crew, waiting for the Norge, Bernt Balchen, who was and expert plane engineer, and an authority of skis, did help Byrd, only when seriously needed by the American Commander . . .
>
> Byrd never forgot the help Balchen gave him, when he was having trouble with the skis, so when he was about to return to America, he invited Balchen to come along. Since Balchen was waiting to go back to his Norway, instead he accepted Byrd's invitation to come aboard the *Chantier* that was about to return to New York, and that's the true story about Bernt Balchen. (Konter, R. W. [Undated]. *Adventure Ahoy! Part II*, National Archives and Records Administration, Konter Files, College Park, Maryland).

Other expressions of cooperation were evident between the rival expeditions. Amundsen's genuine admiration for the determination exhibited by Byrd and the other American expedition members is illustrated in a photograph, one of Konter's most treasured possessions.

As mentioned above, Byrd tried to pare the plane's cargo and fuel load before the polar flight. So, imagine his surprise when Konter's ukulele made in onto the plane, nevertheless:

> One little discovery I made was interesting, also characteristic of the truly boyish spirit that prevailed throughout. In searching the plane for gear with which we might dispense and so lighten her, I found that nearly every man on the expedition had hidden some souvenir aboard. No doubt this weight was a factor in keeping us from taking off. However, I never did find a ukelele [sic] secreted aboard by the

notorious "Ukelele Ike" [sic] Konter. He produced it out of the plane after we returned from the Pole and now has it back home as a wonderful souvenir of the trip (Byrd 1928:182).

Byrd mistakenly referred to Konter as "Ukulele Ike," unaware that nickname belonged to another player, Cliff Edwards (who helped make the song "Singin' in the Rain" famous). Ukulele Dick didn't mind the notoriety, though. Byrd's account of discovering souvenirs on the *Josephine Ford* leaves out one important detail—how pilot Floyd Bennett managed to get the ukulele on the plane. Konter fills in the story:

One day just before the flight to the pole, was to take place I confidentially asked Bennett, if he would take my ukulele aboard the plane, with him on the coming adventure. I remained aboard the *Chantier* while he took the uke ashore with him, and hid it somewhere in the plane, this was one of the best Ukuleles of all times, it was made by Martin. Just before the take off, all the volunteers went ashore to see the start of what we all hoped would be a historical flight, with Bennett at the stick. We all stood at points of vantage, at the base up on the

"As for Amundsen, and his secret feeling against Byrd, we felt that perhaps it included us also, but we found that we were badly mistaken, for he was very friendly towards us volunteers. One day he joined us in a friendly conversation, and I asked him if he would pose with me in a picture, I would like to take of him, he warmly replied, 'Why certainly my man; where do you want me to stand'? This picture is now one of my treasured memories of him, and more so because he is holding my arm in a friendly gesture." —Richard Konter. Left to right: Willard Van der Veer (?), Charles Kessler, Amundsen, Frank Fritzon, Richard Konter, Robert McKay. *Courtesy of Jean Neptune.*

hill, and when the plane started moving we didn't cheer, and little did we realize that we were about to see an almost disaster (R. W. Konter, *Adventure Ahoy! Part II*, Konter Files, National Archives and Records Administration, College Park, Maryland).

In this passage, Konter's regard for Martin's instruments is clear. So is the manner by which the ukulele got back on the plane after Byrd had previously lightened the load. After a few false starts, the *Josephine Ford* was airborne, carrying pilot Bennett, navigator Byrd, and Konter's Martin ukulele into history.

Much has been written about Byrd's polar flight concerning the most fundamental controversy of the expedition: Did the *Josephine Ford* actually make it to 90° north? In our opinion, the most comprehensive overview is presented by Sheldon Bart in his excellent book *The Race to the Top of the World*. In conducting research for his book, Bart reviewed personally everything that Byrd's detractors had seen and much they had not. Chapters 22 and 23 of his book ("The Grassy Knoll of Aviation I" and "The Grassy Knoll of Aviation II") are an exposition of the origins of the controversy, the protagonists, the relevant evidence, and why, in the end, Bart concludes the veracity of Byrd's assertion that he and Bennett reached the North Pole. We agree with his conclusion.

Upon the return of the flyers, celebration reigned in King's Bay even among the crew of the *Norge*. Konter recalls:

The next morning a little after six oclock we were awakened by one blast after the other of the *Chantier's* big steam whistles that the mate up on the bridge blew, which told us that the plane had been sighted, and bedlam broke loose among us. We all jumped out of our bunks and without stopping to fully dressed, we ran out onto the exposed cold deck. Here we were now a rather amusing sight for no one was wearing trousers, and a few had on sweaters or overcoats, while we were all standing in our underwear. But the sight was worth it for in the distance, we saw the returning plane, heading for the *Chantier*, whose steam whistle kept blasting away.

The Norweigan gunboat Heimdahl's steam whistle also kept blowing as did a small donkey engine up on a nearby hill, that sounded like a peanut whistle, In 1908, I was aboard the New Jersey, when the 16 American battleships made the famous world cruise, and when the fleet entered some ports every thing ashore, and afloat that had a whistle, blew them, but it couldn't beat the enthusiasm that now prevailed here at Kings Bay's three whistles, that welcomed Byrd's return from the North Pole.

Just now I was frantic because I couldn't sight the plane in my camera, as Byrd flew directly over the *Chantier*, so I pointed the camera skyward blindly and snapped the trigger, and hoped! Days later while the ship was on her way home, we stopped at London, where I had the roll developed, and lo, the plane was almost in the center of the film, and the picture is now a part of history.

As noted above, Konter had not been at the landing site, but was on the *Chantier* when the polar aviators returned. After Byrd and Bennett's flight, the aviators were returned by boat to the *Chantier,* whose crew was ecstatic at their achievement. After the celebration died down, the two aviators took some much-needed rest. Konter described the moment when, hours after the flight, Floyd Bennett returned the ukulele to him. Konter continues:

Richard Byrd and Floyd Bennett being ferried to the *Chantier* for some well-deserved sleep after their successful polar flight. Photo by Richard Konter. *Courtesy of Jean Neptune.*

About eight hours later Bennett arose, and invited me to go ashore with him, for a very good reason and one that thrilled me, or, to get my ukulele that was now famous as the only musical instrument that had been to the north pole. When Byrd saw the uke, he congradulated me and autographed it, as other famous men eventually did, such as Thomas Edison, President cooledge, and plently of others, and they all said the same thing "That they were proud to put their names on such a famous instrument" (R. W. Konter, *Adventure Ahoy! Part II*, Konter Files, National Archives and Records Administration, College Park, Maryland).

Floyd Bennett (in reindeer coat) returns the polar ukulele to Richard Konter after the successful polar flight. Charles Kessler (at left, also in a reindeer coat) and Leo M. Peterson (at right) look on off the *Josephine Ford. Courtesy of Jean Neptune.*

After the successful polar flight, the Byrd Arctic Expedition stopped in London for a few days to catch up on messages. They departed London on June 4, and the voyage home was uneventful. Konter wrote:

After the ship left Kings Bay, she finally reached a point off the northwestern coast of Norway, around midnight, where we saw one of the world's most interesting sights that proved we were in the land of the Midnight Sun" There on the crest of a low mountain was the sun, a big, red ball of fire, with no glare, so that we could look right into it, the sight of a life time, or the sun at midnight.

The *Chantier* headed for England where she stopped at London, for a few days, then headed for America The Beautiful, and while crossing the Atlantic Ocean, the fast British passenger steamer Muritania, passed us, not once, but four times. The *Chantier*, was lucky if she could make nine knots, and first time the Muritana, passed us was on her way to New York Bay, and the second time, she was on her way back to England. And the third time, was on her way to New York again, and the fourth time was returning to England.

Because the expedition was to break up, after our return to New York City the *Chantier's* captain invited us volunteers to the cabin, and asked me to bring along my Ukulele. We first had community singing,

Spruced up for a night on the town. Some of the crew of the *Chantier* upon their arrival in London, a few days before June 4, 1926. Photo shows: Thomas Kinkade, Robb C. Oertel, Floyd Bennett, William C. Haines, unknown sailor, Thomas Mulroy, Capt. Michael Brennan, and James Madison. *Used with permission, Admiral Richard E. Byrd Papers, The Ohio State University, Byrd Polar and Climate Research Center Archival Program. PA.2012.12_82.*

Richard Konter, seaman, aboard the *Chantier*. *Used with permission,* Expeditions: North Pole Flight, *Admiral Richard E. Byrd Papers, The Ohio State University, Byrd Polar and Climate Research Center Archival Program. PA.2012.12_284.*

during which the captain made us smile, for he couldn't carry a tune, and a frog in his throat made him sound as if he was croaking.

The gathering turned out to be more pleasant than we had expected for the captain gave us a nice talk, and thanked us for our loyalty to the expedition and Byrd, and to him also. He wound up his talk and flattered us by saying that we had made the expedition the success it was, after which. we left with the kindliest feeling of good will, toward him.

Konter was photographed on board the *Chantier* with Igloo in his lap, a Hohner chromatic harmonica in his mouth, and strumming the ukulele that now clearly bears signatures of some of the Norwegian expedition members.

As the *Chantier* reached U. S. waters and steamed toward New York Harbor, the first greetings came on the morning of June 22 from the tugboat *Aries*, carrying representatives of Acme Newspictures. The *Aries* met the *Chantier* near Ambrose Light in lower New York Bay (40.46°N 73.83°W) to get the first photos of the returning heroes. In the photograph, the crew seems delighted at the attention, with many shouting and waving to the photographers and crew on the *Aries* off their port side. Even Igloo looks on from on deck, standing at Geisler's feet.

Richard Konter and Igloo, on the deck of the *Chantier*. Konter plays a Hohner Chromonica and the partially signed ukulele. *Acme Press photo. Courtesy of Tom Walsh.*

The *Chantier* arriving at the mouth of New York Harbor near Ambrose Light after the successful expedition. The ship is greeted by the tugboat *Aries*, hired by Acme Newspictures to photograph the expedition's return. June 22, 1926. *Public domain. Acme Press photo from C. F. Martin & Co. archives.*

The *Chantier* entered New York Harbor later that morning. She was met by the steamer *Macom*, the mayor of New York's tug/yacht. The *Macom* had been built in 1894 at Sparrow's Point, Maryland. Formerly a New York police boat called the *Patrol*, her new name was short for "Mayor's Committee," an outfit that planned many celebrations around the city, especially for Mayor James J. Walker (Cudahy 1997). On board the *Macom*, Byrd handed over to a representative of the Navy Department his records of the polar flight who, in turn, presented them to a representative of the National Geographic Society for their internal review.

The *Chantier* and some of its crew, including Igloo, greeting the *Aries*. June 22, 1926. *Public domain. Acme Press photo from C. F. Martin & Co. archives. Public domain.*

At the battery pier, mayhem ruled. The festivities began at about 10 a.m. when the *Macom* tied up next to the *Chantier*. Konter received one of the most touching honors of all—probably the most memorable and definitely the most musical welcome, as the Associated Press put it (from the Rochester, New York *Democrat and Chronicle* of June 25, 1926): ". . . 20 girls playing 20 ukes for 20 minutes greeted him at the pier." Konter made quite an impression. The following day's *New York Times* included extended coverage of Konter's reception:

"Ukulele Dick" Greeted.

While Byrd and Bennett were starting for the City Hall with their escort, other members of the Byrd expedition who had come on the *Macom* were being greeted. The greatest of these individual receptions came to Dick Konter, known as "Ukulele Dick" and author of "Dick's Ukulele Guide." Twenty young women who were formerly his pupils were lined up near Pier A playing violently on twenty ukuleles in honor of the return of their master. Dick came running off the pier flourishing in his hand a ukulele which had flown over the North Pole. Yes, sir, Dick had hidden away his ukulele inside the *Josephine Ford* and sent it as a stowaway on the trip to the top of the world and back. This distinguished instrument has not only been to North Latitude 90, but it is covered with the signatures of the world's greatest explorers—Byrd and Bennett, Amundsen, Ellsworth and Nobile and all the members of their respective parties. But still the ukulele master did not accomplish his mission and he came home unhappy. His purpose in joining the Byrd expedition was to introduce the ukulele to the Eskimos. It was not until he arrived at Spitzbergen that he learned that there was not an Eskimo on the whole blessed island. However, he organized the first ukulele class in the Arctic Circle, composed of members of the crew of the *Chantier* and of some of the Norwegian residents.

The steamer *Macom*, official yacht of the city of New York. *Used with permission,* Expeditions: North Pole Flight, *Admiral Richard E. Byrd Papers, The Ohio State University, Byrd Polar and Climate Research Center Archival Program. PA.2012.12_418.*

A ticker-tape parade ensued up lower Broadway. Byrd and Bennett marched ahead of hundreds of VIPs toward City Hall. There, Mayor Walker held forth in august company that included five U. S. senators and five U. S. representatives. After greetings and photo ops, it was off to luncheon at the Advertising Club at 23rd Street and Park Avenue.

Konter writes,

The *Chantier* finally tied up at The Battery, at the foot of New York City, where a committee of prominent citizens escorted Byrd, and Bennett, in an auto parade up Broadway, where they received the usual ticker tape reception, then met the mayor, and his staff. Byrd, and Bennett, then returned to the ship, where we volunteers were thanked for making the expedition the success it was. The expedition then broke up, and that was the last we saw of the *Chantier* . . . (R. W. Konter, *Adventure Ahoy! Part II*, Konter Files, National Archives and Records Administration, College Park, Maryland)

As challenging as the Arctic expedition had been for Byrd and his men, their return to the United States was also demanding, especially for Byrd and the expedition's leaders. Nearly everybody wanted a piece of Byrd, from fans of exploration who'd take anything they could get—an autograph or photo—to politicians hoping for a photo op, to entrepreneurial types who knew a good thing when they saw it.

By the evening of their arrival in New York City, Byrd and Bennett had already been whisked away to Washington, D. C., to receive the National Geographic Society's Hubbard Medal, presented to them by President Coolidge.

On June 25, Carnegie Hall was packed with people excited to see the polar heroes Byrd, Bennett, and most of the crew of the *Chantier*. After being introduced by the president of the American Geographical Society, Dr. John H. Finley, Byrd was given a special honorary degree, "Doctor of Latitude and Longitude."

Byrd then lectured and showed motion pictures to the assembled crowd. Afterward, many of the attendees repaired to the Winter Garden on the 24th floor of the Hotel McAlpin, where Admiral Charles Plunkett of the Navy held a reception. Konter, no doubt, had his ukulele along at Carnegie Hall.

The greatest personal recognition Konter received for his role on the successful expedition was held four days after the Carnegie Hall event. On June 29, 1926, *The New York Times* said the event that evening would be a "homecoming dinner" held in Konter's honor by the Greenwich Village

Historical Society at Gonfarone's, a restaurant-hotel at the southwest corner of MacDougal and Eighth streets (40 West 8th Street) in Greenwich Village. Konter's prescience for historical moments in his own travels, photographs, and writings might have resulted in an association with the Greenwich Village Historical Society about which, ironically, we know nothing today, but the two seem like a good fit. In any case, the society clearly thought enough of Konter to throw a big party in his honor. *The New York Times* article notes that

Mr. Konter's hobby is teaching young people how to play the ukulele. Fifty of the young people known as "Konter's Ukulele Players" will be at the Greenwich Village dinner.

Gonfarone's had a storied history. It was opened in 1894 by Catherine Gazetta Gonfarone, who started a modest restaurant in the house on the corner. The restaurant originally catered to Italian-Americans, but with the help of good prices, good food, and sound management, it attracted a wider clientele and grew to include adjoining houses. At the turn of the century, it became a favorite of neighborhood artists and writers looking for value (Harris 2003). Among them was O. Henry, who wrote of it in a 1904 short story, "A Philistine in Bohemia." He wrote, "Eating places are literary landmarks," especially inexpensive ones that were cordial to starving artists and writers.

President Calvin Coolidge with Commander Richard E. Byrd and Floyd Bennett. Washington, D. C., on June 2, 1926. Byrd received the Hubbard Gold Medal at this event. *Public domain. Photo by Harris & Ewing. Library of Congress Prints and Photographs Division. Call Number: LC-H2- B-333 [P&P] Harris & Ewing, Library of Congress.*

Interestingly, Gonfarone's also had an important role in popularizing spaghetti in America, precisely because of its bohemian associations. Jan Whitaker wrote:

> The bohemian fad for spaghetti grew stronger in the early 20th century, particularly in lower Manhattan and San Francisco. Diners flocked to Gonfarone's in Greenwich Village.

Hotel Gonfarone, 38 West 8th Street at MacDougal Street, circa 1913. *Public domain.*

Despite its low prices, the restaurant made money because a 50-cent dinner with a complimentary glass of wine cost but pennies to put on the table (Whitaker 2009).

No one could question the value of a meal at Gonfarone's. Fifty cents would get you

> [a] pint of California red wine, assorted antipasto, minestrone or spaghetti with meat or tomato sauce, choice of main dishes (boiled salmon with caper sauce; sweetbread with mushroom gravy; broiled spring chicken or roast prime ribs of beef), vegetables and salads (spinach, potatoes, green salad), a dessert (biscuit, tortoni or spumoni), fresh fruit, assorted cheeses, and coffee [a 'demi-tasse'] (Gabbacia 1998:100).

In his book on the history of bohemianism in America, Albert Parry called Gonfarone's, "a resort of scribes, artists, cranks and lovers" (Parry, et al. 1960)—just the kind of place one could imagine the globe-trotting Richard Konter would have especially enjoyed.

In their review of the event the next day, the *Times* noted that some five hundred people had attended, including Bennett and Byrd, who agreed to speak. Their arrival, and that of Konter, was greeted by sustained applause and "the ringing of miniature sleigh bells" likely to conjure associations to Santa's home. In his remarks about the quality of the crew, Byrd noted that "Konter was one of the best of the crowd and deserves the honors you are giving him tonight." Konter responded in kind, graciously telling the crowd that

We of the crew knew he (Byrd) had his troubles, and we agreed that we would keep our troubles to ourselves. So throughout the trip the crew retained its worries and tried to help. Commander Byrd always praises us, but I ask if any one who looks at these leaders can imagine a man being unwilling to follow their leadership. We got some satisfaction transporting the fliers to their point of departure, of course, but our real thrill came when we saw them returning, having accomplished their great feat.

Also in attendance at Konter's fete was the scandalous couple Edward W. Browning and his young, really young, wife, "Peaches," who were the subject of relentless tabloid scrutiny (Greenburg 2008). "Daddy and Peaches" had met at the Hotel McAlpin (Byrd's New York headquarters) on March 5, 1926, just before the expedition.

It is likely that signatures were added to the ukulele this night—*The New York Times* reported that Konter had the ukulele with him that evening:

Konter became known as the ukulele player of the crew, and carried last evening the ukulele which he took on the trip and which he hid in the plane, thus making it the first ukulele to cross the Pole.

There can be little doubt that the dinner at Gonfarone's must have been one of the proudest evenings of Konter's life. From his perspective, it probably seemed that, despite his humble origins, there was little he couldn't accomplish.

6

Between the Expeditions

DICK KONTER FOUND HIMSELF back home in New York. He was riding high on the adulation of the crowds that welcomed home the expedition members. He returned to recruiting duty as a reservist, but found time to deliver talks and musical performances on his newly autographed ukulele. He continued to seek autographs for it, a job made ever-easier by the gradual accumulation of celebrity signatures. Who wouldn't want their signature in such famous company?

Dick Konter, (aka Ukulele Dick), entertaining Pathe Film Executives, circa 1920's. *Alamy Photos.*

The day after Konter was photographed with his ukulele in Brooklyn, Byrd commended Konter's performance (NARA, Konter Archives):

Hotel McAlpin
New York City

July
Second
1926.

My dear Konter:

As our expedition is about to disband I feel that before doing so it is my duty as well as my keen pleasure to record in a letter your splendid services incident to our flight to the North Pole.

I find that one of the peculiarities of Arctic expeditions is that mens' qualities and true natures soon show themselves.

Where, in civilization, one may never really learn to know his neighbor in years of acquaintanceship, in the Arctic it is extremely difficult to cloak one's true nature even for a short time.

You came along and volunteered for this work and the fine spirit of patriotism which prompted you to do this has been evident throughout.

I shall not easily forget the splendid sportsmanship which prompted you to take a hand along with the other fellows in a hundred and one difficult jobs all of which were over and above the call of duty. The spirit of the members of our expedition is an epic in American adventure.

I, and all members of the Expedition, Konter, are greatly indebted to you. You have proved an able worker, a fine sport and a loyal gentleman and by your work and spirit have merited the wholehearted thanks of every member of the Expedition.

Yours very sincerely,

RE Byrd

On September 16, 1927, Konter received an honorable discharge from the Navy. Although he was still enjoying his celebrity as a member of the Byrd

Arctic Expedition, he was at a turning point in his career and needed to make ends meet. So, he had an idea—he would parlay his reputation as a ukulele player, arranger, writer, and bandleader into a career as an instrument retailer. To this end, on October 10, 1927, Konter wrote a letter to C. F. Martin III:

44 Berkeley Pl.,
Brooklyn, N.Y.,
Oct. 10th, '27.

Mr. Fred Martin,
Nazareth, Penna.,

Dear Sir:-

    Thru several business friends of yours in New York, who were trying to bring us together during your visits here, and who referred you to me, I am writing for a bit of very confidential information.

    I have just quit the U.S. Navy after 30 years and am very well known here in N.Y., and quite well known thruout the United States also, for several reasons. (Retired SEPT. 27, '27).

    My idea is to go into the MUSICAL INSTRUMENT GAME and I am trying to get in touch with the manufacturers who handly the better grade of instrument, and I am SPECIALIZING in the UKULELE, for regardless of all the warning I am getting from all dealers, salesmen, etc., that it is a DYING GAME, or INSTRUMENT, I SAY, IT IS NOT and I have that confidence in the UKE that I KNOW I CAN MAKE IT A GO.

    What I am after, how could I get about $500.00 worth of ukes, with a few guitars, tiples and taropatches, DIRECT FROM YOU, WITHOUT HAVING TO GO THRU THE JOBBER.

    While I can get some of the best references in the world, I am NOT after credit, as I pay as I go, and altho' there are quite a few fairly good instruments on the market, I know I am not afraid to recommend your instruments.

    Perhaps you heard of the UKULELE that was taken over the NORTH POLE by COMMANDER "BYRD" last MAY 9th, 1926? It is my uke and is creating quite a sensation even to this day as I do a great deal of entertaining and the UKE with its many autographs is a very big drawing card and ad, for it happens to be your uke. I had smuggled the uke in the plane before it took off, as I was a member of the expedition.

    I am NOT looking for any SPECIAL FAVOR, ior as I said before, I PAY AS I GO, but as the market is going backward, and with the following I have developed, I am not afraid to tackle the game and make it a go.

    Hoping that you will keep this letter confidential, as I will anything I may get from you, and hoping that I hear from you at the earliest possible date, I beg to remain,

        Very truly and sincerely,

        R. Konter

October 10, 1927 letter from Richard Konter to C. F. Martin III. *Courtesy of C. F. Martin & Co. archives.*

In this charmingly naive letter, Konter does his best to drum up support for his idea of going into business and dealing in Martin ukuleles, using his fame on the instrument as a selling point for both Martin and future customers. He stresses three points. First, he believes, despite compelling evidence to the contrary, that the ukulele is not "a DYING GAME, or INSTRUMENT, I SAY, IT IS NOT and I have that confidence in the UKE that I KNOW I CAN MAKE IT A GO." Second, Konter writes that would like to buy ". . . DIRECT FROM YOU, WITHOUT HAVING TO GO THRU THE JOBBER." Finally, he stresses that he is not after credit, somewhat confusingly writing, "I am NOT looking for any SPECIAL FAVOR, for as I said before, I PAY AS I GO, but as the market is going backward, and with the following I have developed, I am not afraid to tackle the game and make it a go."

A couple of weeks later Martin replied to Konter with the following letter:

October 26, 1927

Mr. R. W. Konter
44 Berkeley Place
Brooklyn, N.Y.

Dear Sir:

Your letters addressed to the writer personally were held until his return yesterday from an extended Western trip.

We are interested to learn that you are planning to go into the musical instrument business, and, of course, we are pleased that you wish to handle Martin instruments.

We prefer to do business direct with the dealer rather than with the distributor and will, therefore, be very glad to arrange to sell you whatever you may need whenever you are properly established. We cannot, of course, allow dealers' discount to anyone except he be regularly engaged in the retail music business and recognized as a dealer by the commercial agencies.

Perhaps you could let us know something more about your immediate plans. Have you a good location for your store, and how much capital do you expect to have available to begin your business?

We will be glad to hear further from you.

Yours very truly,

C. F. MARTIN & CO. INC.

This reply was probably all it took to take the wind out of Konter's retail sails. Retail musical instrument sales, to Martin, clearly involved more than a performer with a dream—it seemed to require a brick-and-mortar store and a bank account. Nevertheless, C. F. Martin replied to Konter on November 1 to say that he expected to be "in New York City tomorrow and will probably be in the Wurlitzer Store about four o'clock in the afternoon. Should you wish to be there about that time we will be glad to meet you and talk with you about your business plans." There is no evidence the meeting ever took place nor of Konter ever opening a retail shop.

Ukulele sales were indeed waning by the end of 1927, and Konter was back working at the bank.

On December 29, 1927, Byrd wrote to Konter with some bad news and some good news:

Byrd Antarctic Expedition
9 Brimmer Street
Boston, Mass.

December 29, 1927

Mr. R. W. Konter
44 Berkeley Place
Brooklyn, N.Y.

My dear Mr. Konter:

I am very sorry about the loss of your photographs. We went through everything I had and sent the collection among which we thought you might find yours.

I will consider very seriously taking you along on our Antarctic expedition, but cannot take you as official photographer. You would have to go in some other capacity but if I can fit you in on this expedition I will write you at a later date.

Very sincerely yours,
(Signed) RE Byrd

7

Byrd's First Antarctic Expedition

AT ITS CORE, THE FIRST Byrd Antarctic Expedition had a familiar goal: to make Americans the very first to fly above the geographic South Pole. Byrd's emerging identity as the world's foremost explorer allowed him to fund and staff the expedition, and he took the high ground when he stated that science was "the primary object of the expedition" (Rose 2008:215). Still, Byrd knew that much of the public excitement about expeditions had little to do with scientific advancement and far more to do with their danger and adventure.

In any case, the 1928–1930 expedition's agenda was more ambitious and the challenges more formidable and complex than those of the Byrd Arctic Expedition of 1926. Byrd wrote his account of the expedition as *Little America* (Byrd and Gould 1930). A more frank, historical account of the expedition based on Byrd's papers is provided in *Beyond the Barrier*, by Eugene Rodgers (Rodgers 1990). Most of the account that follows is drawn from Rodgers's excellent book.

Because of the positive impressions Konter had made on expedition leaders during the Byrd Arctic Expedition, Byrd invited Konter to join the first Byrd Antarctic Expedition team. Konter accepted, again quitting his bank job to join a second history-making effort at the ends of the earth. In Konter's words:

Before I resigned from the bank, I had been working for, as its outside man, who had to take, and pick up large sums of money, to and from, other banking institutions. Because of the great popularity of my Childrens Ukulele Club, which gave me lots of prestage, with all the offices of these banks, all of whom were very warm, and friendly to me. Now that I had been a volunteer member of Byrd's Artic Expedition,

I was all the more popular, and since the bank officers knew rich men who readily donated to worthy causes, they wanted to help Byrd, by giving me the names of these prominent people, but Byrd was not interested, when I put the proposition to him.

Konter seems puzzled and perhaps mildly annoyed that Byrd would not welcome his potential donations. He felt as if he was an integral part of Byrd's team, even if Byrd didn't regard him in the same spirit. Despite Konter's efforts to help, the class distinctions between the two men were beginning to show.

Transporting men, dogs, planes, equipment, and supplies to Antarctica was complicated and time-consuming. Four ships were required to move the expedition's men and gear into place.

The 170-foot, three-masted *City of New York* was the expedition's flagship. She was built in Arendal, Norway, in 1885 as a sealing barquentine named the *Sampson*. She was purchased by Byrd in 1927, rebuilt in New York, rerigged as a barque, and renamed. Konter was assigned by Byrd to duty on the *City of New York*. She would transport Konter and many other members of the expedition south to the Antarctic continent.

(After the expedition, the *City of New York* became a polar exploration museum, touring the Atlantic coast and the Great Lakes. In 1944, she entered service between Nova Scotia and the West Indies, and was fitted with a motor in 1947. She sank in 1962 outside Yarmouth Harbor, Nova Scotia.)

The *City of New York* under full sail. *Public domain. Photographs of Epaminondas J. Demas, 1926–1979, National Archives. National Archives Identifier 45648677.*

The master of the *City of New York* was forty-three-year old Captain F. C. Melville, a skipper who had previous experience with square-riggers. *Moby Dick's* author was a cousin of Captain Melville's father. Byrd came to dislike Captain Melville, thinking him sloppy and careless. Konter, by contrast, wrote of Melville respectfully. The latter two men probably hit it off because of Konter's own personal familiarity with wooden square-riggers of the kind first encountered in the Navy. Indeed, some years later recalling the expedition, Konter wrote:

All during my career aboard the CNY, her skipper, the chief engineer, and me, a seaman, were like three brothers, and it is with pride that I show the captain's testimonial to me. (R. W. Konter, *Adventure Ahoy! Part III*, Konter Files, National Archives and Records Administration, College Park, Maryland)

The *City of New York* left New York Harbor on August 25, 1928, arriving in Colón, Panama, on September 16. After running into engine trouble (and running out of money to pay the canal fee), she finally made it through the canal and out into the Pacific Ocean. The next leg of her voyage took her to Tahiti for re-coaling before she sailed on to New Zealand. Relatively slow, the *City of New York* was the last to arrive in Port Chalmers, New Zealand, the harbor of the South Island town of Dunedin, on November 26, 1928.

Byrd Antarctic Expedition flagship *City of New York*, Dunedin Bay, New Zealand. *Courtesy of Jean Neptune.*

Another of the expedition's four ships, the *Eleanor Bolling* (named for Byrd's mother), and her twenty-nine-man crew left New York on September 16, 1928, for Norfolk, Virginia. Due to a massive storm encountered on the way to Norfolk, the *Bolling* sailed for Tahiti on September 26, after needed repairs were completed. She met the *City of New York* in Papeete. After a three-day Tahitian layover to take on coal and other supplies, she departed for New Zealand (Rodgers 1990).

The *Eleanor Bolling*, Byrd Antarctic Expedition supply ship, off Dunedin Bay, New Zealand. *Courtesy of Jean Neptune.*

In Norfolk, the *Bolling* met the massive *C. A. Larsen*, a Norwegian whaling mother ship that Byrd had enlisted to help ferry supplies as deck load to New Zealand. The *C. A. Larsen* would sail through the canal and then north to Los Angeles. There, she would collect Byrd, fourteen men, and more supplies. She arrived in Wellington, New Zealand, on November 5, 1928. Afterward, she would hunt whales in the Southern Ocean off Antarctica, under contract to the U. S. company Procter & Gamble. The final ship was the whaler *Ross*. The fastest, she was the first of the expedition's ships to arrive at Port Chalmers. She also carried the expedition's precious dogs. Despite their importance to the expedition's success, many of the dogs suffered from diarrhea and distemper on the voyage, and several died. It was discovered later that mistakes had been made in the manufacturing of the dog food. Luckily, Igloo, Byrd's dog, had traveled with his master on the *C. A. Larsen*.

With men and supplies finally together in New Zealand, the expedition's ships left for Antarctica early Sunday morning, December 2, 1928.

The *City of New York* was towed part of the way south across the Southern Ocean by the *C. A. Larsen*, the larger ship acting as an icebreaker. Konter was a keen observer of what was happening around him, and the activities of the whalers captured his attention. In describing what he saw, including the suffering of whales who refused to leave their harpooned mates, only to die themselves, Konter wrote:

Today, with the help of chasers, factory ships return home in about four months with a load oil from 16,000 to 18,000 tons of whale oil, so, how much longer are whales going to last at that rate? Think that over . . . (R. W. Konter, *Adventure Ahoy! Part III*, Konter Files, National Archives and Records Administration, College Park, Maryland)

Perhaps annoyed by C. F. Martin & Co.'s reluctance to honor Konter's request to sell their instruments or simply because he lacked the funds,

Richard Konter (*right*) playing a Favilla harp guitar aboard the *City of New York* with expedition physician Francis Coman (*left*), who plays a Favilla ukulele, 1928. *National Archives and Records Administration, Richard W. Konter Papers, XRWK - A1 131 (2 boxes).*

Konter brought no Martin instruments with him on the southern voyage. In a photograph taken on the deck of the *City of New York* with Dr. Francis D. Coman, the expedition's physician, Konter is playing a Favilla harp guitar and Coman is strumming a Favilla ukulele.

On November 7, 1928, Konter wrote a radiogram from WFBT (the *City of New York*) to Favilla Brothers, requesting that they rush three Style 5 ukuleles and twelve Style 1 ukuleles, providing a phone number for payment and instructions.

On May 3, 1929, Konter wrote from Dunedin, New Zealand, to Favilla Brothers at 161 Bowery in New York City. He wanted to report how pleased he was with the Favilla instruments (ukuleles and bass guitar) that he'd either brought along or perhaps just received:

> Most of the cheap ones are still intact and in very fine condition several being on the ice with the commander, yours being the only ukuleles there and I am very sorry I am not there with them.

He continued:

> I have played your better grade uke against many of the high priced foreign ukes and so far I have always been able to hold my own or best the other ukes as far as tone was concerned even if they were more expensive ukes.

The *City of New York*, tied up at the edge of the Ross Ice Shelf, Bay of Whales, Antarctica. *Courtesy of Jean Neptune.*

Aerial photograph of the *City of New York*, tied up at the edge of the Ross Ice Shelf, Bay of Whales, Antarctica. Unloading tracks from crew visible to left of ship. *Courtesy of Jean Neptune.*

After reaching Antarctica at the margin of the Ross Ice Shelf at the Bay of Whales on December 28, 1928, the members of the expedition worked like slaves to unload and transport the expedition's cargo and establish the wintering-over camp of the expedition that Byrd named "Little America." (Byrd and Gould 1930).

After nearly two months of backbreaking work, Dick Konter received one of the biggest disappointments of his life: on February 22, 1929, Byrd informed Konter and others they would be leaving the winter base of Little America to sail back to Dunedin, rather than remain on "the barrier" (i.e., the Ross Ice Shelf). In *Beyond the Barrier*, Eugene Rodgers recounts the decisions facing the expedition leaders:

On 21 February, the sun dodged briefly below the horizon at midnight, signaling the beginning of a two –month-long dusk. The next day, Byrd and Gould had to carry out one of their more disagreeable tasks. It was time to cut the squad, for the *New York* would leave that day. Of the 62 men there, close to half knew whether they were staying or going—they had virtually indispensable roles at Little America or on the *New York*. The others, who longed to remain, had suffered in anguish during the final days of unloading. The men had sweated in the Battle of New York City, made plans to winter over, endured the hardships of voyaging to the ice and building Little America, and faced down the perils of sea and ice. These men had all sacrificed a substantial part of their lives for Byrd and science. Now, with most of the expedition's prizes still to be claimed, 20 men—one out of every three—had to leave.

A few of the crew were lazy, untrustworthy, selfish, or incompetent—clearly unsuitable. Some just rubbed others the wrong way, ordinarily a tolerable deficiency but a serious problem in a closely confined group. Some could well have stayed, but Byrd felt they were more useful on the ship or judged that others were better suited or had more desirable skills (Rodgers 1990:81).

Konter found himself among the twenty men who were told they would not be spending the Antarctic winter at Little America.

Why was Konter not chosen to winter over?

First, it was entirely reasonable for Byrd to regard Konter, who had spent thirty years in the Navy, first and foremost a seaman, and it was in that role that he offered the greatest value to the crew of the *City of New York* during its potentially perilous crossings of the Southern Ocean. Konter's service at the helm of the *Chantier* was probably not forgotten by Byrd, either.

Dunedin from Maori Hill, N.Z

Color postcard showing the town of Dunedin from Maori Hill, New Zealand; cancellation date unclear. Reverse includes manuscript address and message. Black ink postage cancellation and RETURN ADDRESS Aux-Bark "City of New York: Byrd Antarctic Expedition. *Public domain. Little America Antarctica (Konter) Collection, National Air and Space Museum Archives, NASM-NASM-9A12358.*

Second, the *City of New York* was a wooden, square-rigged barque. Konter had first learned his maritime skills on similar wooden sailing ships, like the *Constitution* and the *Essex*. Indeed, his days before the mast would later be a point of some pride with Konter when, in 1968, he served the U. S. Naval Ex-Apprentices Association as the editor of *Trade Winds*, the organization's newsletter for "The Survivors of Our Navy's Square-Rigger Days." Byrd, as Rodgers wrote, had to "cut the squad," and Konter's ukulele playing didn't trump his identity as a sailor. The very lives of those who were to remain at Little America depended upon the safe passage of the *City of New York* to and from New Zealand.

Third, Konter had, according to his own account, made an extremely favorable impression on the "colonial" (i.e., non-Maori) community in Dunedin, New Zealand. Thus, Byrd's decision could also have been influenced by the positive impression Konter seems to have made on the British colonial population in New Zealand upon the expedition's initial arrival from the U. S. Konter would later write:

> While here some of the expedition members imbibing a little too much, and unfortunately it left a bad impression among the colonials, which Byrd noticed. He always noticed the attentions I was receiving from colonial families, and confidentially told me to keep up my good work, because it was giving the expedition a good reputation, and promoting his name. (R. W. Konter, *Adventure Ahoy! Part III*, Konter Files, National Archives and Records Administration, College Park, Maryland)

Also, according to Konter, while at Little America, Byrd asked Konter for a special favor:

> Before we left for New Zealand, Byrd called me aside, and told me because I was a high type of man, and a strick tetotaller, he was taking me into his strickest confidence. I'm not ordering you to go back to Dunedin, and wait for us there, you have made a big hit with the colonials and the Britishers, they like you, and I want you to hold the good word for our expedition, we sure need it. He then shook my hand, and paid me other high compliments, and thanked me for being loyal to him, so I agreed to go back to Dunedin. (R. W. Konter, *Adventure Ahoy! Part III*, Konter Files, National Archives and Records Administration, College Park, Maryland)

Did this private conversation actually occur, or is it Konter trying to explain to history and himself why he was not chosen to remain and entertain the men through the long Antarctic winter? By invoking Byrd's "strickest confidence" in the passage above, was Konter trying to lessen the devastating toll his mandatory departure from the ice was taking on him?

There was also likely a fourth reason for Byrd's decision. Laura Kissel of the OSU Byrd Polar Archives told us that, later in life, Konter had suffered a breakdown and a falling-out with Byrd. Even after digging deeper into the archival record, the precise details of what happened aren't entirely clear, but the result is documented in letters both to and from Konter. For example:

We, the undersigned shipmates of Mr. Konter on the last Byrd Antarctic Expedition, know that his accusations are in the nature of spiteful complaints against personal disappointments he received on the trip.

When we left for Antarctica in 1928, Mr. Konter had his heart set on remaining over winter at Little America, but upon arrival at the ice his physical and emotional characteristics were considered not quite up to the standard required of those picked for barrier billets. The principal deciding factor that he should remain on the ship that returned to New Zealand was his unpopularity with the men. He had been given the title of Morale Officer, but his unpopularity often caused him to feel dejected and morose, a condition decidedly in antithesis to his title. It was quite apparent to all that he was under a delusion of grandeur that fluctuated to the depths of mental depression. A statement of his was to the effect that "my life is ruined because I was not allowed to stay on the ice". Every member of the expedition well knew that the conditions under which he joined specified that his chance to stay at Little America depended upon his ability to fill a useful post and to get along with his companions. No one had a right to believe that he had a definite promise to winter on the ice, and he decision as to who should remain was not made until the final sailing day of the *CITY OF NEW YORK*.

Mr. Konter's statements are decidedly unfair, and his absence from the ice party does not give him a balanced picture of the Expedition sufficient for him to comment upon all its phases.

Unfortunately, we do not know exactly who the "undersigned shipmates" were. Nor do we know when the letter was sent, nor whether it was written in response to a particular letter from Konter, or because of comments Byrd had made to certain members of the expedition.

Konter on the foredeck of the Byrd Antarctic Expedition's flagship, the *City of New York*. *Courtesy of Jean Neptune*.

We are not sure how Byrd was feeling about Konter on the day he and Gould "cut the squad," but it is likely that both Konter's excellent seamanship and the grumbling evidenced in the letter played a role in Byrd's decision to send Konter to New Zealand on the *City of New York*. As it turned out, Byrd's decision was a good one, for the passage north was difficult and Konter's sailor's skill was needed. In fact, Byrd sent Konter a radiogram from Little America on February 28, 1928 (NARA, Konter folders). It reads:

> To: Dick Konter
> WFBT
>
> Heartiest congratulations for the part you played in winning the battle through the ice and storms stop I was with you in thought throughout your fight stop I know what you went through stop I am proud of you stop Best of good wishes
>
> Byrd
>
> WFA 2/28 0730 WM

Despite these warm words from Byrd, it is clear from letters Konter wrote during the summer of 1930 to Byrd and others that Konter was personally devastated by Byrd's decision to send him sailing. Some years later, though, Konter attempted to put a happier face on the situation. It should also be clear that he was trying to protect his legacy and ensure that history remembered him as a man of quality, despite being asked to leave Little America:

Byrd was sending a number of members back home, and some said, they were not wanted by Byrd, but he let them know that these were all good men, but he had no room for them on the ice. It so happened these men were good loyal workers. Many of these men were very depressed, for they felt that they were getting a raw deal, after working so hard unloading the two ships. (R. W. Konter, *Adventure Ahoy! Part III*, Konter Files, National Archives and Records Administration, College Park, Maryland)

Although his passage avoids saying it directly, Konter was surely among the "very depressed."

He made the best of his time in New Zealand, though. He traveled extensively, revisiting places he'd been with the Great White Fleet. He was a big hit with the locals—this is well documented. In our interview with Konter's stepdaughter, Jean Neptune, she told us of a kiwi carved of black onyx, now lost, that had been given to Konter by grateful New Zealanders. Byrd was impressed by the affection the Kiwis had for Konter. Describing their arrival in New Zealand after the conclusion of the expedition, Konter wrote:

Up near the North Pole "Ukelel ?" Dick Konter found that eskimos exchange greetings by rubbing noses so he tried to introduce this custom down near the South Pole. The young lady in the picture is a New Zealand belle—and she seems quite pleased with her lesson in—shall we say—polar manners.

Dick Konter rubbing noses with a Maori woman, New Zealand. From article titled "To the Poles of the Earth" about Konter from the mid-May 1933 issue of *Our Navy*. *National Archives and Records Administration, Richard W. Konter Papers, XRWK - A1 131 (2 boxes)*.

With the help of her sails and a favorable wind, and her old engine, *The City Of New York*, soon reached New Zealand and when she arrived in Dunedin, there were several thousand colonials standing on the waterfront wharf. At the time I was standing alongside of Byrd. There were hundreds of colonial women, men, and children, standing there.

Seeing many of my friends among them, I waved my hand at them, and I as well as Byrd was surprised at the reaction, hundreds of arms arose and waved back at me. When Byrd saw this he smiled and said, "Gee; who don't know you here?"

The next day Byrd sent for me and asked me to meet him at his headquarters in one of Dunedin's leading hotels, where he greeted me warmly, as he shook my hand. He said "Dick, I'm hearing great things about you, from Dunedin's most promiment colonials". Today I'm talking to Dunedin's school children and I want you with me at my side. As an enliste I was quite surprised to receive that honor from an admiral; for only commissioned officers get that appointment. (R. W. Konter, *Adventure Ahoy! Part III*, Konter Files, National Archives and Records Administration, College Park, Maryland)

Richard Konter playing the ukulele in New Zealand, circa 1929. *National Archives and Records Administration, Richard W. Konter Papers, XRWK - A1 131 (2 boxes).*

Konter appeared in a 1933 feature on him in the Mid-May issue of *Our Navy* magazine. The picture is captioned:

Up near the North Pole "Ukulele" Dick Konter found that eskimos exchange greetings by rubbing noses so he tried to introduce this custom down near the South Pole. The young lady in the picture is a New Zealand belle—and she seems quite pleased with her lesson in— shall we say—polar manners (Page 6).

Despite the article's assertion (and Konter's own statements) that he had hoped to introduce Inuit people to the ukulele while in Spitsbergen, there were no Inuit people there.

Further evidence of Konter's reputation can be found in an April 24, 1930 letter to him (NARA, Konter files), in which the mayor of Dunedin, R. S. Black, thanks him for his contributions to the community. He wrote, "You have left a loving memory behind you, particularly in the hearts of all the children in New Zealand. As Mayor of the City, I appreciate this very highly." The mayor also says that he "will be particularly delighted" if he could have the autographs "of all the Members of the Expeditions put on a hard white paper so that I can frame it . . ."

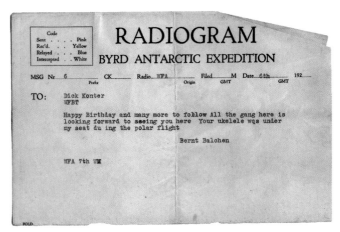

Birthday wishes from Bernt Balchen in Antarctica to Richard Konter in New Zealand in a January 6, 1929 radiogram. *National Archives and Records Administration, Richard W. Konter Papers, XRWK - A1 131 (2 boxes).*

Overall, while he was in New Zealand, Konter seems to have kept his disappointment about not spending the Antarctic winter with the crew on the barrier to himself, keeping busy with travel and musical appearances.

In the same way Konter took Floyd Bennett, the pilot of the *Josephine Ford*, into his confidence to get his Martin ukulele aboard the 1926 North Polar flight, it is clear that on the South Pole flight, Konter, all the way from New Zealand, was still up to his old tricks. Bernt Balchen was the pilot of the *Floyd Bennett* on Byrd's successful South Polar flight on November 29, 1929. It is clear that Konter and Balchen were friends and likewise in cahoots.

On January 6, 1929, Balchen sent a radiogram to Konter in New Zealand:

TO: Dick Konter
WFBT

Happy Birthday and many more to follow All the gang here is looking forward to seeing you here Your ukelele wqs under my seat du
ing the polar flight

Bernt Balchen
WFA 7th WM

WFBT are the radio call letters for the *City of New York*. The radiogram
originated at Little America, whose call letters were WFA.

This time, of course, the ukulele was a Favilla, not a Martin.

After Byrd's successful South Pole flight on November 29, 1929, and
the completion of the expedition's scientific work, the expedition departed
Antarctica on February 9, 1930 (Rodgers 1990). Most of the men traveled
home on the *City of New York* or the *Eleanor Bolling,* but Konter was invited
by Byrd to accompany him, meteorologist William C. Haines, Charles E.
Lofgren, Russell Owen of *The New York Times*, and Lloyd V. Berkner back to
Panama on the RMS *Rangitiki*.

Konter wrote:

I received a rather pleasant surprise when Byrd said to me, "Dick, you
are not going back on the *City Of New York*, for I'm keeping you on

Postcard of the RMS *Rangitiki* autographed by Konter, Byrd, Haines, and Lofgren in
1930 on their way from New Zealand to the Panama Canal Zone. *Public domain.*

my staff, and you are returning with me, as my aide." This was rather a nice compliment as an enlistee, to be a member of the admiral's staff, that was usually a commissioned officers honors.

The *Rangitiki* was a nearly seventeen-thousand-ton commercial liner of the New Zealand Shipping Company, launched in 1929, and much speedier than the expedition's own ships. The *Rangitiki* left Wellington, New Zealand, after April 3 and arrived on May 14, 1930, at the Panama Canal Zone, ahead of the *City of New York* and the *Eleanor Bolling*. Despite leaving New Zealand earlier, the slower ships took longer to reach Balboa. The *Bolling* arrived on May 22, re-coaled, and went to sea again to offer the *City of New York* a tow. They both reached the canal zone on May 31, 1930.

The voyage on the *Rangitiki* was pleasant for Konter. He recalled:

. . . when we boarded her, for some reason known only to themselves, most of Byrd's staff officers immediately retired to their rooms, and avoided everybody for they were never seen all during the 18 days, only at meal times.

The S. S. *City of New York* at Dock 6, Balboa, Panama Canal Zone, June 1, 1930. *Public domain. Courtesy of the Panama Canal Museum Collection, George A. Smathers Libraries, University of Florida, Gainesville.*

There was a little going on aboard the Rangatiki, to help pass the time, so about three times a week I gathered the children or the cabin passengers together and entertained them.

Eventually their parents joined them, and finally so did the other pasengers, and soon I was well known by everybody, most of whom were English. Among them were high Army Officers, and two Lords, all of whom couldn't have been nicer to me, which I felt keenly, as an enlistee.

One afternoon I went up forward and entertained the children of the immigrant passenger, for which I was well paid, not in money, but sentiment. When I was through a ten year old Scotch boy first made a speech of appreciation, then led the children in not three, but ten cheers for me. I'll never forget the colonials, and Britishers, of New Zealand, for their kindness towards me, especially those aboard the Rangatiki, for the last night aboard they threw a farewell party in my honor.

The official New York City yacht *Macom* tied up to the *City of New York*, probably 1930, on the Byrd Antarctic Expedition's return to New York. Black "X" is beneath William Pool, Johanna Cohen to the right. *Courtesy of Jean Neptune.*

After a brief stay in Panama, both the expedition's ships negotiated the Panama Canal and on June 3 sailed into the Atlantic Ocean for home. Despite making excellent time, they were held back from arriving in New York Harbor until Thursday morning, June 19, 1930, the date for which New York City's welcome had been planned, when Mayor Walker would again steam out to meet returning heroes on the *Macom*, and lead them to City Hall through the now-inevitable ticker-tape blizzard. On board the *Macom* was Konter's old shipmate William Pool, with his fiancé, Johanna Cohen. They were to be married in two days.

Konter described the homecoming:

When the two expedition ships reached New York Bay, they were met by a big tug full of high city officials, who escorted us to the Battery, at the foot of New York City. Here the expedition members landed and boarded large open autos, in which we were driven up Broadway, where we received the famous ticker - tape reception, where great crowds greeted us. When the parade finally reached City Hall, we were met and greeted by the mayor, who presented each member with city's medals. The next night at a dinner in one of the City's hotels, each member was presented with special congressional medal of solid gold, each costing about $50.00.

8

Konter's
Later
Years

THE SUMMER OF 1930 WAS one of the most confusing and difficult times in Richard Konter's life. Between June and August, he made a harsh and emotionally charged about-face—from gratefully accepting Byrd's compliments and letter of recommendation to dramatically cutting his ties with Byrd and both of the expeditions of which he had been a part. He went so far as to write to Byrd a vicious tirade, telling Byrd that his missives to Konter "were well meant, but each one I received from you seems more like a stab-wound," and demanding "you block me out of your life, forget me, forget that I exist, for I am doing everything I can to forget you and the expedition."

What happened to cause Konter to so suddenly reach this point of no return after such celebrated adventure and success? First, we know well the disappointment Konter felt when he was not chosen as part of the Antarctic wintering-over party. And apparently things were not quite as rosy at Little America as Byrd had depicted them in his own expedition memoir (Byrd and Gould 1930). Although we do not know the precise nature or extent of the abuses Konter had endured from other members of the party, we know that he felt victimized, characterizing some of the crew as "degenerates" who "knocked and ratted him."

Was it simply that he was seen by the mostly younger crew as old and out of touch? Perhaps Konter's brand of entertainment had become outmoded and unwelcome, and even the ukulele, the instrument to which he had devoted so much of himself, was becoming passé.

His pride took another hit after a meeting with President Hoover: On the morning of June 20, 1930, the expedition members took a train chartered by the National Geographic Society to Washington, D. C. After a stop at

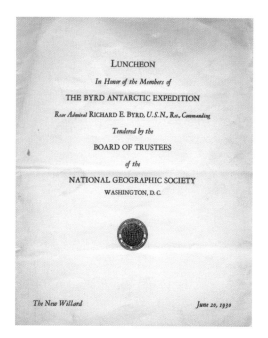

Cover to the program of the luncheon hosted by the National Geographic Society on June 20, 1930, for the Byrd Antarctic Expedition members. *National Archives and Records Administration, Richard W. Konter Papers, XRWK - A1 131 (2 boxes).*

the White House to meet the president, the society's board of trustees held a luncheon for the expedition and VIPs at the New Willard Hotel, and then it was off to greet members of Congress on Capitol Hill.

A copy of the luncheon program in the National Archives, begins with the statement "EVERY MEMBER OF THE BYRD ANTARCTIC EXPEDITION IS PRESENT." The members of the expedition are listed in categories, beginning with "The 'Little America' Detachment," followed by "The Crew of the 'City of New York,'" and "The Crew of the' S. S. Eleanor Bolling.'" Following these were a list of the guests at the luncheon. Konter was, of course, not included in the coveted "Little America' Detachment," the first-stringers, so to speak. He was, however, listed among the crew of the *City of New York*. His name, however, was, again, misspelled "Kontor."

Konter must have felt as if he were on some sort of roller coaster, alternately the victim of ennui and the object of great kindness. After the train returned to New York the next day, Byrd wrote a letter of introduction on Konter's behalf (Byrd Polar Archives, OSU). It reads:

Hotel Biltmore
New York
July 2, 1930

TO WHOM IT MAY CONCERN:

This letter will introduce Mr. Richard W. Konter who served as a volunteer member of the Byrd Antarctic Expedition from May 1928 to June 1930.

Mr. Konter was with me also on the North Pole Expedition in 1926, and was selected for the South Pole Expedition because of his loyalty and efficiency.

He served in various capacities as a member of the crew of the Barque "City of New York", making two voyages from Dunedin, New Zealand to the Bay of Whales, Antarctica and return.

Konter had been tentatively selected to spend the winter on the ice barrier, but after it was explained to him that certain men were urgently needed to return the vessel to New Zealand, he showed a fine sense of loyalty and courage in electing to return to New Zealand in the face of a difficult passage through the unusual ice conditions known to exist at that time in the Ross Sea.

When the expedition returned to Dunedin I learned with much satisfaction that Mr. Konter had been an able representative of the expedition in New Zealand, and had made a host of friends.

Konter was retired from the United States Navy after thirty years' service, and is in all respects a sober and industrious man, and a perfect gentleman.

I take great pleasure in recommending him to anyone requiring his services.

(Signed)
RE Byrd

Konter was handed the letter by Byrd, having been at expedition headquarters. Konter stated,

At my last meeting with Byrd, he warmly shook my hand and pattered me on the shoulder, and flattered me by saying that I was the most trusted man on the expedition, then he gave me this letter . . .

That same day, Konter replied to Byrd on Byrd Arctic Expedition stationery:

2 July 1930

Admiral Richard E. Byrd
Hotel Biltmore
New York City

Dear Admiral Byrd:

I want to thank you very much for your letter of July 2. It is a very generous expression of your appreciation of my services as a volunteer member of the Byrd Antarctic expedition from May, 1928, to June, 1930, and I thank you also for your recognition of my services as a volunteer on the Byrd Arctic Expedition in 1926.

It was a very great disappointment to me that I did not serve with you on the Barrier, but it gave me the keenest pride to serve you in New Zealand, where, you made clear to me, my duties were equally important. The experience of the expedition has meant a great deal to me as has my association with you. I thank you for all you have done and I wish you good luck

Sincerely yours
Richard W Konter

RK:S

Later that same evening, a dinner was held in Konter's honor at the home of Commander Albert Mortiz, U. S. Navy (Retired). Mortiz had graduated from Annapolis in 1881 and spent fifty-three years in the Navy, and Konter had served under him on the *Yosemite* off Guam (*Brooklyn Daily Eagle*, July 3, 1930). While it was not as splendid as the evening he'd enjoyed two years earlier at Gonfarone's, fifteen dinner guests and some fifty neighbors stopped in to hear Konter's playing and stories, and to see about one hundred photos he'd brought along of his recent Antarctic adventure.

However, the aftermath of the expedition felt underwhelming. Konter was clearly not himself. His return was ultimately another disappointment, added to the pile of indignities he had experienced during the expedition, and from which he was still smarting. Rather than anticipating a triumphal dinner for five hundred to be held in his honor, as he had after the Arctic expedition, Konter now felt somewhat forgotten.

Another matter was bothering Konter, and badly. Closer to his heart, Johanna Cohen, the talented musician to whom he'd earlier proposed, had married William Pool on June 16, 1930, just two days after Konter and the South Pole expedition steamed into New York Harbor. The couple had greeted Konter and company as guests on the mayor of New York's steamer, *Macom*, on their arrival back.

Konter's final break with Byrd happened on August 14, 1930. He wrote three letters on that day—one to Captain H. H. Railey; one to Ashley McKinley, an expert in aerial photography and survey who went with Byrd on the South Pole flight; and one to Byrd:

Aug. 14th, 1930

Captain H. H. Railey,
Byrd Antarctic Expedition

Dear sir:-

Aa I was one of the few real volunteers of the expedition, one who did not put the dollar before loyalty, decency, or trust, I feel that I must return any allowance, or expense which the Admiral or the expedition went thru for me, for the more I think of certain things the more I want my life blotted out of any connection whatsoever with the expedition.

My passenger trip on the Rangatiki was somewhere around $350.00, I received about $100.00 allowance during my stay in New Zealand and there was a dental bill for about $2.50, but as there may be an item or two which I cannot remember, I am sending a check for $500.00 to cover everything, so please accept this as a reimbursement for any expense the expedition may have gone thru for me.

Please scratch me off the expedition list and forget that I ever connected with it and if things get any worse than they have been getting, I think I can defend myself.

I have nothing against you captain and I think had they more like you on the expedition, things may have been a bit happier and I don't happen to be along [sic] in thinking as I do.

With my personal regards to you, I'll remain,

very sincerely,
Richard W Konter

P.S. A letter from the Admiral will do no good. I would rather not hear from or about him anymore. I am writing to him under separate cover and hope my letter will not get in other hands than his, if so, it will not be my fault.

R. W. K.

Konter was just as direct to Byrd:

44 Berkeley Place
Brooklyn, N. Y.
Aug. 14th, 1930

R. E. Byrd
Rear Admiral
U. S. N., (ret.)

Sir:- It is with heartfelt regrets that I have to write as I do, but I feel justified and would do anything to be able to blot out the past four or more years of my life.

This is a request that you block me out of your life, forget me, forget that I exist, for I am doing everything I can to forget you and the expedition.

Perhaps your letters were well meant, but each one I received from you seems more like a stab-wound, a reminder of the most bitter experiences of my life, so I want nothing, letters presents, recommendations, or anything.

Although some of us fellows of the Arctic expedition had some justified grievances, we smiled through everything instead by you and I
defy anyone to face me and say that I did not always have the best in
the world to save for you, but what a wonderful reward I got?

You say you always stood by me. If so, why did you not call me
before you and give me a chance to defend myself when I was being
tattled, ratted and knocked by some of your degenerates. You just lis-
ten to them and never gave me the first chance of a hearing, although
I did not know at the time that I was being knocked.

You knocked all the loyalty, faithfulness, trust and anything else I ever
had for you, out of me, so I am asking you to just scratch me off your
list, get me out of your life, forget me is I am trying to forget you and
as for your gang, I don't care what they think of me, for or against
me.

There is only one request I would like to make:- I would like to break
my contract with you and the expedition concerning my pictures
which were rejected and which I wish to use as soon as I am allowed
to. I would also like to do some writing, but only that part of the
expedition in which I took an active part, the polar flight, or the year
on the ice I am not interested in, and last, I would like to do a little
lecturing, but only of my own experiences with the expeditions.

(Signed) Richard W Konter

We don't know if Byrd responded to Konter's request, but Konter continued
lecturing in both formal and informal settings about his experiences with
both expeditions.

We can only speculate about what caused Konter to become so
overwhelmingly depressed upon his return from Antarctica. That the uplifting
personal momentum he felt upon his return from the Byrd Arctic Expedition
was not repeated must have been a huge blow. Konter's disappointments,
whether real or imagined, took a heavy toll on him; it seems to have clouded
his judgment. It made no sense for Konter to alienate himself from Byrd
and the undeniable contributions he'd made to both polar expeditions. The
recipients of Konter's letters during this dark period were genuinely confused
by his behavior.

Psychological diagnoses conducted by amateurs decades after the fact aren't likely to be accurate. But it is difficult to resist the temptation to assemble what we've learned into a hypothesis to explain Konter's depression. Several forces and events were probably at play in the mind and heart of this sensitive man.

First, Johanna Cohen (or her father, at least) had spurned Dick Konter's marriage proposal—and just two days after his return from the Antarctic, she married Bill Pool, a former shipmate and friend who was a decade his junior, which made Konter feel old and unloved. It is easy to imagine how, a generation earlier, a comparable feeling of loss led Konter's father to attempt to take his own life after the death of his beloved wife. Son and father undoubtedly shared some personality characteristics; the loss of love may have affected them similarly.

Second, it's easy to imagine Konter having a difficult time coming to terms with the harsh realities of class distinctions in America after living for so long within the formalized ranking between officers and sailors in the Navy. Within that structure, he'd worked tirelessly to earn the respect of those around him. Upon leaving the Navy, it seems as if Konter expected that civilian society would recognize achievement and confer status based upon it, and that status would

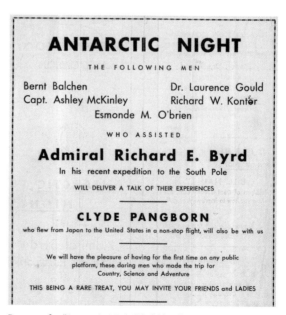

Program for "Antarctic Night" held by the Grand Street Boys Association. Speakers included Konter, Gould, and Clyde Pangborn. *National Archives and Records Administration, Richard W. Konter Papers, XRWK - A1 131 (2 boxes).*

be just as meaningful as family or political ties. But Konter was a commoner, not a child of privilege—no politician, no blue blood like Byrd—and despite his extensive travels, his formal education ended before graduating high school. It must have seemed unfair to him that many doors he felt should have been opened to a man of his accomplishment remained closed.

Finally, the ukulele "mania" he had ridden high upon had cooled, and to make matters even worse, the country was gripped by the early years of the Great Depression. After his retirement from the Navy, Dick Konter would never again hold a steady job.

Konter was clearly torn between the pride he felt about his association with the expeditions, and his personal animosity toward Byrd and certain other members of the expedition. He seemed to tiptoe the line, carefully choosing topics and personnel in lectures and ukulele performances to various organizations throughout the 1930s.

During the early 1930s, Konter's activities still seemed focused on his association with Byrd's expeditions, plus a few musical performances. For example, on December 15, 1931, Konter spoke to the Grand Street Boys Association's "Antarctic Night" with Bernt Balchen, Laurence Gould, Ashley McKinley, and Esmonde O'Brien, joined by flyer Clyde Pangborn (NARA, Konter Files. Also see entry for Pangborn). In the program, however, his name was again misspelled as "Kontor."

Announcement for a benefit presentation held in Plainfield, New Jersey, by Richard Konter recounting his adventures. *National Archives and Records Administration, Richard W. Konter Papers, XRWK - A1 131 (2 boxes).*

Konter made two presentations on March 8, 1935, in Plainfield, New Jersey, for the benefit of Troop 8 of the Boy Scouts of America, that also included a movie about Alaskan adventures.

We asked Jean Neptune if there was any jealousy between her dad, Bill Pool, and Dick Konter. Jean replied, "Evidently not, although . . . (but) after my mom and dad got married, they kind of lost contact with Dick. He never married." We know from *The Brooklyn Daily Eagle* for Friday, November 10, 1933, that "Battleship Bill" and Dick Konter, "retired sailors," performed ukulele selections the previous evening for two hundred people at a YMCA event for the "Three Score and Ten Club." From this we can infer that the men probably remained friends, at least at first, but Johanna and Bill were busy with their new family, and contact with Konter probably became infrequent as time went by.

Konter, however, hung on to old grudges. As late as 1936 he was still troubled with Byrd when he wrote the following letter:

Mr. R. E. Byrd,
9 Brimmer Street
Boston, Mass.

Sir:-

Quite some time ago I requested that you take me off your mailing list and get me out of your life as I am trying to do to you and both your expeditions.

There are many things I am not going to forget so I want no reminders. Any mail, packages, medals, or anything else you send will be returned. I want nothing from you.

I gave you plenty but got nothing but abuse for my loyalty and faithfulness and I'll always live in the fact that I always shot square and worked harder than most of those you favored, yes, and cited.

Well I'm not going into a tirade. You may call it a spell. And do me only one favor. Don't ever tell anyone that I was on the verge of a nervous breakdown. Just tell them that you just busted my heart like you did others.

Don't make me write any more letters for we both may regret it if I do, for I don't care if I land in the gutter. You started me there and I'll help you make a good job of it.

Take this from a busted heart and with heartfelt regrets I will remain,

Your once loyal follower,

R. W. Konter

PS: Tell the one who got the $100 I was supposed to get upon our return last spring, that he can keep it, for I would have returned it anyway. It was typical expedition spirit. (I understand every man got $100).

R. W. K.

One might question the sincerity of Konter's request to "get me out of your life as I am trying to do to you and both your expeditions" while he was still using his association with Byrd and his expeditions to draw crowds (albeit for charitable causes), yet his frustration is palpable.

The World-Telegram article mentioned above, written by Herbert Kurz, notes that, "He made one more try for the old life when he attempted to re-enlist in the Navy during World War II. He was turned down." Indeed, we know from Konter's military service records that he attempted to come out of retirement and volunteer his service with the Navy. His request was denied on medical grounds. On June 21, 1940, the examining medical officer found that the fifty-eight-year-old Konter was "disqualified for enlistment in the Navy or Marine Corps by reason of the following disability, viz: defective vision, chronic bronchitis, chronic myocarditis, hemorrhoids, (and) chronic urethritis."

Kurz's *World-Telegram* article also says that, "Failing to find work during the great depression he turned to his guitar and uke." Kurz continued, "The trip to the Antarctic ended Mr. Konter's adventures on the sea. He came back to Brooklyn and found that life during the depression could be as tough as anything he'd gone through." Konter remained determined. On April 24, 1942, Konter wrote to the morale officer, Navy Department, to propose the formation of "an all-electric string orchestra, to be composed of naval personnel . . ." Rear Admiral Randall Jacobs, U. S. N. replied:

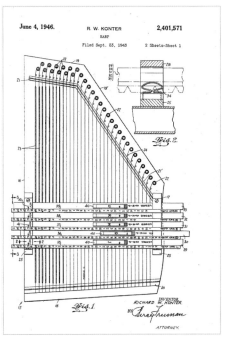

Illustration of Richard Konter's patent for improvements to the autoharp. U. S. Patent 2401571 A, June 4, 1946. *Public domain. U. S. Patent Office.*

"it is regretted that compliance cannot be made with your proposal, and that physical disability precludes your efforts to re-enlist in the naval service. It is noted, however, that your letter refers to a background of considerable entertainment and, in view of this circumstance, it is suggested that you might be interested in communicating with Camp Shows, Inc., 8 West 40th Street, New York, New York."

Konter's address is listed in the letter, on his draft card, and in a 1943 Manhattan, New York, City Directory, as 161 Madison Avenue, less than two blocks east of the Empire State Building. This is the address of the Hotel Warrington, a residential hotel. On his draft card, he indicated that he was unemployed. He was fifty-eight, down but not out, and he kept busy. It almost seems as if he knew that he had nearly forty more years ahead of him. Even though his "all-electric string orchestra" wasn't going to materialize, his curiosity and industry had not waned. So, like his father had before him, he applied for a patent, for an improvement he'd devised for the Autoharp. He was awarded patent US 2,401,571 A on June 4, 1946.

The next we hear from Dick Konter is in 1952, an important year for our story. It seems that living for twenty-six years with the North Pole ukulele had been enough. It had served him well. He'd given countless performances and lectures with it, and the ukulele was a reliable conversation piece. It had gained him notoriety and entrée to the realm of celebrities, but both the ukulele and its signatures seemed to be losing contemporary relevance. Like a car not yet old enough to be a classic, it had lost its magic and just sat there, waiting to become one.

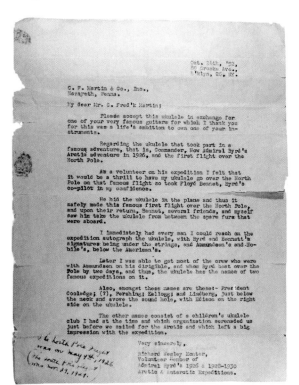

October 24, 1952 letter to C. F. Martin III from Konter, accompanying his donation of his North Pole ukulele to the company in exchange for a Martin guitar. *C. F. Martin & Co. archives.*

Konter had an idea. He reconnected with Bill Pool and Johanna ("Josie"). The trio took a road trip together to Nazareth, Pennsylvania, to the C. F. Martin & Co. factory because Konter had also reconnected with the company and struck a deal. In addition to seeing the home of instruments with which they were all familiar, the goal of their excursion was to deliver Konter's North Pole Martin ukulele back to its birthplace in exchange for a Martin guitar. To Konter, the trade was a steal. The guitar was a popular instrument on which he was already an accomplished player. In this way, Konter's North Pole ukulele had found its way home, accompanied by a one-page letter explaining its significance.

Johanna (on Favilla Model U-2 ukulele) and Dick (on Favilla Model F-6 guitar) performing. Konter wears an Italian tricolor pin. Date unknown. *Courtesy of Lee Feist.*

Only about ten months later, Bill Pool died, on August 26, 1953. Konter's first love was now a widow. The untimely death of Battleship Bill Pool would lead to, eventually, another unexpected but welcome turn in Dick Konter's life.

The article about Konter that appeared in the *World-Telegram* puts Konter's residence (in about 1962) as a "cluttered room-and-a-half at 89 Crooke Ave., Flatbush." There, the then eighty-year old plugged in his electric guitar for the writer, Kurz, and played songs and told stories. Kurz wrote of Konter that, "Today he makes the rounds of homes for the aged and veterans hospitals with a group of elderly musicians trying to take some cheer into those places."

It was around this time of the *World-Telegram* piece, nine years or so after Battleship Bill died, that Konter began a new courtship with Johanna. Jean Neptune told us about how she learned of their engagement:

I met Dick when he was eighty. After my dad passed away, it was quite a few years later that my mom reconnected with Dick and they started going out to dinner, and she brought him over to the house. My children were small at the time; that was when we called him "Uncle Dick." One day she came to me and she said, "I have to tell you something. I'm getting married." I said, "What?" She said, "I'm getting married to Dick."

Richard Konter and his band, Camp Dix, New Jersey, 1967. Johanna behind him at right, playing ukulele. *National Archives and Records Administration, Richard W. Konter Papers.*

Dick Konter proposed to Johanna for a second time. This time, she accepted. "I said, 'Mom, he's eighty years old,'" Jean said. "She said, 'I know.' She was maybe fifty-two, around there, but I said, 'How much longer can he last?'" Jean continues the story:

Well, seventeen years . . . they had a wonderful seventeen years together. He adored her. He treated her like a queen. He was so happy that after all those years of being a single man he finally had a family, with grandchildren. Unbelievable.

And he loved to talk to the kids. And he'd tell them jokes, *corny* jokes, but my mom laughed every time he told one. . . . He'd say, "You know what kind of flower you have on your face?" And they'd say, "No, what?" And he'd say, "Two lips."

The couple married in June 1962. Dick Konter was once again a happy man.

Konter enjoyed his married life immensely and kept active, continuing to play music and lead bands. They performed mainly for a variety of charitable organizations, including hospitals and retirement homes.

In a 1968 copy of *Trade Winds*, a newsletter Konter edited for the U. S. Naval Ex-Apprentices Association—the group's bylaws were mercifully short:

"Loyalty-Service-Common Sense-The Golden Rule and Dues"—he recounts playing for newly arrived Vietnam veterans at the Veteran's Hospital on First Avenue in New York City with his "Jolly Troupers" Novelty Orchestra.

Here are the names and talent of my members and now you can see why we are a Novelty Orchestra: Clara Adams sits at a piano, backwards, and plays real tunes on it; George Reichold and Saul Gumpers, both 88 and Ex-Vaudeville singers of years ago: Harriet Higgins who plays and old, rusty, steel carpenter's saw beautifully; Anton Cottone, my Italian violinist; Bill Horn, a WWI-casualty, sings and plays the violin; George Bauers, a novelty whistler who imitates all kinds of birds; Martha Gutin a pinch hit pianist who helped me organize the Jolly Troupers, which we call ourselves; George Walker, my Scotch concertina player; Elizabeth Gilfallan our 88-year old member who sings, dances and plays guitar at the same time; Al Bluhm, my banjoist only 74 who was once with Buffalo Bills shows. Karl Brown, my pinch hit pianist who once had his own orchestra; Alan Correlli, a born comedian; Rose Rivero, a blues singer; My dear wife Jo, who plays the ukulele

Richard Konter speaking in his role as grand marshal of the United War Veterans of King's County, Brooklyn, New York. The logo on the lectern is that of the New York City Department of Parks & Recreation. Photo from sometime after May 30, 1970. *National Archives and Records Administration, Richard W. Konter Papers.*

beautifully and renders such solos as Rubenstein's melody In F on it, with me, Richard accompanying her on the guitar; Ralph Valente, a fine electric mandolinist; and Judy Stahlman, our Sophy Tucker, and a wonderful blues singers who the veterans and the other patients love. (NARA, Biographical Materials folder, Konter files).

The orchestra performed a show in March of 1968 for the "Survivors of the Great Blizzard of 1888." It was taped and broadcast later that evening, allowing Konter to see himself on television. "Rather novel," he put it.

While serving as the editor of *Trade Winds*, Konter was able to stay in touch with former Navy shipmates and their families. He was called upon frequently to revisit his long-ago adventures (which he did with gusto), and he received many accolades in later life. For example, in another 1968 *Trade Winds* piece, Konter tells of his invitation and attendance at the rechristening

U. S. NAVAL SUPPORT FORCE, ANTARCTICA
HISTORICAL OFFICER
CENTER FOR POLAR ARCHIVES, 8E
NATIONAL ARCHIVES AND RECORDS SERVICE
WASHINGTON, D. C. 20408

28 March 1974

Mr. Richard W. Konter
89 Crooke Avenue
Brooklyn, New York 10226

Dear Mr. Konter:

The Advisory Committee on Antarctic Names, of which I am Chairman, recommended, on March 1974, the name Konter Cliffs for some ice covered promontories at approximately 75° 06'S, 137° 48' West of the coast of Marie Byrd Land. These cliffs will appear on a map (SS 7-9/14) now in preparation by the U. S. Geological Survey at the scale of 1:250,000.

This name will not be official until reviewed by the United States Board on Geographic Names and approved by the Secretary of the Interior. There are formalities and names recommended by the Advisory Committee are usually accepted without further question. You will be glad to learn that, at a previous meeting of the Advisory Committee a geographic feature was also named for Captain Melville who had been neglected all these years.

Best of sailing and we wish you many years to continue to enjoy this honor.

Sincerely,

HENRY M. DATER
Chairman, Advisory Committee on Antarctic Names

HMD:mew

Letter informing Konter of the official recommendation that "Konter Cliffs" be added to the list of official place names of Antarctica. *National Archives and Records Administration, Richard W. Konter Papers.*

of the modern battleship *New Jersey* at the Philadelphia Navy Yard. He attended with his wife, about whom he writes:

When I mention Jo, it is my wonderful wife whom I married when I was 80, and its been five wonderful years for me, and beautiful ones also.

In 1963, Konter self-published *Shipmates, Ahoy,* a work of historical fiction that drew heavily on his own experiences at sea. Konter called it a novel for "boys and girls 10 to 100."

As he approached the end of his active life, Konter received many honors and accolades (NARA, Biographical Material folder, Konter papers). On May 4, 1970, Konter was informed by the United War Veterans of King's County, Brooklyn, New

Richard Konter in his later years. Undated photo. *Courtesy of Lee Feist.*

York, that he had been appointed to the grand marshal's staff for the 103rd Annual Observance on Saturday, May 30, 1970. Konter would himself later serve at least four times as grand marshal of the parade.

Also in 1970, the Radio Club of America gave Konter an honorary membership. Other honorary RCA members include Walter Cronkite and Andy Rooney. In 1975, the club would bestow on Konter its first annual Edgar F. Johnson Pioneer Citation. According to the club: "Established in 1975, this award recognizes long-time RCA members who have either made noteworthy contributions to the success of RCA or to the radio industry."

On March 28, 1974, Henry M. Dater, chairman of the Advisory Committee on Antarctic Names, wrote to Konter that he was to receive a special honor:

The Advisory Committee on Antarctic Names, of which I am Chairman, recommended, on March 1974, the name Konter Cliffs for some ice covered promontories at approximately 75° 06' S, 137° 48' West of the coast of Marie Byrd Land. These cliffs will appear on a map (SS 7-9/14) now in preparation by the U. S. Geological Survey at the scale of 1: 250,000.

In 1975, Konter received the Honors of the Society from the Society of Old Brooklynites (NARA, Konter folders). Dick Konter was finally receiving the recognition he'd craved for so long. Much of it was for his musicianship and his Navy career. He'd acknowledge his participation on Byrd's expeditions, but, in the words of his stepdaughter, "He had no time for Byrd."

Richard Wesley Konter passed away August 25, 1979, at the Veterans Administration Hospital in Fort Hamilton, Brooklyn, right next to the *Chantier's* first anchorage on its voyage north. He was ninety-seven. Johanna continued to reside in Brooklyn but lived not even three years after her husband's passing. She was seventy-five.

Four separate memorial services were held in Konter's honor, among them by the Fleet Services Association and the Reliance Masonic Lodge of Queens, New York (Konter had been a Mason for over seventy years). Konter's obituary in *The New York Times* notes that, "From about 1930 to 1970, he led a band and a group of entertainers that performed in the New York area at children's shelters and hospitals for the chronically ill and at homes for the aged." He must have felt comfortable in Fort Hamilton at the end of his own voyage, having visited many times before, and bringing music and joy to its residents.

PART TWO

KONTER'S
MARTIN
UKELELES

9

How Konter's North Pole Ukulele Was Examined and What It Revealed

KONTER BROUGHT TWO MARTIN STYLE 1K ukuleles along on the North Pole expedition (R. W. Konter, *Adventure Ahoy! Part II*, Konter Files, National Archives and Records Administration, College Park, Maryland). One of them is the subject of this book.

Konter gave the other ukulele to pilot Floyd Bennett's family after Bennett's untimely death in 1928. That ukulele is now in the hands of a relative of Bennett's. It bears a single inscription written by Konter. As is the case with the ukulele that inspired this book, Konter first prepared the surface by scraping away the factory finish (see below). The inscription on that ukulele is located on the top, on the lower-left lower bout to the bass side of the bridge. It reads

"Ukulele Dick"
Richard W. Konter
Byrd Arctic Expedition
King's Bay Spitzbergen
May 9th–1926

Both ukuleles were Martin Style 1K examples. The "K" in the name designates that the instrument's top, back, and sides are made of koa wood (*Acacia koa*). Koa is a fast-growing tree species endemic to Hawai'i and the second most common tree on the islands. Koa is a desirable tone wood for ukuleles and guitars.

Richard Konter's North Pole ukulele. *Photo by John Sterling Ruth, C. F. Martin & Co. archives.*

"Ukulele Dick"
Richard W. Konter
Byrd Arctic Expedition
King's Bay Spitzbergen
May 9th – 1926

The other ukulele brought along by Richard Konter on the Byrd Arctic
Expedition. *Courtesy of Sandy Kling.*

Walsh and King write:

The original Martin ukulele line introduced at the end of 1915 consisted of soprano ukuleles in three styles designated simply as styles 1, 2, and 3. The style 1 was the plainest model, and it retailed for ten dollars.

Although simply appointed, Konter's Style 1K ukuleles were of excellent quality. Neither of Konter's ukuleles has a serial number. In fact, no Martin ukulele manufactured after 1916 did; the model was discontinued in 1944. Neither instrument has a headstock decal, but both have manufacturer stamps on the back of the headstock and inside the sound hole. Both have fretboard markers at frets five, seven and ten, as well as ebony nuts and ebony bridge saddles. Both also have rosewood binding on the back, but neither have Grover Simplex tuners with black buttons. Together, these construction details indicate that the instruments were manufactured in 1926, the year of the expedition (Walsh and King 2013:134-135). Konter loved them, and considered the model "one of the best ukuleles of all times."

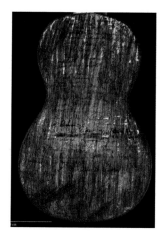

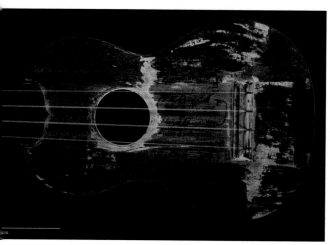

Top: UV-induced visible fluorescence image of the back of the ukulele. What remains of the original finish is clearly visible in infrared light as light-colored areas, despite Konter's scraping to remove the finish of the instrument to promote ink adhesion. *Imaging by E. Keats Webb, Museum Conservation Institute, Smithsonian Institution. June 2014.*

Left: UV-induced visible fluorescence image of the top of the ukulele. *Imaging by E. Keats Webb, Museum Conservation Institute, Smithsonian Institution. June 2014.*

Martin dealer sales records from around the time of the Arctic expedition show only one retailer in New York City who had recently purchased any Style 1K instruments for their retail stock—Fred Gretsch. This suggests to us that Konter purchased both Martin 1K ukuleles from Gretsch, who had two Style 1K examples in stock just before the North Pole voyage (Greig Hutton, personal communication).

Other than the signatures and other inscriptions, and normal wear and tear from playing, the principal modification to the ukulele was the removal of the factory-applied finish. All exterior surfaces of the ukulele were modified in this way except for the back of the neck, the bridge, and the fingerboard. Konter scraped away the finish to better prepare the wood surface to accept the inked signatures. The factory finish presented Konter with surface undesirable for signatures—a slick, relatively nonporous surface. Its removal allowed the ink of autographs to better penetrate the wood and last longer than if they'd been applied to the finished surface.

The most direct and compelling evidence we have for his modifications come from ultraviolet-induced visible fluorescence imaging conducted by E. Keats Webb and her interns at the Museum Conservation Institute of the Smithsonian Institution in June 2014 (Webb, et al. 2014). This technique was employed to see if it would increase the legibility of the signatures. While it wasn't successful at that task, the technique clearly illustrated Konter's method of scraping away the factory finish to give ink signatures a better footing on the instrument and thereby increase their longevity.

Striations suggest to us that the tool used to remove the finish was probably nothing more than a penknife. Except for these extensive modifications to the ukulele's factory finish, there is no evidence that Konter otherwise modified the instrument.

Studying the Ukulele: Resources

We have employed a variety of resources in our research for this book. We have benefited in our attempt to identify the inscriptions and autographs on the ukulele because of a variety of historical sources. Konter's own writings also mention specific persons who signed the ukulele.

For the ukulele itself, we've been fortunate to have access to high-quality photography by John Sterling Ruth available from C. F. Martin & Co. to guide our investigations. Ruth took beautiful full views of the ukulele, plus well-lit detail images of the top, the back, and the right and the left sides, which Dick Boak mentioned in his introduction to this book. These images have proven to be valuable, given that the overall patina and clarity of the signatures have darkened over the since 1997, when the photos were made.

We also contacted members of the Smithsonian Institution's Department of Anthropology with an interest in the Arctic to see if they could help us in conducting multispectral imaging studies of the ukulele that might reveal additional details and help us to identify signatures. (Multispectral imaging refers to photography conducted under controlled conditions using multiple wavelengths of light, some in the visible spectrum, some not.) Our colleague Dennis Stanford put us in touch with Bill Fitzhugh, director of the Smithsonian's Arctic Studies Center. Bill kindly agreed to act as a sponsoring curator for imaging the ukulele at the Smithsonian's Museum Conservation Institute. There, E. Keats Webb and her interns performed the actual imaging, a daylong process. These images have proven valuable in our study.

The imaging performed by the MCI team included the following:

- Reflected infrared digital photography (using a modified DSLR)—IR
- Infrared reflectography (using a specialized IR camera)—IRR
- Ultraviolet-induced visible fluorescence—UV
- Reflectance transformation imaging—RTI
- Visible light RTI of the back of the ukulele and RTI using the modified camera with the 660nm filter for the front and back
- Multispectral imaging (using modified DSLR)—MSI
- Nine bandpass filters for imaging the front of the ukulele—470nm, 525nm, 590nm, 635nm, 660nm, 695nm, 735nm, 800nm, 880nm
- Views of the front, back, and sides with visible light, 660nm and 880nm
- Hyperspectral imaging (using a specialized camera)—HSI
- Visible and IR details of the sound hole

Later, Webb and her crew did post-processing on the resulting images and published a draft report on their work. The images are easily manipulated and enhanced on computers and, in many cases, have helped reveal abraded and faded signatures and clarified other important details. Photographs of subjects other than the ukulele itself have come from other sources. They have helped to clarify details about the signers and their specific historical circumstances.

NARA and the Byrd Polar and Climate Research Center Archival Program

At the National Archives and Records Administration in College Park, Maryland, and at The Ohio State University's Byrd Polar and Climate Research Center Archival Program, we studied and scanned photographs and documents from Konter's and Byrd's personal files for clues about who some of the unidentified signatures might belong to and where and when they were added.

Our Identification Process

Using the resources listed above, we got down to the work of identifying the signers. We should mention, however, one important but not always apparent fact that is easy to miss when looking at photographs: the ukulele is really tiny. It presents only a diminutive surface for signatures. Because of this and the large number of autographs, most of the signatures are smaller than what would result from someone normally signing a document.

Also, as mentioned, time and the wear and tear of Konter's strumming have not been kind to many of the ukulele's autographs. Some signatures are clear and dark, but a much larger number are partially obscured by varying degrees of surficial erosion or ink loss, and some preserve only the faintest traces of the originals. Although one of the main goals of our study of the ukulele was to identify the individual signatures, simply being able to read what was preserved proved challenging. We feel, however, that we have been mostly successful.

Yet another of our original goals proved far more elusive—determining where and when particular signatures were added. Our (limited) success here depended on the availability to us of documentary information, information which often went unrecorded or which is inaccessible to us.

Reading the Signatures

"To identify the individual signatures" is trickier than it sounds, because that job actually involves several distinct tasks, any one of which can slow or halt progress. To study each autograph we used available digital images, and consulted the ukulele itself as required. The use of digital photographs allowed us to conveniently manipulate the images to best effect.

The first step was detecting residual ink traces. For many signatures, this was easy; at other times, it was diabolically difficult. Some signatures have simply vanished, while others are obviously present but remain maddeningly illegible. The grain of the koa wood of the ukulele often obscured letter shapes, as well.

Second, we needed to identify and string together individual letters to form a name. Indistinct letters made this process difficult in some instances, but for more common names, the interpolation was obvious.

Third, the name had to "make sense." Some of our initial efforts resulted in some "names" that we are increasingly confident have never been bestowed (at least on a human being) in recorded history. Cadoka Schirker? Paul Arpinnsten? Some name identifications in which we are now confident have been through some pretty humorous "drafts."

"Inking" the Signatures

As Dick Boak described in his introduction, once signatures were located on the ukulele, he carefully traced over them on a digital tablet that resulted in a digital rendering of the autograph or message. We then colored each rendering to reflect our confidence attributions. Collectively, these digitally "inked" signatures and messages represent a milestone of the progress we made toward identifying the signatures preserved on the instrument.

Narrowing the Field with Documentary Sources

Finally, once confident of our transcriptions, we tried to link the name to a known person. Here, we surprised ourselves by our success rate. Some names, however, have evaded our searches to date. Several perfectly legible signatures—such as those of Lil Richmond and Kay Golding, for example— belong to individuals for whom we have been unable to locate reliable information. Child members of Dick's Ukulele Club, or local friends of Konter's who may have signed the ukulele come to mind here.

Identifying the Signers

At the conclusion of our efforts, we were able to identify a total of 158 signatures on the various surfaces of the ukulele. We are confident that there were once more than this number. We say this because several signatures are visible in historic photography in places where only traces of ink remain today. Also, there are the faintest traces of ink elsewhere on the instrument, which were once signatures that have been so abraded as to be unreadable. However, we are confident that both of these categories of illegibility constitute a minor fraction of the total number of signatures once present on the ukulele.

SIGNATURE SUMMARY

	Certain	Probable	Possible	TOTAL
Top	86%	0%	14%	100%
Left Side	92%	6%	2%	100%
Right Side	89%	8%	4%	100%
Back	59%	17%	24%	100%
Headstock	100%	0%	0%	100%

The table above shows the number of autographs on each surface of the instrument by confidence category. Not included are the signatures we know existed but that are so thoroughly obliterated as to be completely unreadable. Additional signatures of which no trace of any kind remains are obviously not included, either.

The same confidence data, presented as percentages of signatures on each major surface, is shown in the table above. Percentage values allow meaningful comparisons between surfaces with different numbers of signatures.

	Certain	Probable	Possible	TOTAL
Top	19	0	3	22
Left Side	46	3	1	50
Right Side	23	2	1	26
Back	35	10	14	59
Headstock	1	0	0	1
TOTAL	123	16	19	158

NMAH Glass-Plate Negatives: One Mystery Solved, Another Created

During our research, we discovered the existence of two glass-plate negatives in the archives of the Smithsonian's National Museum of American History. We know now that these two images were made within moments of one another, just nine days after the *Chantier* steamed into New York Harbor after the successful North Pole flight.

The first of the glass-plate images shows Konter looking sharp in his uniform. He wears the insignia of a chief petty officer, with twenty-eight years' worth of service stripes (with good conduct) on his sleeve. He also appears to wear the specialty mark of an electrician's mate, but this is not completely visible in this image.

Richard Konter with the North Pole ukulele in New York City, July 1, 1926. *Photographer unknown, Underwood & Underwood Glass Stereograph Collection, Archives Center, National Museum of American History, Smithsonian Institution.*

He is seated outdoors at what may be a café or bar. He sits near a table at the bottom of a staircase, his chair in front of a curved flower box planted with what look like geraniums. The triangular area under the staircase is protected by a decorative wooden lattice. Shadow angles and Konter's squint suggest the picture was taken near midday in the open sun.

Konter holds his ukulele by its neck, and the instrument rests on his left leg. The ukulele's top, headstock, and lower part of its right side are clearly visible in the photograph. The top is partially signed, and there is an inscription between the four tuning machines on the headstock. The large autograph "Marie," present at the top of the headstock today, is not there in this picture. No signatures appear to be present on the right side. Little is recorded about this image, but what *is* recorded is incomplete (e.g., "Seated man holding ukulele") and/or incorrect (e.g., "Photographs—1900–1910").

122

The second image (right) shows only the ukulele standing against the very same background, a wooden lattice, in the same light. This suggests strongly the two photographs were taken just moments apart at the same session. The ukulele stands on the edge of a table, leaning against the lattice, photographed head on. The entire image is slightly overexposed, and the headstock is completely blown out because of its angle relative to the overhead sun; it is impossible to read in this image. The body of the ukulele is clearly legible, however. In fact, the image is so clear that it is easy to see where Konter intentionally removed the finish  from the ukulele to provide a writing surface better for ink. At the time of this photograph, he had removed the original finish from the top (by abrasion) only below the waist on the right side, and below the top of the sound hole in the central and left parts of the upper bout.

An important detail in this image provides us with information that allowed us to solve a mystery posed in a different historic photograph—but it has also created another. Let us turn first to the mystery it solved.

Insignia of the U. S. Navy and related services., circa 1940. Navy Department.

Both images provide enough detail for us to see clearly that the ukulele is the same, and in the same condition—carrying the same signatures. Interestingly, an inscription that is easily visible in the image is now gone from the top of the instrument. The inscription is visible in the photograph below the bridge near the bottom of the top of the instrument. It reads:

INCLUDED WITH THIS UKE
TO THE POLE WAS A COVER, STRINGS,
A HONOR [sic] HARMONICA AND A
PICTURE OF DICK'S UKULELE CLUB

We surmise that Konter erased this inscription sometime after the date of these images (July 1, 1926) to make room for what he deemed a more "important" inscription or signature. Were it not for this glass-plate negative, much of the information contained in this inscription would be lost. One bit survived, however, but elsewhere: it is the mention of the ukulele club, now seen on the back at the ukulele at the top near the heel of the neck.

Yet this inscription, now gone, provided us the information needed to make sense of another photograph, one made at the moment Floyd Bennett returned the ukulele to Konter after the polar flight. That photo shows Bennett in his reindeer coat facing Konter, who holds the ukulele, which Bennett just handed to him (See image on page 60). Charles Kessler (at left, in a reindeer coat) and Leo M. Peterson (at right) look on in front of the open cargo door of the *Josephine Ford*. If we zoom in on the ukulele in that image, we see several interesting items that probably would be impossible to understand without the information provided in the inscription only preserved in the silver gelatin glass-plate negative at the National Museum of American History.

First, the interior of the ukulele viewed through the sound hole is brilliant white in the photograph made next to the *Josephine Ford*. This is not what one would expect. Instead, it should be in deep shadow or blackness. A comparison of the two National Museum of American History images shows the difference. The brilliant white is clearly from something placed inside the uke—likely papers, or "A picture of Dick's Ukulele Club," as mentioned in the message below the bridge that has been erased. Still, the existing inscription at the top of the back of the ukulele reads:

Konter's North Pole ukulele.
Photographed in New York
City, July 1, 1926. Cropped
from a scan of the original
glass negative. *Photographer
unknown, Underwood &
Underwood Glass Stereograph
Collection 1895-1921,
Archives Center, National
Museum of American History,
Smithsonian Institution.*

[DICK'S UKULELE CLUB]
WHOSE PICTURES OR NAMES
WERE TAKEN TO THE
NORTH POLE
BY
COM'DR BYRD & CHIEF BENNETT

Thus, it is likely that Konter placed photographs and perhaps signatures on paper of the ukulele club members inside the instrument through the sound hole before the flight, so that these tokens would be along for the flight over the pole. It is these white documents, reflecting the Arctic sun, that we see through the sound hole. We do not know if any or all of the ukulele club members had signed the back of the ukulele in advance of the expedition, because no images exist of the back of the instrument, but it seems unlikely based on this evidence. Children's signatures on the instrument before the polar flight might have convinced Floyd Bennett to bring it along, but this is only conjecture on our part.

Detail of Ukulele from picture on page 60 showing brilliant white inside sound hole and harmonica tied to back of neck. *Courtesy of Jean Neptune.*

Second, zooming in on the neck of the ukulele reveals several distinct and unusual features. First, there is an object attached to or held against the back of the neck. Visible also is string or twine that is clearly not the ukulele's strings. Rather, this twine was used to bind the item on the back of the neck. At first, we thought the object might be a small notebook. However, close inspection reveals that this object is the harmonica mentioned in the (deleted) inscription—a Hohner harmonica (misspelled "Honor" by Konter in the original inscription). In fact, enough of the harmonica's structure is visible that we know it to be an example of the "Chromonica" model by Hohner. In another well-known photograph of Konter taken on the deck of the *Chantier*, he has Igloo the dog on his lap, his ukulele in his hands, and a chromatic harmonica in his mouth. (See image on page 62). The engraving on that harmonica can be easily read. It is a Hohner Chromonica, and perhaps it is the same one in both photographs. Thus, we'd like to set the record straight: the ukulele was not alone as the first musical instrument to reach the North Pole—a Hohner Chromonica arrived at precisely the same time.

Autographing Instruments

Before discussing Konter's "mental template" about how autographs should be positioned on the ukulele, first we should ask: Why sign an instrument at all? When did the practice begin? Indeed, why do people collect autographs in the first place?

People collect autographs for a number of reasons. A feeling of respect or emotional attachment to the signer probably lies at the core of most autograph collecting. David Lowenherz of Lion Heart Autographs told us that he thinks many autograph collectors feel that there is "no way to get closer to a person, especially a deceased person, than through their signature." Echoing this sentiment, Steven Raab remarked that Thomas Madigan, a renowned autograph collector, wrote that, "Between the present and the past there exists no more intimate personal connection than an autograph. It is the living symbol of its author." (Raab 2012, https://www.raabcollection.com/blog/why-autographs-matter-and-people-collect-them) It seems that Richard Konter, a keen observer of history in the making, felt this way, too. Moreover, he appreciated that the autographs he was collecting on his ukulele would transform it into a conversation piece and lend authenticity and some serious mojo to the stories he so loved to tell.

Once an autograph is obtained, a collector's focus can turn easily from an autograph or two to a collection. For example, what may have started as pitcher Bob Gibson's lone signature might end up as an obsessive hunt for autographs of all the 1964 St. Louis Cardinals. Collecting signatures of a certain "kind" of person (e.g., cabinet members, astronauts, musicians, etc.) often ends in completism. Richard Konter certainly felt this way about the autographs of the crew of the *Chantier*.

We contacted a number of auctioneers and dealers of antique musical instruments and asked them about autographed instruments that had passed through their hands or with which they were familiar. Perhaps surprisingly, none could recall specific examples of stringed instruments that pre-dated Konter's North Pole ukulele. They did mention autographed piano soundboards and Civil War drumheads, but not smaller stringed instruments like guitars, mandolins, or ukuleles older than Konter's. While this was an informal and certainly not exhaustive survey, it made us wonder if Konter was one of the first to collect autographs in this way. Indeed, how many musicians would be willing to "deface" their instrument's finish, as Konter did, to accommodate autographs? Probably not the owner of a Guarneri violin. Perhaps this simple fact explains the rarity of autographed stringed instruments.

Visibility

Konter used an organizational framework to position the autographs on the ukulele. Despite variations in size, ink, and angle, the signatures were not written haphazardly, in just any location. As a player, Konter was keenly aware of differences in the relative visibility of the ukulele's surfaces during performance. This, no doubt, influenced his selection of the areas where he would ask different individuals to sign. By requesting signers to ink their autographs in specific places on the instrument, Konter was able to group signatures that he felt belonged together, and to spotlight the signatures he thought were the most impressive.

From our admittedly small sample of photographic evidence showing the sequence in which signatures were applied, it seems Konter's organizational scheme varied only slightly over time. Unfortunately, the only definitive photographic evidence we have is of the front of the instrument, especially the top.

In addition to grouping signatures, in some cases Konter also used inscriptions to illuminate for the viewer the kinds of signatures present in a particular area. For example, just above the bass side of the bridge, Konter wrote, "ORIGINAL SIGNATURES OF NORTH POLE FLYERS," and along the top side binding on the left side of the instrument he wrote, "MEMBERS OF BYRD ARCTIC EXPEDITION U. S. S. B. S. S. *Chantier*."

Konter's "Fences"

Moreover, Konter occasionally used a visual device we've come to call "fences." Fences are simply inked boundary lines drawn to enclose areas of varying sizes for the purpose of segregating signatures and/or inscriptions from others in the same area. The best examples are to be found on the top of the ukulele, where Konter enclosed signatures he intended to be identified as a group because they share certain characteristics.

Re-Inking

As Konter continued to play this ukulele as his primary instrument, many of the signatures and messages on the instrument began to fade. In many cases, Konter had no hesitation about going over them with fresh ink to enhance their visibility.

Postprocessed multispectral image of the top of the ukulele. Evidence of re-inking of signatures by Konter is clearly visible. *Imaging by E. Keats Webb, Museum Conservation Institute, Smithsonian Institution. June 2014.*

Multispectral images captured at the Smithsonian's Museum Conservation Institute are able to show the re-inking well with digital manipulation. In the image, re-inking is especially evident on the lower-right bout, where the times and date of the polar flight are listed, as well on the signatures above the sound hole. Other examples are apparent in the image, as well.

The Instrument's Surfaces

The Top

The top of the ukulele was reserved by Konter for signatures and inscriptions that he deemed to be of the utmost importance. Of the twenty-two signatures we are able to read, we have given a confidence attribution of "certain" to nineteen of them, "probable" to none, and "possible" to three. The autographs on the top are mainly of leaders—from the Byrd Arctic and first Antarctic Expeditions, the *Norge* Expedition, and of aviators, military and political leaders, and, perhaps a little out of place but of some celebrity, the daughter of Admiral Robert Peary, Marie.

The top of Konter's North Pole ukulele, June 2014. *Imaging by E. Keats Webb, Museum Conservation Institute, Smithsonian Institution.*

Signature tracings overlaid on image of the top of the ukulele. Color-coded by confidence category (black = certain, red = possible). *C. F. Martin & Co. archives.*

We can see, but not read, an additional five signatures on the top of the ukulele, one on the upper-left bout, and four on the upper-right bout. Both of these areas, but especially the right upper bout, are heavily abraded from Konter's strumming. We have not counted these signatures in our totals.

Of the perhaps ten "messages" that appear on the instrument, used by Konter to illuminate the meaning of particular groups of signatures, six appear (or in the case of one, now erased, appeared) on the top. All of the messages still present on the instrument are oriented to be read from the perspective of a right-handed player holding the instrument in playing position. In other words, the message read left to right from the fingerboard to the bridge.

Message 1

The first message found on the top is located immediately below the bridge and reads:

THIS UKE
WAS TAKEN
TO THE
NORTH POLE
ON THE
FOKKER
PLANE
BY
CMDR BYRD
AND
CHIEF BENNETT
() PETTY OFFICER

Message 2

It is then "signed" by the ukulele's owner:

UKULELE DICK
(R. W. KONTER)

We have counted the "R. W. Konter" part of this message as his signature on the instrument. The self-explanatory message above his signature is followed immediately by a second message that appears on the lower-left bout that reads:

Message 3

The above is
Certified
as true

Konter was concerned about authenticating the statements and signatures
collected on his ukulele. Here, he had the North Pole fliers and their
mechanic certify the signed ukulele's authenticity.

With this certification, Konter was attempting to ensure for posterity
that the statement above his signature was "authenticated" by important
expedition members, thereby conferring legitimacy upon it. The fact that
this statement appears on the top in a prominent location is no accident;
the location on the top of the ukulele was important to Konter. Thus, it is
followed by three signatures (the second occurrence of Byrd and Bennett on
the instrument, and the only occurrence of Leo Peterson's autograph):

R E Byrd
Floyd Bennett
L M Peterson

Message 4

The longest message on the top is located below the waist of ukulele and extends onto the lower-right bout. The inscription is enclosed in a single-line "fence" that extends from the right edge of the top and across the waist to the right edge of the bridge. The line stops on the lower part of the top so the right edge of the inscription is not enclosed by the line. The inscription concerns the flight of the *Josephine Ford:*

LEFT KING'S BAY
SPITSBERGEN FOR NORTH POLE
MAY 9TH '26; 1.28 AM : RETURNED
5.38 PM
(SAME) DATE.
15 HRS & 52 MINS.
1520 MILES
ROUND TRIP

The inscription is more clearly legible on the July 1, 1926 glass-plate negative from the National Museum of American History than it is on the ukulele today. The possible implications of this inscription are discussed on pages 147–149, under "North Pole Flight Controversy and Konter's Role."

Message 5

Beneath the sound hole and under the strings are found the signatures of Richard Byrd and Floyd Bennett, along with their Navy ranks and roles on the flight, added by Konter.

Commander & Navigator
(Signed) RE Byrd
Lt. Com'dr U.S.N.
&
(Signed) Floyd Bennett
NAVAL AIR PILOT, USN
PILOT & ENGINEER

ORIGINAL SIGNATURES OF NORTH POLE FLYERS

Below the last line of the inscription is a single "fence," a line to keep Byrd and Bennett separate from the *Norge* expedition members on the lower-left bout.

Message 6

The final message still visible on the top of the ukulele reads:

"NORGE"
Spitsbergen
May 10 '26

The message is directly to the left of the sound hole (or, to a right-handed player in playing position, above it). Today, the message and four signatures are enclosed in a single-line "fence" that serves to segregate the *Norge* expedition leaders from the other signatures in the area. The signatures present today belong to Umberto Nobile, Roald Amundsen, Lincoln Ellsworth, and Hjalmar Riiser-Larsen.

Puzzlingly, Nobile's signature is missing from the ukulele in the July 1, 1926 NMAH glass-plate negative. This can only mean that Konter left Spitsbergen without Nobile's signature on the instrument. It also means that either Nobile signed the instrument some time after the expedition's return to New York City, or Konter forged the Italian airship designer's autograph for completeness sake.

In *First Crossing of the Polar Sea*, Amundsen and Ellsworth recount that after their successful flight across the Arctic Ocean in the *Norge*, they traveled from Alaska to Seattle by sea on the *Victoria*, then by train to New York:

On the 3rd of July [1926] at 9 A.M., three hours before the departure of the *Bergensfjord*, we came into New York. Here a splendid reception awaited us, and what in particular moved us deeply here was to see our good friend of Svalbard, Commander Richard Byrd, at the head of the great procession that came with resounding music into the Grand Central Station, and offered us a hearty welcome (Amundsen and Ellsworth 1927).

Was Konter was there with Byrd to greet the *Norge* crew? Perhaps the "resounding music" Amundsen and his team heard was ukulele music. Although we cannot prove it, it seems likely that Konter got Nobile to sign the instrument at Grand Central Station, two days after the ukulele was photographed without Nobile's signature.

In whatever way Nobile's signature was imprinted, its details, especially the distinctive initial "N" of the surname, are rendered accurately when compared to other examples of his autograph. We believe the signature is authentic.

Message 7

The final message is no longer visible on the instrument today. It is discussed below in the section titled "NMAH Glass-Plate Negatives: One Mystery Solved, Another Created"

Relatively large areas of the top were still un-inked upon Konter's return to the USA after the Byrd Arctic Expedition, especially the upper bout of the ukulele.

The Left Side

We are able to identify fifty signatures on the left (bass) side of the ukulele. Of them, we attribute "certain" confidence to forty-six of them, "probable" to three, and "possible" to one. The vast majority (forty-eight) of the signatures on the left side are of the members of the Byrd Arctic Expedition.

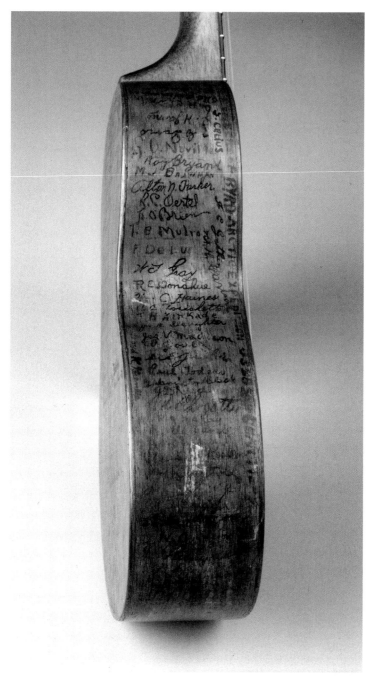

Richard Konter's North Pole ukulele, left side. *Photo by John Sterling Ruth,*
C. F. Martin & Co. archives.

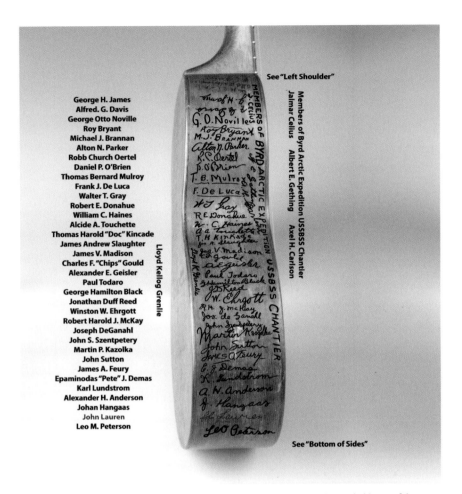

Signature tracings overlaid on image of the left side of the ukulele. Color-coded by confidence category (black = certain, red = possible). *C. F. Martin & Co. archives.*

Message 8

Also on the left side along the waist of the ukulele near the top, and at a ninety-degree angle to the signatures, Konter wrote an identifying message that reads,

"Members of Byrd Arctic Expedition U. S. S.B S. S. Chantier."

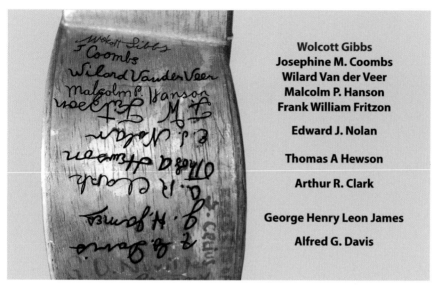

Wolcott Gibbs
Josephine M. Coombs
Wilard Van der Veer
Malcolm P. Hanson
Frank William Fritzon

Edward J. Nolan

Thomas A Hewson

Arthur R. Clark

George Henry Leon James

Alfred G. Davis

Signature tracings overlaid on image of the left shoulder of the ukulele. Color-coded by confidence category (black = certain, blue = probable). *C. F. Martin & Co. archives.*

The Right Side

We have identified twenty-six signatures on the right (treble) side of the instrument. Of them, we attribute twenty-three of them to "certain" confidence, two to "probable," and one to "possible." Fully half (thirteen) of the autographs on this side are of the Norwegian and Italian members of the *Norge* crew. The signatures of the expedition's leaders, Amundsen, Ellsworth, Nobile, and Riiser-Larsen, do not appear here because Konter had asked them to sign on the front of the instrument. Among the autographs on this side are five of journalists, authors, and cinematographers, four are of expedition sponsors, and two are by politicians, plus one nearly unreadable signature and one pretty famous inventor—Thomas Alva Edison.

The bottom of the instrument, with signatures grouped on the left and right sides, can be seen in the following figure.

Richard Konter's North Pole ukulele, right side. *Photo by John Sterling Ruth, C. F. Martin & Co. archives.*

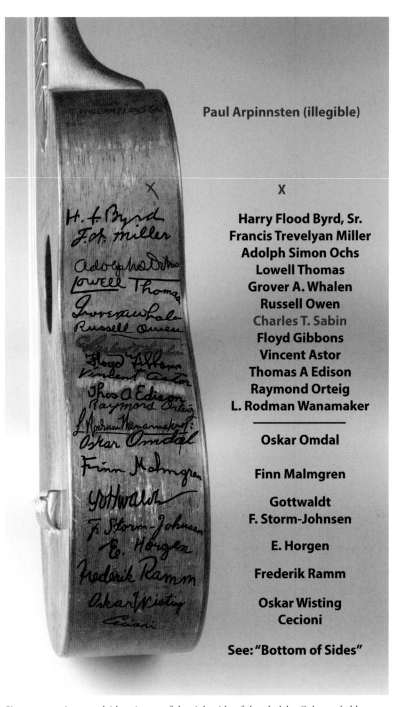

Paul Arpinnsten (illegible)

X

Harry Flood Byrd, Sr.
Francis Trevelyan Miller
Adolph Simon Ochs
Lowell Thomas
Grover A. Whalen
Russell Owen
Charles T. Sabin
Floyd Gibbons
Vincent Astor
Thomas A Edison
Raymond Orteig
L. Rodman Wanamaker

Oskar Omdal

Finn Malmgren

Gottwaldt
F. Storm-Johnsen

E. Horgen

Frederik Ramm

Oskar Wisting
Cecioni

See: "Bottom of Sides"

Signature tracings overlaid on image of the right side of the ukulele. Color-coded by confidence category (black = certain, blue = probable). *C. F. Martin & Co. archives.*

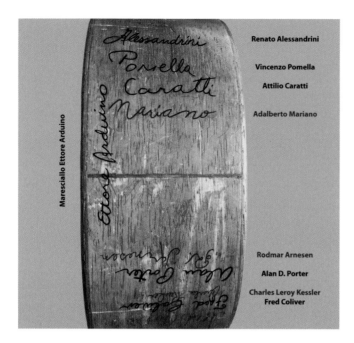

Renato Alessandrini

Vincenzo Pomella

Attilio Caratti

Adalberto Mariano

Maresciallo Ettore Arduino

Rodmar Arnesen

Alan D. Porter

Charles Leroy Kessler
Fred Coliver

Signature tracings overlaid on image of the bottom of the ukulele. Color-coded by confidence category (black = certain, blue = probable). *C. F. Martin & Co. archives.*

The Back

The largest continuous flat surface of the instrument contains a large and diverse collection of autographs. As he did elsewhere, Konter segregated similar signatures in particular areas of the back. Roughly the top half of the back includes a large collection of signatures by members of Dick's Ukulele Club and persons associated with it. Toward the waist are found a diverse collection of personalities including politicians and athletes. Toward the bottom of the back are entertainers and musicians not affiliated with the Ukulele Club, as well as a prominent polar explorer, Captain Bob Bartlett, and other military men and friends of Konter.

We have identified fifty-nine autographs on the back of the ukulele. Of them, we have designated thirty-five with "certain" confidence, ten as "probable," and fourteen as "possible."

The signatures on the back of the instrument had a relatively hard life. There is a large number of autographs in the least confident categories (66.7 percent of the total of our "probable" confidence attributions, and 73.7 percent of all of our "possible" attributions on the entire ukulele are found on the back). Such a drop in confidence probably reflects the years of soft abrasion and polishing that the signatures on the back of the instrument received as it was played by Konter. Unlike the top, where strumming has completely obliterated signatures, the gentler polishing and abrasion that happened to the signatures on the back preserved enough of them to be tantalizing, encouraging us to speculate, but not enough to be certain.

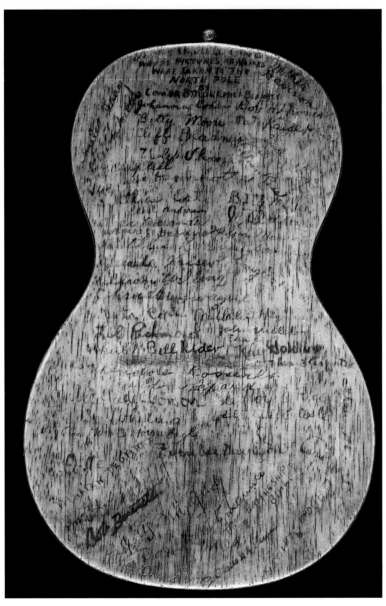

Richard Konter's North Pole ukulele, back. June 2014. *Photo by E. Keats Webb, Museum Conservation Institute, Smithsonian Institution.*

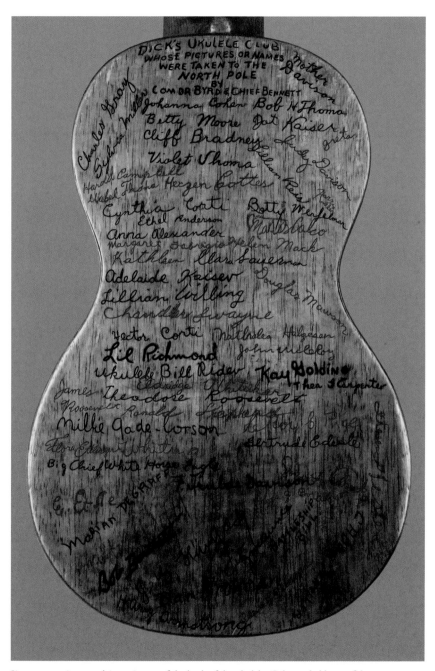

Signature tracings overlain on image of the back of the ukulele. Color-coded by confidence category (black = certain, blue = probable, red = possible). *C. F. Martin & Co. archives.*

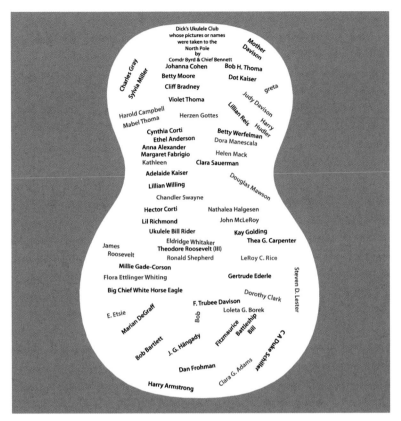

Key to the names on the back of the ukulele. Color-coded by confidence category (black = certain, blue = probable, red = possible). *C. F. Martin & Co. archives.*

Message 9

Discussed above, the message

[DICK'S UKULELE CLUB]
WHOSE PICTURES OR NAMES
WERE TAKEN TO THE
NORTH POLE
BY
COM'DR BYRD & CHIEF BENNETT

appears at the top of the back of the instrument.

The Headstock

The headstock of the ukulele contains a message and a signature, both on the front, and both are fully readable.

Message 10

This message reads simply:

> R.W. KONTER
> AN.
> USSB SHIP
> CHANTIER
> BYRD
> ARCTIC
> EXPEDITION

It seems to be another owner's label on a prominent surface, one shared only with royalty.

Inside the Sound Hole

Inside the sound hole of the ukulele we find a single inscription and a partially torn label. The ukulele's sound hole allows a limited view of the interior of the instrument. An area of the interior surface of the back of the ukulele is easily visible directly beneath the sound hole. In this location, the manufacturer's stamp "C. F. Martin & Co." is printed in an arc, with "Nazareth, PA." beneath it, running parallel to a back brace. On the unfinished koa wood in this location, Richard Konter also wrote, "Property of R. W. Konter S. S. Chantier.

We know from photographic evidence (NMAH glass negative) that, also in this location, sometime before July 1, 1926, a strip of paper with adhesive was attached that

Looking into the sound hole of Richard Konter's North Pole ukulele, June 2014. *Photo by E. Keats Webb, Museum Conservation Institute, Smithsonian Institution.*

bore the logo and address of Clarence Williams Music Publishing Co. Inc. (also see entry on Clarence Williams). This label, or "sticker," completely obscured the C. F. Martin factory stamp.

This Clarence Williams Music Publishing, Co. label is positioned inside the ukulele in a location often used by instrument retailers to affix their own labels. However, the label is positioned oddly, at an angle almost one hundred eighty degrees from what one would expect if it were a retailer's label. We do not know if Clarence Williams Music Publishing sold musical instruments, but we feel it is unlikely.

Inscription tracing overlaid on image of the sound hole (interior surface of the back of the ukulele). Color-coded by confidence category (black = certain). *C. F. Martin & Co. archives.*

So why is the Clarence Williams label in that position, and at such an odd angle? We speculate that Konter may have placed his publishing colleague's label inside the sound hole for the North Pole flight, as he had done with photographs of the members of Dick's Ukulele Chorus. If the label had an adhesive backing, it is likely that humidity and condensation caused it to stick on the unfinished wood, obscuring Konter's original inked statement of ownership. We think this is likely to be the case. If the label had no adhesive, it is difficult to imagine Konter or anyone else affixing it in this position. Because of the current state of the label and the lack of adequate photographic evidence, at some later date Konter or another person tried to remove the label and peeled it back to its current state, where well enough was left alone.

Logo of Clarence Williams Music Publishing Co. Inc.

North Pole Flight Controversy and Konter's Role

As mentioned earlier, those who have attempted to judge Byrd's claim have relied upon a variety of available evidence (e.g., logbooks, eyewitness accounts) and the understanding that it must make sense within the basic physical requirements of the flight, such as the distance to the pole from King's Bay, the capabilities of the plane itself, the effect of temperature on engine and aeronautic performance, and the effect of tailwinds and headwinds on airspeed.

One of the most basic statistics about the flight turns out to be one of the most elusive—the duration of the flight itself. In fact, several different flight durations have been reported. Bart (2014:357) concludes that this critical information is unavailable for a simple reason: those who were most likely to collect and record it were otherwise occupied at the *Josephine Ford*'s takeoff—and they were getting drunk. Bart notes that many of the Norwegian, Italian, and American crews were toasting one another on the *Heimdahl*, the Norwegian gunship that had tied up at the pier where Byrd hoped earlier to dock the *Chantier*. Several reports cited by Bart indicate that the roar of engines in the distance as Bennett and Byrd tried repeatedly to lift off was enough to bring some of the revelers to the *Heimdahl*'s portholes for a look, but after a few unsuccessful attempts, it was well after midnight local time, and the flight wasn't looking likely enough to keep the reporters paying close attention.

One person who may have been unimpressed by the revelry, Richard Konter, was a teetotaler and on board the *Chantier* when the *Josephine Ford* finally rose off the makeshift runway. His ukulele is inscribed with data about the flight time that Bart does not cite. It may provide important information unavailable elsewhere.

The relevant inscription is located on top of the ukulele at the right lower bout. It is a message enclosed in one of Konter's ink "fences." It reads

LEFT KING'S BAY
SPITSBERGEN FOR NORTH POLE
MAY 9TH '26; 1.28 AM : RETURNED
5.38 PM
(SAME) DATE
15 HRS & 52 MINS.
1520 MILES
ROUND TRIP

The original inscription may be actually more legible in the 1926 glass-plate negative from the National Museum of American History because, unlike the ukulele today, it had not been partially re-inked at the time of the photograph.

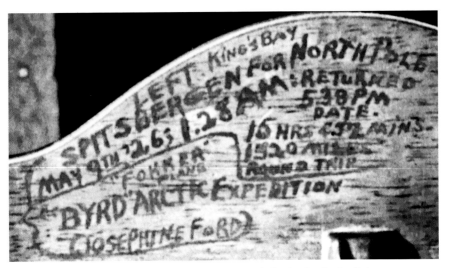

Close-up of waist and lower-right bout. Inscription includes details of polar flight. Photographed in New York City, July 1, 1926. Cropped from a scan of the original glass negative. *Photographer unknown, Underwood & Underwood Glass Stereograph Collection 1895-1921, Archives Center, National Museum of American History, Smithsonian Institution.*

Interestingly, the departure and arrival times in Konter's message do not result in the total flight time that appears in the same inscription. We suspect this was due either to Konter's own (erroneous) calculation, or else someone with an independent "official" time conveyed it to him. Using Konter's departure and arrival times, the flight would have lasted 16 hours and 10 minutes, some 18 minutes longer than the flight time of "15 HRS & 52 MINS." Although the clarity of the total flight time inscription leaves a little to be desired, the departure and arrival times are perfectly legible. We can only speculate about the source of this discrepancy, but one thing is clear: Konter didn't drink.

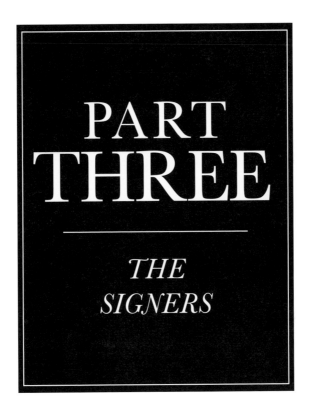

PART THREE

THE SIGNERS

What follows are the results of our efforts to identify the men and women who signed the ukulele. We've organized the presentation of their signatures according to the surface of the ukulele they signed. For each autograph, we've included our identification, a photograph of the person (if available), their dates of birth and death (if available), a rendering of their signature, and some interesting bits of what we've learned about their lives and their relevance to Konter.

10

Signers
on the
Top

THE TOP OF THE UKULELE WAS signed by at least twenty-two individuals. These are listed below, first by "confidence category," and then alphabetically by our database category "signer category" (a purely synthetic designation we have used to lump similar kinds of individuals together).

Confidence = Certain:

Floyd Bennett	Byrd Arctic Expedition
Richard Evelyn Byrd	Byrd Arctic Expedition
Leo McKinley Peterson	Byrd Arctic Expedition
Bernt Balchen	Explorers & Aviators
Charles A. Lindbergh	Explorers & Aviators
Captain Ashley Chadbourne McKinley	Explorers & Aviators
Clyde Edward Pangborn	Explorers & Aviators
Marie Ahnighito Peary	Explorers & Aviators
Roald Engelbregt Gravning Amundsen	*Norge* Dirigible Crew
Lincoln Ellsworth	*Norge* Dirigible Crew
General Umberto Nobile	*Norge* Dirigible Crew
1st Lieut. Hjalmar Riiser-Larsen	*Norge* Dirigible Crew
President John Calvin Coolidge	Politicians & Military
Vice Pres. Charles Gates Dawes	Politicians & Military
Secretary Frank Billings Kellogg	Politicians & Military
General John Joseph Pershing	Politicians & Military
Captain Lewis Broughton Porterfield	Politicians & Military

Mayor James John Walker
Laurence McKinley Gould

Politicians & Military
Scientists

Confidence = Possible:

Dr. Clarence Julian Easterling Owens
Amelia Mary Earhart
Mayor Edward H. Larkin

Dignitaries
Explorers & Aviators
Politicians & Military

We now present each signer, illustrated with their inked signature and, if available, a photograph.

Confidence = Certain:

Floyd Bennett (October 25, 1890–April 25, 1928)

B, stands for Bennett, we see him each night,
the rest of the day he keeps out of sight.

—From *The Chantier Shovelful* (informal ship's newsletter)

From Warrensburg, New York, Bennett was a desperately impoverished child from a family of five children. After trying to run away with the circus, he became fascinated with cars at fifteen and worked in a lumber camp all winter to pay the tuition required to became an auto mechanic. During the first World War in 1917, Bennett enlisted in the Navy and attended flight school. There, the talented mechanic became a pilot of legendary skill.

Exactly two years younger than Richard Byrd, Bennett served with him in 1925 on an aviation survey of Greenland. It was there that Byrd became familiar with Bennett's abilities

Lieutenant Floyd Bennett. Undated. Original image by Bain News Service. *Library of Congress Prints and Photographs Division Washington, D.C. LC-B2- 6358- 18 [P&P].*

and the two men forged a close friendship. Bennett is famous as Byrd's pilot on the polar flight of May 9, 1926. Both he and Byrd received, by a special act passed on December 21, 1926, the Congressional Medal of Honor for their achievement. Bennett's Medal of Honor citation reads:

For distinguishing himself conspicuously by courage and intrepidity at the risk of his life as a member of the Byrd Arctic Expedition and thus contributing largely to the success of the first heavier-than-air flight to the North Pole and return.

Bennett was quiet, hardworking, and adventurous. Bennett and Bernt Balchen flew to offer relief to the crew of the *Bremen*, which had completed the first successful transatlantic airplane flight from east to west, between April 12 and 13, 1928. The fliers were stuck on Greenly Island, in Canada, following their nonstop flight. The three crew members of the *Bremen* included the Irish Major James Fitzmaurice, also a signer of the ukulele. Bennett died during the flight from pneumonia he had contracted previously. He was given a funeral in New York City, whose first municipal airport was known as Floyd Bennett Field. In Bennett's memory, Byrd dropped a stone from Bennett's grave over the South Pole on the flight that he and Bennett had originally planned. Bennett's body is buried in Arlington National Cemetery.

The ukulele was stowed with Floyd Bennett's cooperation under the pilot's seat on the *Josephine Ford*. Konter subsequently made a second, much simpler ukulele for Bennett (possibly for his widow or family). His signature is located prominently with R. E. Byrd's on the top between the sound hole and bridge.

Commander Richard Evelyn Byrd, Jr.
(October 25, 1888–March 11, 1957)

R. E. Byrd was one of the United States' premier polar explorers. His life up until the North Pole expedition is summarized in Chapter 3. Byrd and pilot Floyd Bennett were awarded the Congressional Medal of Honor for their North Pole flight. Byrd went on to lead a number of Antarctic expeditions, as well. Byrd invited Konter to be part of both his first Arctic and first Antarctic expeditions. Byrd ended his career with the Navy as a rear admiral. He is buried in Arlington National Cemetery. Byrd's life is the subject of Lisle Rose's excellent biography *Explorer: The Life of Richard E. Byrd* (2008).

R. E. Byrd with Laurence Gould. *Courtesy of Carleton College Archives.*

Byrd signed the top of the ukulele in two separate locations—one between the sound hole and the bridge, another in the left lower bout in the "certification area."

Leo M. Peterson (May 13, 1901–April 22, 1995)

Leo Peterson was born in Alabama. In 1916, he was one of six flyers employed for the season by the Northern Aircraft Company of Bay City, Michigan. The company booked appearances at "fairs, carnivals and homecomings," and were advertised as "A Sure-Fire Attraction . . . Will draw more paid admissions than any Attraction ever offered." It was likely in this air show capacity that Peterson became intimately familiar with airplane engines. He joined the Navy at seventeen years of age in 1919, serving seven years including in World War I, and later in the reserves. When Byrd hired him, he was a Naval Air Service mechanic in Anacostia, Virginia. In *Skyward*, Byrd writes, "Aviation Machinist's Mate Leo M. Peterson was given leave from the Navy" to accompany the expedition. Peterson was Byrd's trusted engine expert and mechanic for the 1929 expedition to the North Pole. Peterson was the first person to greet Bennett and Byrd upon their landing back at King's Bay. He died in Duplin County, North Carolina, at the age of ninety-three.

Leo M. Peterson, Byrd's mechanic. *Courtesy of Jean Neptune.*

His signature appears twice on the ukulele. On the lower-left area of the top, Peterson joined Byrd and Bennett in certifying the accuracy of Konter's inscription ("This uke was taken to the North Pole . . .") below the bridge. His barely discernible signature also appears with the *Chantier* crew on the left (bass) side below the lower bout. Comparison of Peterson's autograph with signatures from the *Chantier's* crew list at the Byrd Polar Archives appears to confirm our attribution to Peterson.

Bernt Balchen (October 23, 1899–October 17, 1973)

Bernt Balchen was Norwegian, later becoming a U. S. citizen. Balchen served as a cavalryman in the Finnish Army against the Russians in WWI. In 1921, he became a pilot in the Norwegian Naval Air Force, where he had his first Arctic flying experience. He was an early polar aviator, navigator, aircraft mechanical engineer, and military leader. He was later awarded the U. S. Distinguished Flying Cross. Balchen was a member of the *Norge* ground crew at King's Bay, and he may have been instrumental in saving Byrd's flight to the North Pole by repairing a broken ski on the *Josephine Ford* (see above). Following the expedition, Balchen did return to the United States on the *Chantier*. In New York,

Norwegian pioneer Arctic aviator Bernt Balchen. *Public domain.*

department store owner Joseph Wanamaker offered Balchen a job in his store, where the *Josephine Ford* was on display. Balchen hated the job, but was relieved to be given the job of co-pilot and navigator while flying the *Josephine Ford* on a tour of more than fifty American cities with pilot Floyd Bennett. Their task: to promote commercial aviation as a safe, reliable, and practical means of transportation. Following their air tour, Anthony Fokker hired Balchen as a test pilot for the Fokker Aircraft Company in Teterboro, New Jersey.

Balchen was with Floyd Bennett in late April of 1928 when Bennett died of pneumonia, in flight, on a mission to rescue the crew of the *Bremen*. Balchen flew the remaining eight hours and was paid $10,000 for his efforts. He gave the sum to Bennett's widow.

On November 29, 1929, Balchen became one of the first four men to fly over the South Pole. On that flight Balchen served as chief pilot, Harold June was co-pilot and radio operator, Ashley McKinley was the photographer, and Richard Byrd was the navigator and expedition leader. The flight was considered one the greatest aviation achievements in history. A Byrd Antarctic Expedition radiogram dated January 6, 1930, from Balchen to Konter (in New Zealand), confirmed that Balchen had Konter's Favilla ukulele under his seat for the Antarctic flight.

Due to his reputation as a polar, transatlantic, and aviation expert, Balchen was hired in 1931 by Amelia Earhart as a technical adviser for her planned solo transatlantic flight. She later wrote in a letter to G. P. Putnam:

Please tell Bernt Balchen how deeply I appreciate all that he did to make this flight possible. Of course he is about the finest flyer and technical expert in the world but beyond that it was his confidence in my ability which helped so much." Amelia Earhart, 22 May 1932.

A scan of the original letter can be seen at: http://e-archives.lib.purdue. edu/cdm/singleitem/collection/earhart/id/920

Balchen's Arctic exploration expertise service helped the U. S. Army Air Forces and the Allies during World War II over Scandinavia and Northern Europe. After the war, Balchen continued to be an influential leader in the U. S. Air Force, as well as a highly regarded private consultant in projects involving polar regions and aviation.

Somewhat inexplicably, in his 1958 autobiography, *Come North with Me,* Balchen contended that, in the fall of 1926 while on their tour with the *Josephine Ford,* Floyd Bennett had confided in him that he and Byrd had never reached the North Pole, but had simply flown the Fokker plane out of sight and circled for fifteen hours before returning. Balchen's story was never confirmed and all available evidence refutes it convincingly, but it has stoked the rumor mill for decades. Was Balchen feeling that Byrd had not adequately appreciated his contributions?

Balchen died of bone cancer in 1973. He was buried at Arlington National Cemetery in Virginia. He is buried in Section 2, Grave 4969, near Admiral Richard E. Byrd. His incised signature is located on the lower right-hand area of the top, below the bridge.

Charles Augustus Lindbergh
(February 4, 1902–August 26, 1974)

Richard Konter saved a prestigious spot on the top of the ukulele directly above the sound hole for aviator Charles A. Lindbergh. Because "Lucky Lindy" was a relatively unknown airmail carrier prior to his legendary transatlantic flight on May 20–21, 1927, we surmise that he autographed the ukulele after he achieved fame. Lindbergh had applied in 1925 to serve as a pilot on Byrd's North

Aviator Charles A. Lindbergh with the *Spirit of St. Louis. Library of Congress Prints and Photographs Division Washington, D. C.*

Pole expedition but apparently his bid came too late—Floyd Bennett, who'd known Byrd previously, had already accepted the job. The New York hotel owner who eventually awarded the $25,000 prize for flying nonstop from New York to Paris (or vice versa), Raymond Orteig, also signed the ukulele on the right (treble) side. Byrd had also entered the competition, but Lindbergh won it. Lindbergh's signature is directly below the group that includes (top to bottom) Calvin Coolidge, Vice President Dawes, General "Black Jack" Pershing, and Secretary of State Kellogg.

It is possible that Lindbergh's signature (nearly completely faded) also appears with what could be Amelia Earhart's (also nearly completely faded) at the bottom center of the top, above Lowell Thomas's autograph (certain) and below that of Medford, Massachusetts Mayor Edward H. Larkin (possible). These three signatures were possibly added together in Boston at the Ritz-Carlton Hotel celebration honoring Earhart on July 9, 1928, three months before Byrd (with Konter) would depart on the first Byrd Antarctic Expedition, although we cannot place Konter at the event.

Ashley Chadbourne McKinley
(June 23, 1896–February 11, 1970)

After concluding his military service in the Army in 1926, Ashley McKinley established an aerial photographic and surveying service that gave him particular expertise in this unique field. Though not a participant on the 1926 North Pole expedition, he was responsible for photography on Byrd's 1928–1929 Antarctic expedition to the South Pole. In fact, he was

Ashley McKinley. *Public domain. Press photo from C. F. Martin & Co. archives.*

on the plane at the South Pole with Byrd, June, and Balchen. In the war years that followed, he was specifically recognized with the U. S. Air Corps' Legion of Merit award for his exceptional service in testing and developing cold-weather equipment. He was promoted eventually to colonel.

His slightly faded signature appears on the top next to Bernt Balchen's below the right side of the bridge. McKinley's, Balchen's, and Larry Gould's autographs were almost certainly added to the top of the ukulele at the same time. Although it could have been at the National Geographic Luncheon of June 20, 1930, that Konter attended, another possibility is that McKinley signed at the Grand Street Boys Benefit "Antarctic Night," held on December 15, 1931. These three signatures were also probably signed with the same pen, each showing a remarkable impression in the surface of the wood compared to the surrounding signatures.

Clyde Edward Pangborn
(October 28, 1895–March 29, 1958)

Clyde Pangborn was the first person to fly nonstop across the Pacific Ocean. He was an American aviator and barnstormer, also known as "Upside-Down Pangborn," who performed aerial stunts in the 1920s. Together with Ivan Gates, he co-owned Gates Flying Circus and became nationally famous for

Clyde Pangborn.
Public domain.

daring stunts like moving from plane to plane in midair. In 1931, Pangborn and co-pilot Hugh Herndon Jr. attempted to break the record for flying around the world. Later that year, the pair embarked on the first nonstop trans-Pacific flight. They flew from Siberia to Japan, where they planned to embark for the U. S. mainland, but instead were jailed in Japan for espionage, their detailed flight maps confiscated. After many adventures, they finally took off from Sabishiro Beach, Japan, and landed in East Wenatchee, Washington, forty-one hours and thirteen minutes later. Pangborn observed Japanese military aviation power and warned in 1935 of a potential Japanese attack after realizing the capability of Japan's air force. During World War II, Pangborn served in the Royal Air Force, and after the war was a commercial pilot. He was instrument-rated to fly any aircraft.

Pangborn's signature follows the shoulder of the instrument along the lower left.

Marie Ahnighito Peary (Stafford)
(September 12, 1893–April 16, 1978)

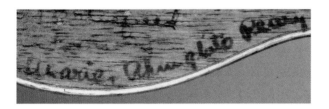

Marie Ahnighito Peary, daughter of Rear Admiral Robert E. Peary, was born in Greenland on one of her father's expeditions in 1893. She became known worldwide as the "Snow Baby." An Inuit woman who made Marie her first fur suit gave her the nickname, never before having seen a baby with such light skin. Marie was sixteen when her father discovered the North Pole. She became famous overnight as the beautiful debutante daughter of a major international hero. In 1917, Marie married Edward Stafford, a Washington attorney with whom she had two sons. Admiral Peary died in 1920 and, in 1932, Marie returned to the Arctic to erect a monument to memorialize her father's accomplishments.

Mrs. Stafford evidently had a bit of a crush on Richard Byrd, writing him on January 27, 1927, "If it is at all possible to arrange it, it would be the biggest thing that ever happened to me if I could make my first flight with you, whom I admire more than anyone except Dad. It would be a memory to treasure forever." (BP, Folder 4317).

Marie Ahnighito Peary Stafford with her father's (Robert Peary) flag. *Public domain. National Photo Company Collection, Library of Congress, Washington, D. C.*

She later became an important figure in international politics. During World War II, she served on the Danish-American Commission that stabilized the dollar and established security for Denmark and Greenland. Marie was awarded the Liberation Medal by the Danish government for her contributions to the commission. In 1950, she was awarded the Henry B. Bryant medal for her contributions to geographical information.

After her husband and mother both passed away in 1955, Marie lived in Bowdoin, Maine. In 1967, she married her second husband, William Kuhne, a retired seaman. She lived in Bowdoin until her death. Her signature is clear and prominent along the binding of the upper-left bout of the top.

Marie Ahnighito Peary, "The Snow Baby." *Public domain.* George Grantham Bain Collection, Library of Congress, Washington, D.C.

Roald Engelbregt Amundsen
(July 16, 1872–June 18, 1928)

Arguably Norway's (and the world's) most famous polar explorer, Roald Amundsen is associated with the most significant polar expeditions of his time. Amundsen was born in Borge, Norway, to a family of seafarers. His mother implored Roald, her fourth son, to pursue a different path in life, that of a medical man. Upon his mother's death when he was twenty-one years of age, he quit the university for a career in seafaring, exploration, and aviation. In 1914, he took airplane pilot training and was awarded the first pilot's license issued in Norway.

During 1903–1906, he was the first mariner to navigate the Northwest Passage. On the voyage, he demonstrated that the geomagnetic North Pole wanders over time. In December 1911, his Antarctic expedition beat Robert Falcon Scott's team in reaching the ninety-degree latitude of the South Pole. In 1925, Amundsen, Lincoln Ellsworth, pilot Hjalmar Riiser-Larsen, and three other team members were the first to reach the northernmost latitude to date (87° 44 north) aboard two Dornier flying boats. With one of the planes badly damaged upon landing, Amundsen and crew shoveled six hundred tons

Roald Amundsen,
Ny-Ålesund,
Svalbard, 1925.
*Preus Museum
c/o Paul Berge.
Creative Commons
Attribution 2.0
Generic license.*

of ice over a period of several weeks with brutal temperatures and limited food to prepare a suitable airstrip. All six returned triumphant on the remaining plane when the world thought they had been lost forever. In 1926, following Byrd and Bennett, Amundsen led the expedition with Umberto Nobile and the crew of the airship *Norge* in overflying the North Pole and crossing the Arctic Ocean. In 1928 Amundsen accompanied a French air mission to rescue any survivors of Nobile's crashed airship, the *Italia*. Tragically, the rescue plane too crashed and the bodies of the six, including Amundsen's, were never found.

All three previous claims to have arrived at the North Pole—Frederick Cook's in 1908; Robert Peary's in 1909; and Richard E. Byrd's in 1926 (just a few days before the *Norge's*)—are all disputed. If the *Norge* expedition was the first to reach the North Pole, Roald Amundsen and Oscar Wisting are the first men to reach both the North and South poles, by ground or by air.

Amundsen's signature (with many letters most likely re-inked by Konter) is the largest of any on the ukulele. It appears just beneath Umberto Nobile's on the top of the ukulele, just above the bass side of the bridge. We can assume that both Nobile and Amundsen signed the ukulele in Spitsbergen prior to Byrd's and Bennett's flight departure.

Lincoln Ellsworth (May 12, 1880–May 26, 1951)

Lincoln Ellsworth was a polar explorer from the United States and a major benefactor of the American Museum of Natural History. Ellsworth's father, James, was a wealthy coal mine owner. He was responsible for the construction of the Ellsworth Building at 537 South Dearborn Street in Chicago, one of the city's first "skyscrapers" (fourteen stories and a basement). Lincoln's mother Eva died in 1888, so Lincoln and his sister lived much of their childhood with their grandmother in Hudson, Ohio. The elder Ellsworth's business interests often kept him away, so young Lincoln saw much less of his father than he would have liked. Despite this, Lincoln developed a strong admiration for his father and, later in life, was determined to name a tract of Antarctica after him. Both father and son had an interest in exploration. As a young man,

Lincoln Ellsworth, 1938.
Photograph by Acme
Newspictures Inc. *Public domain.*

Lincoln explored and hunted in Canada in the first years of the twentieth century, including staking out railway lines.

After meeting Roald Amundsen in person in New York City in late 1924, James Ellsworth agreed to contribute $85,000 to Roald Amundsen's 1925 attempt to fly from Svalbard to the North Pole. The money was given on the condition that his son, who was to be a navigator in one two Dornier Wal flying boats, the N24, would stop smoking. Together, father and son contributed $95,000 of the $130,000 cost of Amundsen's 1925 expedition. The N24 and N25 took off from Svalbard on May 21, 1925. When one airplane lost power, both made forced landings and, as a result, became separated. It took three days for the crews to regroup and seven takeoff attempts before they were able to return in the N25 to Svalbard on June 15, 1925. It was soon thereafter that Lincoln learned his father had passed away on June 2, 1925, without the knowledge his son had returned safely.

In early March of 1926, under the headline "Across the Pole by Dirigible," *The New York Times* announced the "The Amundsen-Ellsworth-Nobile Transpolar Flight" from Svalbard to Alaska. This was Amundsen's second effort to fly over the pole. Lincoln Ellsworth, now in control of his own fortune, contributed with $100 000 to the effort and was appointed navigator of the expedition. The airship *Norge* left Ny-Ålesund at 9:55 a.m. on May 11, 1926, and was over the North Pole at 1:25 a.m. on the 12th, Ellsworth's birthday. This was the first undisputed sighting of the area. They landed safely in Teller, Alaska, seventy-two hours after leaving Svalbard.

Ellsworth died in New York City on May 26, 1951. His 1938 autobiography is titled *Beyond Horizons*. Ellsworth's signature appears on the face of the ukulele directly below Amundsen's.

Umberto Nobile (January 21, 1885–July 30, 1978)

Italian aeronautical engineer and Arctic explorer Umberto Nobile is primarily known for the development of dirigibles in the 1920s. He designed and piloted the airship *Norge* that was the first aircraft of any kind to fly "From Rome to Nome" across the Arctic Ocean via the North Pole, leaving just two days after Byrd's 1926 polar flight. Nobile's dog, Titina, a fox terrier like Byrd's dog Igloo, came aboard as the mascot.

Umberto Nobile with Titina. *Public domain.*

Nobile also designed and flew the ill-fated airship *Italia* in 1928 (Cross, W., 2000). Despite the fact that neither Byrd and Bennett nor the *Norge* had found any significant landmass in the Arctic Ocean, the members of the *Italia* expedition had hoped, at the very least, to find undiscovered islands near the coasts. After reaching the North Pole and heading back towards Spitsbergen, the airship iced up in heavy headwinds. They crew struggled to control of the ship, and it crashed about one hundred eighty miles northeast of King's Bay, shattering the cabin and throwing out ten of the sixteen aboard, plus various items of food and equipment. The airship again shot skyward, carrying off the remaining six crew members, including three veterans of the *Norge* expedition who signed the ukulele— Alessandrini, Arduino, and Caratti. The survivors of the first impact later saw a plume of black smoke above the horizon. Among those enlisted to help rescue the survivors of the *Italia* was Roald Amundsen, who perished in the attempt.

Nobile's signature, the first name of which appears to have been re-inked by Konter, shares a position of honor on the face of the ukulele directly above Amundsen's, Ellsworth's and Riiser-Larsen's, with Konter's adjacent attribution: "*Norge*—Spitsbergen May 10, 1926."

As noted above, Nobile's signature does *not* appear on the instrument in the July 1, 1926 glass-plate negative from the National Museum of American History.

Hjalmar Riiser-Larsen (June 7, 1890–June 3, 1965)

Norwegian aviation pioneer Hjalmar Riiser-Larsen piloted the N25 Dornier flying boat for Roald Amundsen, reaching latitude 87° 44 north in 1925. In 1926, Riiser-Larsen was the navigator and the only Norwegian with an airship license aboard the airship *Norge* during the Amundsen-Ellsworth-Nobile flight from Svalbard over the North Pole to Alaska. In 1928, Riiser-Larsen returned to Svalbard to join the rescue effort for Umberto Nobile and the crew of the airship *Italia* that had crashed on the drift ice. He and fellow Norwegian Lützow-Holm flew a number of search flights, and when Amundsen disappeared on the way to Svalbard to join in the search effort, Riiser-Larsen led the expedition that searched (unsuccessfully) for him. Riiser-Larsen's signature accompanies the other significant *Norge* signatures on the top of the ukulele: Amundsen's, Nobile's, and Ellsworth's.

Hjalmar Riiser-Larsen (1890–1965) was a pioneer of Norwegian aviation. He piloted the flying boat N25 for Roald Amundsen in 1925 and was navigator on the airship *Norge* in 1926. Wikimedia Commons, Bundesarchiv, Bild 102-14193 / Foto: Georg Pahl / Wikipedia, Creative Commons CC-BY-SA 3.0 License.

John Calvin Coolidge Jr.
(July 4, 1872–January 5, 1933)

The signature of the thirtieth president of the United States appears on the top of the ukulele between the sound hole and the fingerboard under the strings. Konter reserved this prominent position for signatures he deemed to be of the utmost importance. The first few letters of Coolidge's first name are abraded from Konter's strumming. Coolidge was president at the time of the Byrd Arctic Expedition, in office from August 2, 1923 to March 4, 1929.

It is unlikely that the president and Konter—a mere sailor—would have crossed paths otherwise. A clipping from an unidentified Brooklyn newspaper in the Konter Archive at the National Archives and Records Administration dated November 30, 1927, reads, "Since that expedition, Mr. Konter has had interviews with President Coolidge who also autographed the ukulele . . ." Thus, we know that Coolidge must have signed before that date and after June 23, 1926, when the expedition arrived "officially" back in New York, a seventeen-month interval. Konter was not present when Coolidge presented the Hubbard Medal to Byrd at the Washington Auditorium on the evening of the day of the ticker-tape parade in New York City to honor the returning heroes. That afternoon, Byrd and Bennett had taken the Colonial Express to Washington, D. C.

John Calvin Coolidge, thirtieth president of the United States, 1919. *Public domain. Notman Photo Co., Boston. Library of Congress Prints and Photographs Division Washington, D.C.*

Coolidge had at least one opportunity to autograph Konter's Martin ukulele. Konter's presence at the White House is documented in an undated photograph taken by Harris & Ewing, a photographic studio based in Washington, D. C. In it, Konter is seated outside on the sill of a White House window. Coolidge's signature is visible on the instrument, but the headstock is unsigned. Thus, Konter must have been at the White House after July 1, 1926, the date of the glass-plate negative showing no signature by Coolidge, and before Saturday, October 23, 1926, the day Marie of Romania signed on the headstock. Her signature is not present on the ukulele at the time of the White House photo. For the moment, the exact date and location where the president autographed the ukulele remain a mystery.

Richard Konter with ukulele at the White House, Washington, D. C. *Public domain. Photograph by Harris & Ewing, Washington, D. C.*

Coolidge awarded Byrd the Congressional Medal of Honor at the White House on February 19, 1927, but the ukulele had already been signed by Coolidge as of this date.

Charles Gates Dawes (August 27, 1865–April 23, 1951)

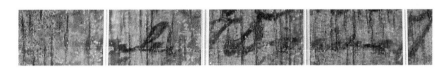

Charles Gates Dawes was an American banker, politician, and thirtieth vice president of the United States (1925–1929). For his work on the Dawes Plan for World War I reparations, he was a co-recipient of the Nobel Peace Prize in 1925. Dawes served in the First World War, was the Comptroller of the Currency, the first director of the Bureau of the Budget, and, in later life, ambassador to the United Kingdom.

He was also a pianist and composer. His work "Melody in A Major" (for piano and violin) became well known in 1912 and was played frequently at his official appearances. In 1951, lyrics were added to "Melody in A Major" by Carl Sigman, turning it into the song "It's All in the Game." Performed by Tommy Edwards, the song went to the top of the *Billboard* charts, where it remained for six weeks in fall 1958. This makes Dawes one of only two persons to have both a No. 1 hit and a Nobel Prize, the other being Bob Dylan. The song has become a standard and has been covered by (among others) the Four Tops, Isaac Hayes, Jackie DeShannon, Van Morrison, Nat "King" Cole, Elton John, Donny and Marie Osmond, Barry Manilow, and Keith Jarrett. Dawes's partial signature is located—appropriately—directly beneath President Calvin Coolidge's, between the bottom of the fingerboard and the sound hole.

The Honorable Charles G. Dawes. *Public domain. Photograph by Harris & Ewing, Washington, D. C. Library of Congress Prints and Photographs Division, Washington, D. C.*

Frank Billings Kellogg
(December 22, 1856–December 21, 1937)

Frank B. Kellogg was born in Potsdam, New York. In 1865, his family moved to Minnesota, where he became a self-educated attorney. He later became a politician and statesman. In 1905, Teddy Roosevelt asked him to prosecute a federal antitrust case. He led the prosecution against the Union Pacific Railroad in 1908, and in 1911 successfully prosecuted Standard Oil Co. of New Jersey. These cases brought him to national prominence. He was elected as president of the American Bar Association in 1912. Kellogg ran as a Republican in 1916 and served as a U. S. senator from Minnesota from 1917 to 1923, and as U. S. Secretary of State (1925–1929).

He is perhaps best remembered as co-author of the Kellogg–Briand Pact, for which he was awarded the Nobel Peace Prize for 1929. The intention of the pact was to provide for "the renunciation of war as an instrument of national policy." He later served as an associate judge on the Permanent Court of International Justice from 1930 to 1935. He died the day before his eighty-first birthday and was buried in the National Cathedral, Washington, D. C.

Konter reserved a premier location, above the sound hole, for the signatures of Coolidge, Dawes, Kellogg, Pershing, and Lindbergh.

Frank B. Kellogg, circa 1912. American politician and statesman and recipient of 1929 Nobel Peace Prize. *Public domain. Photograph by Moffet, Chicago. Library of Congress Prints and Photographs Division Washington, D. C. 20541.*

General John J. Pershing
(September 13, 1860–July 15, 1948)

General John Pershing. General Headquarters, Chaumont France, October 1918. *Public domain.* Photo by 2d Lt. L J. Rode.

General John Joseph "Black Jack" Pershing was a general officer in the United States Army who led the American Expeditionary Force on the Western Front during 1917 and 1918 in World War I. He was born near Laclede, Missouri, where he attended high school and became a teacher of local African-American children. While teaching, he earned a bachelor of science degree in 1880 from what is now Truman State University. After receiving his degree in in Missouri, he was accepted to the United States Military Academy at West Point, from which he graduated in 1886. He went on active duty in the U. S. Army in September 1886 and served in a number of posts in the American West. His marksmanship was renowned; among all the soldiers in the U. S. Army in 1891, he ranked second in pistol and fifth in rifle.

In 1895, Pershing assumed command of the 10th Calvary Regiment, one of the original African-American "Buffalo Soldier" regiments of the Army. His nickname was derived from this assignment. He later taught at West Point and, like Konter, served in the Spanish-American and Philippine-American wars, where he impressed Theodore Roosevelt at San Juan Hill.

In 1915, Pershing lost his wife and three young daughters in a fire at the Presidio in San Francisco, where he had been posted previously, as he awaited their arrival at his new posting in Fort Bliss, Texas. After his wife's death, he had a brief relationship with "Nita," the younger sister of George S. Patton. In 1916, Pershing led the expedition to Mexico to capture Pancho Villa in retaliation for his attacks on U. S. border towns like Columbus, New Mexico. Although Villa's uprising was crippled by the U. S. expedition, Villa evaded capture.

Pershing is best known for his service in World War I. His controversial tactics have been criticized, both by commanders at the time and by modern historians. His reliance on costly frontal assaults was believed by some to have been responsible for unnecessarily high American casualties. Nonetheless, Pershing was regarded as a mentor by the generation of American generals who led the United States Army in Europe during World War II, including George C. Marshall, Dwight D. Eisenhower, Omar N. Bradley, and George S. Patton.

Pershing is the only person to be promoted in his own lifetime to the highest rank in the United States Army—General of the Armies (a retroactive Congressional edict passed in 1976 promoted George Washington to the same rank, but with higher seniority). Pershing was buried in Arlington National Cemetery. His faded signature can be clearly seen with spectral light imaging. It is located below the fingerboard, under Charles Dawes and above Frank Kellogg.

Lewis Broughton Porterfield
(October 30, 1879–April 5, 1942)

Lewis Porterfield was a rear admiral of the United States Navy. He began his career as a page in the House of Representatives. As commander of the *Venetia* during World War I, he received the Distinguished Service Medal for anti-submarine operations. The disabling of submarine U-39 has been credited to the *Venetia*, and earned him the moniker "Avenger of the *Lusitania*." Porterfield had a direct role in securing Richard Konter's place on the Arctic expedition. Konter had been assigned recruitment duty in New York

Lewis B. Porterfield. *Public domain. NavSource Naval History at www. navysource.org.*

City just before the expedition was to depart. Konter informed Byrd of his predicament, and Byrd reached out to Porterfield for his help. Porterfield and his family received a holiday gift of Virginia apples from Byrd in thanks for his help. His faded and partially abraded signature appears on the upper-left shoulder of the top, confirmed with multispectral imagery.

Mayor James John Walker
(June 19, 1881–November 18, 1946)

James J. "Jimmy" Walker (aka "Beau James") was the colorful and controversial mayor of New York City from 1926 to 1932, an era of Prohibition and lawlessness. Walker was a Roaring Twenties Irish dandy from Greenwich Village who took full advantage of what the city had to offer. Prior to his political career, he had achieved some prominence as a songwriter of such pop classics as "Will You Love Me in December As You Do in May?"

New York Mayor James Walker; cropped from photo of Walker with Umberto Nobile. Photo by *New York World-Telegram and Sun* staff photographer. *Library of Congress Prints and Photographs Division. New York World-Telegram and the Sun Newspaper Photograph Collection.*

Walker saw politics early. He was born in Greenwich Village, the son of a lumberyard owner and alderman. He dropped out of college, but eventually graduated, in 1904, from the New York Law School. He passed the bar exam in 1912. He was a member of the New York State Assembly and later the New York State Senate, where he strenuously opposed Prohibition.

Walker was a liberal Democrat whose mentor was Governor Alfred E. "Al" Smith. Walker showed little interest in the work of municipal governance. Nevertheless, he did manage to legalize boxing in New York and helped repeal blue laws that prohibited Sunday baseball games and theater performances. He also championed the eight-hour workday for women, condemned the Ku Klux Klan, and supported workers' compensation and tenement laws.

However, none of his mayoral duties prevented him from sampling a wide range of the city's speakeasies on a nightly basis, earning him the nickname "The Night Mayor." He was embroiled in a staggering number of corruption scandals that ultimately forced Governor Franklin D. Roosevelt to set up hearings to determine whether Walker should be removed from office. When it became clear that Walker had been accepting large sums from local businessmen seeking to secure city contracts, Walker saw the writing on the wall and resigned on September 1, 1932.

Walker loved publicity. Early in his term, he didn't miss out on welcoming home the *Chantier* at the Battery on the Byrd Arctic Expedition's triumphant return from Spitsbergen. That is likely where Konter invited Walker to sign the ukulele. Walker later pursued his musical interests as the head of Majestic Records of New York City. He died at sixty-five years of age and was buried in Hawthorne, New York. His partially faded signature is on the top of the ukulele at an angle, immediately to the right of the bridge.

Laurence McKinley Gould
(August 22, 1896–June 21, 1995)

Laurence McKinley Gould was a renowned glacial geologist. He was appointed as second-in-command on Byrd's first Antarctic expedition in 1928–1930. He later served as president of Carleton College in Northfield, Minnesota, from 1945 to 1962. The college's main library is named in his honor.

A native of Lacota, Michigan, Gould became interested in geology during his time at the University of Michigan, which was interrupted by military service. He graduated in 1921 with a B.S. in geology. He served at Michigan as an instructor of geology while continuing his studies. During the summer of 1926, Gould served as assistant director and geologist on the University of Michigan expedition to Greenland and Baffin Island. It was this experience that brought him to the attention of Byrd, who invited him to serve with him in Antarctica as second-in-command. Gould was excited to explore the geology of the continent. Indeed, he became the first geologist to do so.

Laurence McKinley Gould, geologist and second-in-command, Byrd Antarctic Expedition. 1928 publicity photo. *Courtesy of Carleton College Archives.*

Gould was a strong advocate for science. He led the American delegation to Antarctica during the International Geophysical Year of 1957–1958. He chaired the Committee on Polar Research of the National Academy of Sciences and headed the international Special Committee on Antarctic Research.

During his lifetime, Gould received twenty-six honorary degrees and was awarded a variety of medals in honor of his explorations, including the Congressional Gold Medal, the David Livingstone Gold Medal of the American Geographical Society, the Cross of Saint Olaf (presented to him in 1949 by King Haakon of Norway), the Navy's Distinguished Public Service Medal, the Explorers Club Medal, and the Gold Medal of the Chicago Geographical Society.

His slightly incised signature, the catalyst for this book, appears on the top to the right of the bridge, adjacent to James J. Walker's.

Confidence = Possible:

Dr. Clarence Julian Easterling Owens
(July 4, 1877–February 7, 1941)

Dr. Clarence J. Owens was born in Georgia. He became the director general of the Southern Commercial Congress, Washington, D. C., a pro-business group. He was an authority on issues in U. S. commerce and expert on international trade. He served as the special commissioner of the Sesqui-Centennial International Exposition held in Philadelphia (coincidentally) in 1926. Dr. Smith oversaw a groundbreaking dedication ceremony for the New York State Buildings (we presume on August 11, 1926) with a group of dignitaries that included New York governor Alfred E. Smith. Because of the timing, we think it possible that the faint signature near the upper-left bout of the top between L. B. Porterfield's and Marie Ahnighito Peary's is that of Clarence J. Owens. We know of no connection between Konter and Owens, however.

Clarence J. Owen, 1917. Crop from photo at Pan-American Trade Meeting, Willard Hotel, Washington, D. C. Harris & Ewing, photographer. *Library of Congress Prints and Photographs Division Washington, D. C.*

Amelia Mary Earhart
(July 24, 1897–disappeared July 2, 1937)

Amelia Earhart was one of the most significant pioneers in American aviation. Her 1932 flight from Newfoundland to Northern Ireland made her the first woman aviator to fly solo across the Atlantic Ocean. For her achievement, she received the U. S. Distinguished Flying Cross. She set many other aviation records, authored books about her life experiences, and helped form an organization for female pilots called the Ninety-Nines. Beyond that, she was a tremendous inspiration for the women of her era, counseling women in their careers, encouraging women to pursue aviation as an avocation, endorsing the National Woman's Party, and showing early support for the Equal Rights Amendment. Her 1937 attempt to circumnavigate the globe in 1937 ended over the central Pacific Ocean near

Amelia Earhart standing under the nose of her Lockheed Model 10-E Electra. *Underwood & Underwood, photographers. Gelatin silver print, 1937. National Portrait Gallery, Smithsonian Institution; gift of George R. Rinhart, in memory of Joan Rinhart. Public domain.*

Howland Island. Amelia Earhart's disappearance remains a mystery, but the world's fascination with her life and career is very much alive.

Though this signature is extremely faint, its proximity to the possible, equally faint signatures of Mayor Edward H. Larkin and Charles Lindbergh in this lower central area of the top below the bridge may be suggestive of Earhart. This prominent area on the top of the ukulele would have been reserved by Konter for significant VIPs. As mentioned, a July 1, 1926 photograph of the ukulele now in the National Museum of American History reveals that Konter removed a previous message from this area, possibly to make a space for these signatures or messages that are above that of writer, broadcaster, and traveler Lowell Thomas.

Edward H. Larkin
(December 13, 1876–date of death unknown)

The signature or inscription that appears at the base of the top of the ukulele (see next page) has occupied many hours of inspection by the authors. It is in one of the most prominent locations on the entire instrument and one of the most interesting, because an inscription that formerly occupied this location was, at some point in the instrument's history, erased to make room for whatever is present here. It is smudged and barely readable, even with the advantages afforded by UV, infrared, and visible light

Miss Amelia Earhart and Mayor Edward Larkin of Medford, Massachusetts, leaving the Ritz-Carlton Hotel, July 10, 1928. *Digital Commonwealth.*

photography from the Smithsonian's Museum Conservation Institute.

Mayor Edward H. Larkin was the mayor of Medford, Massachusetts, from 1927 to 1931. Amelia Earhart lived in Medford while she was employed as a social worker in 1925; her mother and sister lived there, as well. This signature is faded, but the word "Major" or "Mayor" seems possible, as does the first name Edward, the middle initial "H," and the first letter of the last name, "L." An internet search yielded Larkin's name and photographs, and he is seen in one standing with Amelia Earhart. This suggested that the name or names immediately below Larkin's may relate to Earhart's. The difficult process suggested the possibility that Charles Lindbergh's and Amelia Earhart's were the two VIP signatures (possibly all three signed at the same event), faded though they are, at the bottom of the top just above what is definitely Lowell Thomas's (second) signature.

False color rendition of the top of the ukulele below the bridge. It shows three rows of signatures or statements important enough to Konter that he erased what was originally inscribed here. Bottom row is clearly Lowell Thomas's (second) signature.

Considerable doubt can be thrown on the accuracy of our "possible" attribution. We do not know why Konter would have dedicated such a prominent place on the ukulele, even going to the extent of erasing a previous inscription, to make room for the signature of a Massachusetts mayor. Nor do we know why his signature would have appeared larger and above those of two of the most famous aviators in history, one of whom had already signed the ukulele elsewhere.

The top of Konter's North Pole ukulele, strung. *Photo by John Sterling Ruth.*

11

Signers on the Right Side

The right side of the ukulele was signed by at least 26 individuals. They are listed below, first by confidence category, then alphabetically by Signer Category.

Confidence = Certain:

Floyd Phillips Gibbons	Journalists, Authors & Cinematographers
Francis Trevelyan Miller	Journalists, Authors & Cinematographers
Adolph Simon Ochs	Journalists, Authors & Cinematographers
Russell Owen	Journalists, Authors & Cinematographers
Lowell Jackson Thomas	Journalists, Authors & Cinematographers
Renato Alessandrini	*Norge* Dirigible Crew
Maresciallo Ettore Arduino	*Norge* Dirigible Crew
Attilio Caratti	*Norge* Dirigible Crew
Natale Cecioni	*Norge* Dirigible Crew
Capt. Birger Lund Gottwaldt	*Norge* Dirigible Crew
1st Lieut. Emil Andreas Horgen	*Norge* Dirigible Crew
Dr. Finn Malmgren	*Norge* Dirigible Crew
Oskar Omdal	*Norge* Dirigible Crew
Vincenzo Pomella	*Norge* Dirigible Crew

Frederik Ramm	*Norge* Dirigible Crew
Fridtjof Storm-Johnsen	*Norge* Dirigible Crew
Oskar Adolf Wisting	*Norge* Dirigible Crew
Harry Flood Byrd, Sr.	Politicians & Military
Grover Aloysius Whalen	Politicians & Military
Thomas Alva Edison	Scientists
William Vincent Astor	Sponsors
Raymond Orteig	Sponsors
Lewis Rodman Wanamaker	Sponsors

Confidence = Probable:

| Captain Adalberto Mariano | *Norge* Dirigible Crew |
| Charles T. Sabin | Sponsors |

Confidence = Possible:

| Paul Arpinnste | Signature Unidentified |

Confidence = Certain:

Floyd Phillips Gibbons
(July 16, 1887–September 23, 1939)

Author, journalist, and one of radio's earliest news reporters and commentators, Floyd Gibbons joined *The Chicago Tribune* in 1912 and was a war correspondent during World War I. His coverage of the retaliatory 1916 U.S . raid on the Mexican revolutionary Pancho Villa brought him notoriety. Between 1919 and 1926 he was chief of *The Chicago Tribune*'s foreign service, and in 1918, he was hit by German fire and lost an eye while attempting the rescue of an American soldier at the Battle of Belleau Wood in France. Thereafter, he was always seen with a distinctive white eye patch. He received France's highest military honor for valor on the field of battle, and after his death in 1939, he was made an honorary member of the Marine Corps, the first time a civilian ever received the distinction. Known for his rapid-fire verbal delivery, Gibbons was the narrator for the 1930 film *With Byrd at the South Pole,* with cinematography by Willard Van der Veer, who also is a signer of the ukulele. The documentary was the very first to win an Academy Award and the only one to win for cinematography. Gibbons's stylized and flamboyant signature appears on the right (treble) side, just below the waist.

Floyd Gibbons, war correspondent, after being wounded, 1918. *Harris & Ewing Collection, Library of Congress Prints and Photographs Division Washington, D. C.*

Francis Trevelyan Miller
(1877–1959)

F. T. Miller was born in Southington, Connecticut. He became a writer and filmmaker, best known for his books about exploration, travel, and photography. He wrote *The Photographic History of the Civil War in Ten Volumes* and the screenplay for *Deliverance,* a 1919 film about Helen Keller. In addition to his books about the Civil War and World Wars I and II, he also authored two books about the Byrd expeditions, *Byrd's Great Adventure* and *The World's Great Adventure,* explaining his inclusion on the ukulele. His signature appears on the right (treble) side below Harry Byrd's.

Cover to *Byrd's Great Adventure,* by Francis Trevelyan Miller.

Adolph Simon Ochs
(March 12, 1858–April 8, 1935)

Adolph S. Ochs was an American newspaper publisher and former owner of *The New York Times* and *The Chattanooga Times.* In 1896, the *Times* was experiencing financial losses and fierce competition. Ochs was able to borrow

the funds to purchase the paper, become the primary shareholder, form the New York Times Corporation, restore the paper to firm financial footing, and in 1904 move the business to a new building in what would become Times Square. In the 1920s, he added the well-known phrase "All the news that's fit to print." to the masthead. Under his leadership, circulation grew from 9,000 to an astonishing 780,000 by the early 1920s. Obviously, he would have traveled in important circles and most likely would have greeted the *Chantier* upon its triumphant return—or at least have attended the celebratory parades and events.

New York Times publisher Adolph Ochs (1858–1935) and his daughter, Iphigene, 1902. *Public domain. Original photograph by Aimé Dupont.*

Later, at Little America in Antarctica, Byrd named the radio station "the Ochs Radio Station, in honor of the friend who has done so much for me." Byrd, R. E. *Little America* (1930:163). His scribbled signature stumped us until we discovered one of his letters at the OSU Byrd Polar Archives that had an identical comparative autograph. His signature appears with other journalists', sponsors', and dignitaries' just above the waist of the right (treble) side.

Russell Owen (January 8, 1889–April 3, 1952)

Russell Owen was an American journalist employed by *The New York Times*. He covered Arctic and Antarctic exploration both as a reporter and as an author of several books. Owen flew with Amundsen aboard the *Norge* to King's Bay on Spitsbergen, where he first met R. E. Byrd. Owen won the 1930 Pulitzer Prize for Reporting in 1930 for his coverage of Byrd's first Antarctic expedition. He appears in the Academy Award–winning film *With Byrd at the South Pole* (Paramount, 1930). He also wrote a book about the expedition, *South of the Sun.*

Russell Owen at typewriter.

In Antarctica he was generally disliked, intensely by Byrd. Indeed, in his Antarctic journal for May 1, 1929, Thomas B. Mulroy wrote, "Owens is the most laziest and useless S of B on the expedition it would give me great pleasure to plant him out on the Barrier." Yet, Owen wrote,

"They belong to a unique fraternity, these fliers. They are a little different from other men in their attitude toward their work. For fliers know that every day they fly death may lurk behind the next cloud; they all feel that some-where, some time, they will meet death quickly. Yet they keep on.

RUSSELL D. OWEN
"OCEAN FLYING TAKES HEAVY TOLL"
(Quoted in Bart 2013).

His signature appears (partially overwritten in pencil) at the waist of the right treble side just below Grover Whalen's. Owen's boss and owner of *The New York Times* Adolph S. Ochs also signed this side of the ukulele.

Lowell Jackson Thomas (April 6, 1892–August 29, 1981)

To many of Konter's contemporaries, Lowell Thomas would have been one of the ukulele's best-known signers. Thomas's journalistic impact made him familiar to the American public through his tales of far-flung lands and peoples. He was born in Woodington, Darke County, Ohio, and grew up in Victor,

Colorado. One of his jobs in Victor was working at the local newspaper. He later attended Princeton University, where he caught the attention of the university president at the time, Woodrow Wilson.

As U. S. president, Wilson enlisted Thomas to drum up public support for American involvement in the deeply unpopular First World War, although his assignment was ostensibly to "compile a history of the conflict." While a war correspondent, Thomas made T. E. Lawrence ("Lawrence of Arabia") known to the world. From the twenties until 1952, Thomas was heard by millions as the narrator of *Movietone* newsreels for Twentieth Century Fox. He also supported and attempted to mainstream the development and popularization of the widescreen "Cinerama" movie format using multiple synchronized projectors. From 1930 until his retirement in 1976, he was a prominent radio newscaster for both CBS and NBC. In 1940, Thomas anchored the first live telecast of a political convention, although he broadcast from a studio in New York while the convention was held in Philadelphia. In 1945, he

Lowell Thomas in 1939.. From the cover of *Magic Dials: The Story of Radio and Television. Public domain*

was honored with the Alfred I. duPont Award for broadcast journalism in the public interest. He was accomplished in so many areas, the Library of Congress had difficulty cataloguing and classifying his memoirs, and so was forced to catalogue them in "CT" ("biographies of subjects who do not fit into any other category").

Thomas's signature appears just above the waist on the right (treble) side. His distinctive signature also appears below the bridge on the top of the ukulele. This area of the instrument is discussed elsewhere in more detail. The presence of Lowell Thomas's signature in this area suggests by its context that he may be attesting to the authenticity of other statements (made in the same area of the top) about the ukulele. Thomas died at home in Pawling, New York, in 1981.

Renato Alessandrini
(August 11, 1890–May 25, 1928)

Alessandrini (signed with last name only, as the Italians did commonly) was a rigger aboard the *Norge* in 1926. He perished in the airship *Italia* disaster on May 25, 1928. He disappeared with the envelope after the gondola was torn off on the ice. His signature appears with his fellow Italians' on the bottom of the left (bass) side above Pomella's.

Renato Alessandrini, 1929.
Public domain.

Maresciallo Ettore Arduino
(1890–1928)

Ettore Arduino of Verona, Italy, was a wing lieutenant in the Italian Military Aeronautical Corps of Engineers. He became an airship engineer and participated in aerial bombing raids during the war with Austria. After the war, Arduino continued to work on airships at the Aeronautical Construction Establishment, where he, like Pomella, was noticed by Umberto Nobile. In 1926, Arduino accepted Nobile's invitation to be a part of the transpolar flight led by Nobile, Amundsen, and Ellsworth. He was one of the crew that flew with the airship for its entire flight from Rome to Teller, Alaska, via London, Leningrad, Vadsø, Svalbard, and the North Pole.

In 1928, Arduino was placed in charge of the engines on Nobile's ill-fated airship *Italia*. When the crew lost control of the airship and it bounced off the ice, the gondola was torn off the *Italia's*

Ettore Arduino, 1926. National Library of Norway. *Public domain.*

upper envelope. Arduino managed to throw critical, life-saving equipment to those on the ice before floating away to his death with the envelope. His remains were never found. The Verona, Italy Aero Club is dedicated to his memory. His signature, surely solicited by Konter in Spitsbergen, appears at the bottom-right (treble) side with his Italian compatriots'.

Attilio Caratti (1895–1928)

Attilio Caratti was born in Rovato, Italy. After World War I and the death of his father, he returned to Rovato to work at the family workshop with his brothers. In 1926, he served as mechanic aboard the airship *Norge*. Caratti's brother helped Umberto Nobile to design the *Norge*. In 1928, Caratti served as the engine mechanic for the port side engine on the airship *Italia*. Like Arduino, he disappeared with the airship envelope after the gondola was torn off on the ice. He was never found. His barely legible signature is at the bottom of the right (treble) side with his fellow Italian crew members'.

Atillio Caratti, 1926.
Public domain.

Natale Cecioni (1888–1960)

Natale Cecioni of Vaglia, Italy, was a motorcycle expert enlisted by Umberto Nobile to be chief mechanic on the airship *Norge*. Cecioni was also the elevator operator/chief technician on the ill-fated airship *Italia*. He survived the *Italia*'s crash in 1928, despite being thrown out onto the ice and breaking both his legs. He played a crucial

Natale Cecioni, 1926.
Public domain. Courtesy of Società Geografica Italia.

role in the crew's eventual rescue by restoring the radio to an operational state after the crash. The 1969 Russian film *The Red Tent* is a not-so-faithful dramatization of the *Italia* expedition, featuring Sean Connery as Amundsen. Cecioni's signature appears at a slight angle on the bottom of the right (treble) side near the autographs of his fellow Italian crew members.

Birger Lund Gottwaldt (August 29, 1880–April 14, 1968)

Gottwaldt (as he signed) grew up in Oslo and, like Konter, went to sea at the age of fifteen. Through extensive study he became well versed in electronics, telegraphy-telephony, signaling, radio technique, mine laying and defense, shipbuilding, and artillery. In 1918, Gottwaldt helped to found the company that introduced wireless telephony to Norway. In 1926, he was in charge of radio service aboard the airship *Norge*; he later was made a Knight of St Olav's Order for his contribution to that flight. As one of Norway's best-known and most well-rounded naval officers, Gottwaldt served in key military commands and is greatly respected as one of the pioneers of radio communications and polar flying.

Birger Lund Gottwaldt.
Public domain. The National Library of Norway.

Gottwaldt's signature is on right side in the midst of the other Norwegian crew members of the *Norge*. It is badly abraded in an area of the widest part of the lower-right bout. However, enough remains to see that it matches the rare images of Gottwaldt's signature we have located, one of which is from an auction of a piece of the *Norge*'s fabric skin containing other crew signatures.

Emil Andreas Horgen (October 21, 1890–1954)

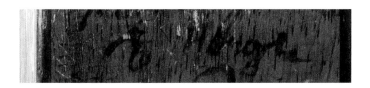

Emil Horgen was 1st Lieutenant, rudder operator, and navigation assistant on the airship *Norge*. He was a 1912 graduate of the Norwegian Naval Academy. Later, Horgen trained as a military pilot in Norway and England. On Roald

Amundsen's 1925 N24/25 expedition, he served as a reserve pilot. He trained in Rome with Umberto Nobile and the Italian crew of the *Norge* along with other members of the Norwegian crew for a month and a half before the *Norge* left for Svalbard. Horgen was to have been on the Latham-47 plane that searched for crew of the missing airship *Italia*, but Horgen's wife was about to give birth, and he did not go. Horgen left the Navy in 1936, but enlisted again in 1940 as second-in-command on the armored ship *Norge*. He was on leave when the Germans invaded April 9, 1940, but he was eventually caught and imprisoned. Horgen was released before the Norwegian officers were sent to prison camps in Poland due to poor health. He left the Norwegian Navy in 1945 at the rank of captain.

Emil Andreas Horgen. *Public domain. The National Library of Norway.*

His signature appears on the right (treble) side just below the lower bout.

Finn Adolf Erik Johan Malmgren (1895–June 1928)

After receiving his bachelor's degree from Uppsala University, Swedish meteorologist and physicist Finn Malmgren continued his affiliation with Uppsala as a professor, eventually gaining expertise in oceanic studies. From 1922 to 1925, Malmgren enlisted with Roald Amundsen for his Arctic exploration aboard the S. S. *Maud* across the Northwest Passage, and in 1926, he joined Amundsen and Umberto Nobile aboard the *Norge* airship's flyover of the North Pole. In 1928, he again joined Nobile as meteorologist on the Arctic expedition of the airship *Italia*, but on its third ill-fated flight, the dirigible crashed, stranding several members of the expedition on floating ice. Malmgren, together with Filippo Zappi and Adalberto Mariano, tried walking back to King's Bay, but with a badly injured shoulder, Malmgren collapsed and asked to be left behind. Boris Chukhnovsky, a Soviet pilot from the icebreaker *Krasin*, sighted Mariano and Zappi with Malmgren's body, and though Mariano and Zappi were rescued the following day, Malmgren's body was never found. The mystery surrounding Malmgren's death was reported in the press, where

Finn Malmgren. *Public domain. The National Library of Norway.*

it was suggested that Zappi and Mariano may have abandoned Malmgren and possibly even engaged in cannibalism. Malmgren's signature is located with those of other dignitaries on the right (treble) side near the lower bout. He must have signed the ukulele in Spitsbergen prior to the departure of the *Norge* airship to the North Pole.

Oskar Omdal (1895–1927)

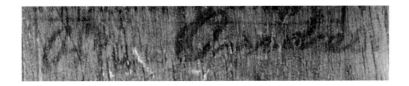

Oskar Omdal was one of Norway's foremost air pioneers. In 1921, Roald Amundsen enlisted Omdal as one of two pilots for his planned North Pole flight from Alaska, but the project seemed jinxed from the start. Omdal damaged one plane in cross-country flight and crashed a second during a test flight. With the sponsorship assistance of American Lincoln Ellsworth, Amundsen made new plans late in 1923. Omdal closely supervised the building of the new Italian-made Dornier Wal flying boats, the N24 and N25, and in the spring of 1925, they were ready. Omdal was the mechanic on the N24, with Leif Dietrichson as pilot and Ellsworth as navigator. The planes landed a few miles apart without radio contact at 87° 44 north. It was the northernmost latitude reached by plane up to that time, but the

N24 was damaged and could not be flown again. Omdal almost died when he fell through the ice on the way from N24 to N25. After twenty-five days of hard work at making a runway in the ice, all six men managed to fly back to Svalbard aboard N25. Omdal made important films during the strenuous expedition. Amundsen wrote later about Omdal that "if he is not present, he is always missed." On July 4, 1925, the expedition members were given an overwhelming hero's welcome in Kristiania (Oslo), Norway. For Omdal, the fame gave him a permanent lieutenant's job in Norway's Naval Air Force.

Oskar Omdal (left) with Roald Amundsen, before their attempt to fly to the North Pole. June 28, 1922. *Public domain.*

Omdal was one of three machinists on the 1926 flight of the airship *Norge* that flew from Spitzbergen over the North Pole to Alaska. A year later, Bernt Balchen enlisted Omdal as reserve pilot on Byrd's South Pole expedition; but prior to the expedition, Omdal accepted a job with Frances Wilson Grayson, a property investor, to cross the Atlantic in a flying boat. Despite bad weather, Omdal took off from New York with Grayson and Brice Goldsborough on board. Having reported heavy icing off the coast of Boston, the plane disappeared without trace.

Omdal's partially faded signature can be found on the right (treble) side of the ukulele, directly above Finn Malmgren's.

Vincenzo Pomella (1896–1928)

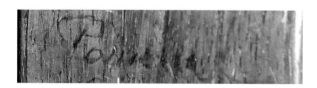

Vincenzo Pomella was an Italian aeronautical engineer with expertise in airship design and their subsequent use in polar exploration. Pomella was born in St. Elias Fiumerapido, Italy. At thirteen, he moved to Rome and developed a passion for engineering. During World War I, he joined the Aeronautical

Engineers in Torino, where he attended mechanics courses for airships. In 1918, he was a crew member on di Calabria's and D'Annunzio's dirigible flight to Vienna. As his skills sharpened, he worked at Rome's Aeronautical Construction Establishment, where he attracted the attention of Umberto Nobile, who chose him for his crew.

In 1926, Pomella joined Nobile's expedition with Amundsen and Ellsworth as a member of the crew of the airship *Norge*. After the successful flight, Pomella stayed with Nobile and, in 1928, he joined Nobile's expedition on the airship *Italia*. When the *Italia* crashed, Pomella was thrown onto the ice and he died of severe head injuries.

He would have signed Konter's ukulele with his fellow Italian *Norge* crew members in Spitsbergen prior to their May 10, 1926 flight over the North Pole. Pomella's signature can be found at the bottom of the right (treble) side.

Vincenzo Pomella, 1926. *Public domain.*

Frederik Ramm (March 11, 1892–November 15, 1943)

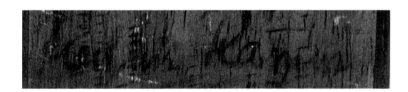

Norwegian newspaper journalist Frederik Ramm went to the Norwegian archipelago of Svalbard in 1924 to report on Roald Amundsen's planned flight to the North Pole with two Dornier air boats. Though the expedition was postponed until 1925, Ramm remained in Svalbard continuing his reporting. In 1926, he joined the Amundsen-Ellsworth-Nobile Arctic flight aboard the airship *Norge* and transmitted regular typed reports by telegraph directly from the dirigible. After the expedition, he submitted a chapter for Amundsen's book about the flight. In the highly politicized

Fredrik Ramm, Norwegian journalist and newspaper editor. *Public domain. The National Library of Norway.*

years preceding World War II, Ramm worked as the editor for the newspaper *Morgenbladet*, where he participated in a widespread Christian movement that resulted in his arrest and life sentence in 1941 by the Germans. Though his sentence was later reduced to ten years, he became ill while incarcerated in Hamburg. Because of the severity of his illness, he was allowed to return home, but died on the way. Frederik Ramm's well-known article "En skitten strøm flyter over landet" ("A dirty current flows over the country"—October 28, 1931) was an attack on the radical intellectual writers of the period, such as Sigurd Hoel. His signature appears with several other *Norge* participants' on the right (treble) side below the lower bout.

Fridtjof Storm-Johnsen
(dates of birth and death unknown)

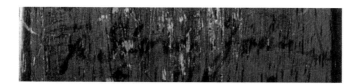

Fridtjof Storm-Johnsen was a Norwegian radio and telegraph operator aboard the 1926 Arctic expedition of the airship *Norge*. Prior to the expedition, Storm-Johnsen held a temporary position at the Kings Bay radio station in Ny-Ålesund. When the S. S. *Maud*'s Russian telegraphist Gennadij Olonkin developed an ear infection, Amundsen replaced him with his fellow Norwegian. Storm-Johnsen assisted Birger Gottwaldt, who was in charge of radio transmission aboard the *Norge*. Storm-Johnsen's faded signature is seen on the right (treble) side of the ukulele near the lower bout.

Storm-Johnsen aboard Ægir. The vessel would carry Fredrik Ramm around Svalbard. *Public domain. The National Library of Norway.*

Oskar Adolf Wisting (June 6, 1871–December 5, 1936)

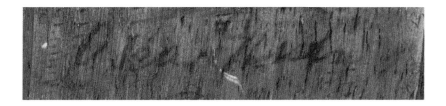

Oskar Adolf Wisting is best known as a Norwegian polar explorer and devoted crew member on many of Roald Amundsen's expeditions. With Amundsen, Wisting was the first person to reach both the North and South poles. From 1918 to 1925, he served as chief officer on the *Maud* in Roald Amundsen's attempt to traverse the Northeast Passage. Between 1923 and 1925, Wisting became the de facto leader of the expedition after Amundsen left to attempt a polar flight. Wisting flew with the airship *Norge* on the flight from Rome to Svalbard and was honored to hoist the Norwegian flag on the airship during the departure ceremony in Rome. On the flight across the Polar Sea, Wisting ran the elevation rudder. It was on the night of May 11–12, 1926, that he and Amundsen became the two first men to reach both poles. In honor of his polar achievements, the Norwegian parliament promoted Chief Gunner Wisting to captain on July 6, 1926. In 1928, Amundsen invited Wisting to join him on the search for the airship *Italia*, but there was no room on the Latham-47 plane to Svalbard. Thus, Wisting survived the ill-fated rescue that claimed Amundsen's life. Wisting led a search expedition with the sealer *Veslekari* for Amundsen, to no avail. This was to be his last expedition.

Original press photo of Amundsen's right-hand man, Oscar Wisting, with "Oberst," the biggest dog in the pack, 1912. *Public domain. Original by Wide World Photos.*

Harry Flood Byrd Sr. (June 10, 1887–October 20, 1966)

The eldest of three Byrd brothers (Tom, Dick, and Harry), Harry F. Byrd was a newspaper publisher, farmer, and politician. He was born in Martinsburg, West Virginia, but his family moved to Winchester, Virginia, in the Shenandoah Valley shortly after his birth. The Byrds were descended from of some of the most socially prominent and wealthy of Virginia's early English families. Byrd's ancestors included William Byrd II of Westover Plantation, who established Richmond; Robert "King" Carter of Corotoman, a colonial governor; and Pocahontas. His younger brother was Richard E. Byrd, Jr.

Byrd married a childhood sweetheart, built a cabin from chestnut logs on a family orchard, and named it Westwood. He sold apples and operated a newspaper, *The Winchester Star.* His business dealings instilled in him a "pay-as-you-go" philosophy that guided his governmental outlook, as well.

Like many of his ancestors, Byrd became a prominent political figure in Virginia. He is known for his reorganization and modernization of Virginia's government. His political machine dominated Virginia Democratic Party politics for much of the first half of the twentieth century. He was elected the fiftieth governor of Virginia in

Governor Harry Flood Byrd Sr. American newspaper publisher, farmer, and politician, taken while governor of Virginia circa 1926–1930. *Harris & Ewing Collection, Library of Congress Prints and Photographs Division Washington, D. C.*

1925 and continued to lead a political movement that became known as the Byrd Organization. He represented Virginia as a United States senator after being appointed in 1933 to fill a vacancy; he was then reelected seven times until his retirement in 1965 due to failing health. He was the leader of the "conservative coalition" in the United States Senate, which blocked much liberal legislation after 1937.

Byrd was an avowed white separatist; he opposed racial desegregation strenuously. He was instrumental in the creation of Shenandoah National Park, Skyline Drive, and the magnificent Blue Ridge Parkway. It must have been convenient for R. E. Byrd to have a brother who wielded so much political power. Harry Sr. was the father of Harry F. Byrd Jr., who was appointed to succeed his father as U. S. senator upon his father's retirement. Harry Sr.'s signature is located on the right (treble) side of the ukulele near the upper bout.

Grover Whalen (1886–1962)

Grover Aloysius Whalen was a New York City politician and businessman. He was a master of public relations and became the official greeter for New York City. He is known as the originator of the ticker-tape parade. He was New York police commissioner when the *Chantier* arrived at the Battery in NYC and was prominent during the parade to honor the expedition. In *Race to the Top of the World: Richard Byrd and the First Flight to the North Pole*, Sheldon Bart notes that "Whalen orchestrated the tumult and hoopla, and was busy concocting even more elaborate fanfare for Queen Marie of Romania" (Marie's autograph is, in fact, on the headstock of the ukulele). Whalen's autobiography is titled *Mr. New York*.

Grover Whalen, commissioner of the New York World's Fair, January 17, 1939. *Harris & Ewing Collection, Library of Congress Prints and Photographs Division Washington, D. C.*

Whalen enforced Prohibition laws ruthlessly and was quoted as having observed that, "There is plenty of law at the end of a nightstick." At the International Unemployment Day demonstration held on March 6, 1930, in New York City, one thousand baton-wielding police set upon some thirty-five thousand demonstrators who were marching down Broadway to City Hall. A contemporary report from *The New York Times* read:

"Hundreds of policemen and detectives, swinging nightsticks, blackjacks, and bare fists, rushed into the crowd, hitting out at all with whom they came into contract, chasing many across the street and into adjacent thoroughfares and pushing hundreds off their feet. From all parts of the scene of battle came the screams of women and cries of men with bloody heads and faces."

Whalen was forced to resign within two months for escalating the violence against the crowd. Nevertheless, he remained a prominent figure of the era.

Whalen's signature appears with dignitaries' and journalists' at the waist of the right side above Russell Owen's.

Thomas Alva Edison
(February 11, 1847–October 18, 1931)

Thomas Alva Edison. *Louis Bachrach, Bachrach Studios, restored by Michel Vuijlsteke - Library of Congress Prints and Photographs Division Washington, D. C.*

Along with Leonardo da Vinci, Thomas Edison ranks among the world's most famous inventors and is one of the best-known signers of the ukulele. He was the recipient of numerous awards and prizes for his work, including membership in the National Academy of Sciences and the Navy Distinguished Service Medal, and was named a commander in the French *Ordre National de la Légion d'Honneur.* His inventions and innovations had a profound influence on nearly every aspect of modern life. These included the phonograph, the incandescent lightbulb, the motion-picture camera, and the industrial research laboratory. Edison was awarded 1,092 more United States patents than Richard Konter, who held exactly one. "The Wizard of Menlo Park" was born in Ohio and grew up in Michigan.

He had scarlet fever as a child, which was thought to be the cause of his partial deafness. He started his career as a telegraph operator. Edison's research and the devices they spawned laid the foundations for modern telecommunications.

As a fellow inventor, Konter surely recognized what a tremendous honor it was to secure Edison's autograph, though we are not certain why he scraped the finish away above his signature. Edison died at his home in West Orange, New Jersey, and was buried on the property.

Edison's autograph is among expedition sponsors', journalists', and other dignitaries', near the waist of the right (treble) side of the ukulele.

William Vincent Astor
(November 15, 1891–February 3, 1959)

A financial donor to the expedition, Vincent Astor came into $70 million when, in 1912, his father, John Jacob Astor IV, perished on the *Titanic*. Vincent's was the largest inheritance in American history, as of that date. At the age of thirty-five, Vincent Astor contributed $5,000 to the expedition. Astor had trained as a pilot and had served as an officer in World War I. He had hoped to attend the Naval Academy, but his father had other plans for him. He remained a naval reservist and served as commodore of the New York Yacht Club from 1928 to 1930. Astor also contributed to Byrd's 1929–1930 Antarctic expedition. Byrd named Antarctica's Mount Astor in the Hays Mountains of the Queen Maud Range in his honor. Astor is buried in Sleepy Hollow Cemetery in Sleepy Hollow, New York. His signature appears in good company on the right (treble) side of the ukulele, just above Thomas Edison's.

Vincent Astor, circa 1912. *Public domain.* New York World-Telegram & Sun *Newspaper Photograph Collection, Library of Congress Prints and Photographs Division Washington, D. C.*

Raymond Orteig (1870–June 6, 1939)

Orteig was born to a rural sheep herding family high in the French Pyrenees. He emigrated to the United States at the age of twelve, taking a job as a bar porter in New York City for $2 per week, but soon found work at the Hotel Martin in Greenwich Village. Orteig worked his way up in the hotel, serving as waiter, head waiter, and hotel manager, and by 1902 he had saved up enough money to buy the hotel. He renamed it the Hotel Lafayette in honor of the Marquis de Lafayette, the young French nobleman who served as George Washington's aide-de-camp. Soon thereafter, Orteig acquired a second property, the Brevoort Hotel in Greenwich Village. Orteig is probably best known as the person who offered the $25,000 prize for a nonstop flight from Paris to New York, or vice versa. Orteig made his offer, valid for five years, on May 22, 1919, in a letter to the president of the Aero Club of America. It went unclaimed, so Orteig reissued the prize on June 1, 1925. Although R.

Mr. and Mrs. Raymond Orteig, May 12, 1932, after passage of R.M.S. *Mauretania* back to New York. *Public domain. Courtesy of http:// www.clos-cot.com.*

E. Byrd entered the competition, the prize was eventually claimed by Charles A. Lindbergh. For his charitable works, including many among the French community in New York City, Orteig was made a chevalier of the *Ordre National de la Légion d'Honneur*, France's highest order for military and civil merits, established in 1802 by Napoleon Bonaparte. His signature is on the right (treble) side of the ukulele, just below Thomas Edison's.

Lewis Rodman Wanamaker
(February 13, 1863–March 9, 1928)

L. Rodman Wanamaker was a department store magnate with stores in Philadelphia, New York, and Paris. He was a significant benefactor to the arts, education, athletics, and Native American scholarship. More significantly to his presence on the ukulele, he was a pioneer in sponsoring record-breaking aviation projects and an early backer of transatlantic flight development.

He was born in Philadelphia, the son of department store owner John Wanamaker and his wife, Mary Brown. Rodman attended Princeton University, from which he graduated in 1886. He joined his father's business and married that same year. He lived abroad for a decade as the Paris resident manager.

Between 1908 and 1913 he sponsored three photographic expeditions to document contemporary Native Americans and their quickly disappearing traditions. He also had interests in aviation. In 1913, his financial contributions encouraged Curtiss Aeroplane and Motor Company

Lewis Rodman Wanamaker in 1927. *Public domain. George Grantham Bain Collection, Library of Congress, Prints & Photographs Division.*

to encourage the development of flying boats robust enough for transatlantic crossings. With the death of his father in 1922, Rodman became the sole owner of the world's largest department store chain.

He also funded the American Trans-Oceanic Company's efforts to increase aircraft range, his intent being to win Raymond Orteig's $25,000 prize for the first nonstop plane flight between New York and Paris. But it was Charles Lindbergh's historic May 1927 flight that won the prize, beating Wanamaker's entry, the Fokker trimotor *America*, flown by Richard E. Byrd, by only a few days. Regardless, Wanamaker's sponsorship and support of aviation had a tremendous impact, helping to launch a new industry and reduce the duration of international flight times.

Wanamaker was also a great fan of music and musical instruments. During his tenure, around 1909, the Wanamaker department stores in New York and

Philadelphia had Martin make some special guitar models; the Wanamaker branded hot stamps still exist in the Martin archives.

Wanamaker suffered from kidney disease during the last decade of his life. He passed away in Atlantic City, New Jersey, and was buried in Philadelphia. His unique signature, ending with a colon ":" is located on the right (treble) side of the ukulele, appropriately right below Raymond Orteig's.

Among the other sponsors of the expedition, there are two notable omissions: Edsel Ford and John D. Rockefeller Jr. If their signatures were present, we would expect both to be located on the right side among the three other expedition sponsors'. However, we have been unable to locate either autograph on the ukulele. The absence of Edsel Ford's signature is understandable, based as he was in Michigan. However, we found an interesting letter at the Byrd Polar Archives from Rockefeller's personal secretary, Robert W. Gumbel, to Byrd. In the letter, Gumbel informs Byrd of a request he received from Konter:

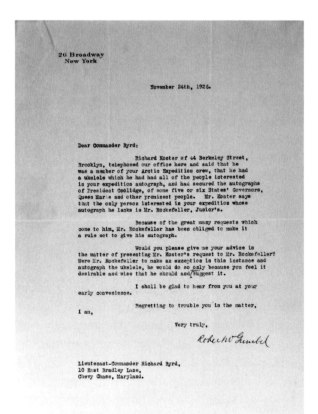

Letter from Robert Gumbel to Richard Byrd, November 24, 1926, inquiring about Konter's request for Rockefeller's signature. *Photo courtesy of* Expeditions: North Pole Flight, *Admiral Richard E. Byrd Papers, The Ohio State University, Byrd Polar and Climate Research Center Archival Program.*

Richard Konter of 44 Berkeley Street, Brooklyn, telephoned our office here and said that he was a member of your Arctic Expedition crew, that he had a ukulele which he had had all of the people interested in your expedition autograph, and had secured the autographs of President Coolidge, of some five or six States' Governors, Queen Marie, and other prominent people. Mr. Konter says that the only person interested in your expedition whose autographs he lacks is Mr. Rockefeller, Junior's.

Because of the great many requests which come to him, Mr. Rockefeller has been obliged to make it a rule not to give his autograph.

Would you please give me your advice in the matter of presenting Mr. Konter's request to Mr. Rockefeller? Were Mr. Rockefeller to make an exception in this instance and autograph the ukulele, he would do so only because you feel it desirable and wise that he should and you suggest it.

We have located no additional correspondence regarding the matter. We see, though, that if Rockefeller's autograph never made it onto the ukulele, it wasn't for Konter's lack of trying.

Confidence = Probable:

Captain Adalberto Mariano
(June 6, 1898–October 27, 1972)

Adalberto Mariano and his wife, the Countess Francesca Bianconcini Persians of Mignano. *Public domain.*

Mariano is *not* listed as a member of the sixteen-man expedition of the *Norge* to the pole. However, Mariano was second-in-command on Umberto Nobile's 1928 airship *Italia* expedition. When the *Italia* crashed, Mariano, Finn Malmgren, and Filippo Zappi attempted to walk back to Kings Bay, but Malmgren, with an injured shoulder, was a casualty. Zappi and Mariano were rescued after being sighted by pilot Boris Chukhnovsky from the icebreaker *Krasin*. (See full story at Index #0031—Nobile.) Due to extreme frostbite, Mariano's leg was amputated and fitted with a prosthesis, but a year after the incident, he married the Countess Francesca Bianconcini Persians of Mignano. They had two sons, one of whom he named Finn, in memory of Malmgren.

His probable signature appears with the other Italians' at the bottom of the right (bass) side. He may have accompanied the expedition to Spitsbergen, but not made the flight. We have found this nowhere documented, but Konter mentions several times that there was a ground crew of about two hundred helping with the *Norge*. Perhaps Mariano was among them. We have found no documentary evidence that Mariano came to the United States, which may suggest that if this is his signature, he must have signed at Kings Bay, Spitsbergen.

Charles T. Sabin (date of birth unknown–1933)

We believe this signature may belong to Charles T. Sabin, vice president of the New York and New England Railroad. If he was twenty years of age at the time he was initiated into the Masons, he would have been eighty-nine years old at the time of Byrd's Arctic expedition. As the railway was highly profitable, it is possible that Sabin, or his company, was in some way a sponsor or donor to the expedition, though we have no documentary evidence of this. It is also possible he was a friend or associate of Byrd's, as the address of the railway is listed as 8 Congress Street, Boston, Massachusetts, less than one mile from Byrd's home at 9 Brimmer Street in downtown Boston. The poorly executed or ink-bled signature appears appropriately with other dignitaries', sponsors', and journalists' on the right (treble) side. This particular Charles Sabin is likely not another man of the same name who was the owner of a slate quarry in Montpelier, Vermont.

Confidence = Possible:

Paul Arpinnste(n) (dates of birth and death unknown)

There is clearly a name in this location on the upper shoulder of the right (treble) side, but it remains indecipherable. The name as shown here must be considered conjecture.

12

Signers on the Left Side

THE LEFT SIDE OF THE UKULELE was signed by at least fifty individuals. They are listed below, first by confidence category, then alphabetically by signer category.

Confidence = Certain:

Alexander H. Anderson	Byrd Arctic Expedition
George Hamilton Black	Byrd Arctic Expedition
Captain Michael Joseph Brennan	Byrd Arctic Expedition
Roy Joseph B. Bryant	Byrd Arctic Expedition
Axel Hildemar Carlson	Byrd Arctic Expedition
Jalmar Celius	Byrd Arctic Expedition
Arthur R. Clark	Byrd Arctic Expedition
Fred Coliver	Byrd Arctic Expedition
Alfred G. Davis	Byrd Arctic Expedition
Joe de Ganahl	Byrd Arctic Expedition
Felice (Frank) J. De Luca	Byrd Arctic Expedition
Epaminodas "Pete" James Demas	Byrd Arctic Expedition
Robert E. Donahue	Byrd Arctic Expedition
Winston Wilder Ehrgott	Byrd Arctic Expedition
James A. Feury	Byrd Arctic Expedition
Frank William Fritzson	Byrd Arctic Expedition
Alexander Edward Geisler	Byrd Arctic Expedition
Albert Edward Gething	Byrd Arctic Expedition

Charles Frederick Gould	Byrd Arctic Expedition
Walter Thomas Gray	Byrd Arctic Expedition
Lloyd Kellog Grenlie	Byrd Arctic Expedition
William Cassius Haines	Byrd Arctic Expedition
Johan Hangaas	Byrd Arctic Expedition
Malcolm P. Hanson	Byrd Arctic Expedition
Thomas A. Hewson	Byrd Arctic Expedition
George Henry Leon James	Byrd Arctic Expedition
Martin P. Kaszolka	Byrd Arctic Expedition
Thomas Harold Kinkade	Byrd Arctic Expedition
Karl Lundstrom	Byrd Arctic Expedition
James V. Madison	Byrd Arctic Expedition
Corporal Robert Harold James McKay	Byrd Arctic Expedition
Thomas Bernard Mulroy	Byrd Arctic Expedition
Edward J. Nolan	Byrd Arctic Expedition
Lieutenant George Otto Noville	Byrd Arctic Expedition
Dr. Daniel Patrick O'Brien	Byrd Arctic Expedition
Lieutenant Robb Church Oertel	Byrd Arctic Expedition
First Lieutenant Alton N. Parker	Byrd Arctic Expedition
Alan D. Porter	Byrd Arctic Expedition
Helmsman Jonathan Duff Reed	Byrd Arctic Expedition
James Andrew Slaughter Jr.	Byrd Arctic Expedition
John L. Sutton	Byrd Arctic Expedition
John S. Szentpetery	Byrd Arctic Expedition
Paul Todaro	Byrd Arctic Expedition
Mr. Alcide A. Touchette	Byrd Arctic Expedition
Willard Van der Veer	Byrd Arctic Expedition
Josephine M. Coombs	Wife

Confidence = Probable:

Rodmar Arnesen	Byrd Arctic Expedition
Charles Leroy Kessler	Byrd Arctic Expedition
Wolcott Gibbs	Journalists, Authors & Cinematographers

Confidence = Possible:

Wieno Johannes Lauren   Byrd Arctic Expedition

Confidence = Certain:

Alexander H. Anderson
(April 22, 1903–October 31, 1976)

Of Finnish ancestry, A. H. Anderson was born in Montana. By the age of six he was living in Trimble, Ohio. When he signed on as a fireman with the Byrd Arctic Expedition, his address was listed as Jacksonville, Ohio. The fireman, or "stoker," on steamships had the job of tending the fire for the running of a steam engine. The United States Navy referred to them as "watertenders." Much of the job was hard physical labor, such as shoveling fuel, typically coal, into the engine's firebox. In fact, the entire crew may have been called upon to do this job at the onset of the trip to Spitsbergen, since the weight distribution of coal in the holds was imbalanced and coal needed to be transferred from the back of the ship to the middle. Anderson's gravestone in Lordstown, Ohio, recalls his service to the 1926 Byrd North Pole expedition. His signature appears below K. Lundstrom's on the bottom of the left (bass) side.

George Hamilton Black (July 11, 1896–July 28, 1965)

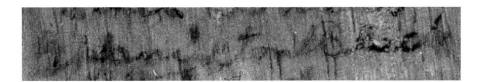

George H. Black (or G. Hamilton Black, as his signature reads) was born in Revere, Massachusetts. He is listed as an able seaman as well as tractor man aboard the *Chantier*. The tractor man was charged with loading or discharging large cargo using the ship's gantry cranes and winches. He served in the Army during both World Wars and was decorated in the European theater. Black also served as a crew member for Byrd's first Antarctic expedition and appeared as a member of the cast in the documentary film *With Byrd at the South Pole*. By 1935 he was working with Byrd's cousin D. H. Byrd at Byrd-

Frost Inc., an oil company in Texas. Later in his life, he lived with his wife in Dallas, Texas, and worked as an apartment manager. Black died in Fort Worth, Texas, in 1965. The first initial and middle name of his signature are only slightly legible, appearing about an inch below the lower bout on the left (bass) side of the ukulele.

Captain Michael J. Brennan
(August 15, 1888–June 23, 1976)

G. H. Black (tentative).

Michael J. Brennan (also spelled Brannan in several sources, and on the ukulele) was born in Kilbaha, County Clare, Ireland. He came to the United States in 1910. He worked on sailing vessels from the age of fifteen, served in World War I as a Navy lieutenant, and afterward in the merchant marine. Brennan was hired by Byrd to serve as captain of the S. S. *Chantier.*

A seasoned mariner, Brennan daily had to face the fact that only nine of his fifty-two-man crew on the *Chantier* had never shipped out previously. The first couple of weeks were especially hard. Byrd recounted in a speech in July 1926 that Brennan was particularly frustrated by the lack of decent helmsmen aboard. He recalled Brennan yelling, "You blankety, blankety landlubber, there isn't a man on the ship who can steer!"

Other tasks were also difficult for the crew. One crew member became agitated when he saw a "light dead ahead," on a collision course with the *Chantier.* The light turned out to be the planet Venus. Samantha Seiple wrote in *Byrd & Igloo*: "While Konter's dog Igloo was busy making mad dashes around the decks, the square-jawed captain of the *Chantier*, Michael Brennan, was struggling to steer the ship. It turned out that the weight from the coal in the after hold was too heavy, causing the rear of the *Chantier* to sink down lower into the ocean. All hands were called

Michael J. Brannan, captain of the *Chantier. Photo courtesy of* Expeditions: North Pole Flight, *Admiral Richard E. Byrd Papers, The Ohio State University, Byrd Polar and Climate Research Center Archival Program.*

on deck. Byrd and his queasy, seasick crew spent days breaking their backs moving the coal from the after hold to the midship coal bunkers. But it didn't dampen their enthusiasm."

Notably, Brennan recorded an exact duration (fifteen hours, fifty-seven minutes) for Byrd and Bennett's flight to the North Pole in the log book of the *Chantier*. He died at the age of eighty-seven, buried with military honors in the U. S. National Cemetery at Pinelawn.

His signature appears with others' of the *Chantier* crew on the upper shoulder of the left (bass) side.

Roy Bryant (November 5, 1894–December 1971)

Roy Bryant was born in Laredo, Texas. By the time he was fifteen, his family was living on La Page Street in the 7th Ward in New Orleans, Louisiana, his mother's home. He was a captain in the Army Reserve during World War I. Both he and Jonathan Duff Reed (see entry below) were heroes and both went on Byrd's North Pole expedition as ordinary seamen. In *Skyward*, Byrd comments that though the two were "utterly without sea experience, they knuckled down and stood hardship and toil like old mariners." Bryant's last known address was in 11373 Flushing, Queens, New York.

Bryant's signature is on the left side at the upper bout. A copy of his signature from his World War I draft registration shows unmistakable similarity in the final letter of his last name. There appears one of Konter's "fences" or demarcation lines associated with or connected to his signature, but we are unsure what Konter is separating. The left side of the ukulele is entirely *Chantier* crew, with the exceptions of Josephine Coombs, Wolcott Gibbs, and Willard Van der Veer up by the neck joint.

Axel H. Carlson
(November 23, 1888–date of death unknown)

A. H. Carlson of Stockholm, Sweden, and later Minneapolis, Minnesota, was second assistant engineer aboard the S. S. *Chantier*. He served in World War I, and his registration identifies him as a marine steam engineer. His World War II draft registration places him in the Bronx, New York, in 1942. The second assistant is typically in charge of boilers, auxiliary engines, and fuel transfer (bunkering). He neatly written signature, signed with fountain pen, appears perpendicular to most of the other signatures on the left (bass) side near the waist, overlapping slightly with A. E. Gething's.

Axel H. Carlson. *Public domain, National Archives and Records Administration; Application for Seaman's Protection Certificates.*

Jalmar Celius (July 18, 1901–date of death unknown)

Jalmar Celius of Osknes, Norway, was a fireman aboard the *Chantier*. He remained on board the *Chantier* on the night of June 23, 1926, while Byrd and Bennett received medals from President Calvin Coolidge. He most likely signed the ukulele after the rest of the crew, as his signature is perpendicular to the others. His signature appears on the left (bass) side along the back binding. After his *Chantier* voyage, Celius enlisted as a sailor on the S. S. *Namasket*, Fleet No. 1, based out of Linoleumville, Staten Island, New York.

Jalmar Celius. *Public domain. National Archives and Records Administration; Washington, D. C. Petitions for Naturalization from the U. S. District Court for the Southern District of New York.*

Arthur R. Clark (June 11, 1904–date of death unknown)

A. R. Clark of Chicago, Illinois, signed on as a mess boy aboard the *Chantier*. The mess boy was charged with odd jobs in a ship's food service, cleaning the crew's mess room, waiting on tables, dishwashing, and pantry work. The *Chantier*'s manifest for the trip home from London to New York has Clark's entry on line five filled in with his details. But, in ink it has been scratched out with the word "DESERTED." We know of no additional details, however.

Clark's birth year is estimated from the crew list at OSU's Byrd Polar Archives and on the *Chantier* manifest. Clark's signature is upside down (in relation to most of the others) on the upper-left shoulder.

Fred Coliver (ca. 1889–date of death unknown)

Fred Coliver, listed with two Brooklyn addresses (1195 Fulton Street and 9 Arlington Place), was an oiler aboard the *Chantier*. The main duty of an oiler (or "greaser") is maintaining, cleaning, and, at times, operating ship engine parts. He was listed as a German national on the crew list at the Byrd Polar Archives. His signature appears below Leo Peterson's at the bottom of the left (bass) side.

Alfred G. Davis (ca. 1884–date of death unknown)

> D, stand for Davis, he's willing and able,
> when the chow bell rings, he is first to the table.
>   —From *The Chantier Shovelful*

A. G. Davis, originally hailing from Massachusetts but later with a Brooklyn address, was the first assistant engineer, as noted in official *New York Times* list. The first assistant engineer is responsible for supervising the daily maintenance and operation of the engine department. His signature, upside down in relation to most other crew members' on the left (treble) side, is above G. O. Noville's on the upper shoulder of the ukulele.

Joe de Ganahl (December 30, 1902–July 21, 1943)

Like several last-minute additions to the *Chantier*'s crew, Joe de Ganahl came aboard with bag and baggage the day the *Chantier* departed from New York. He was born on December 30, 1902, in Tampico, Tamaulipas, Mexico, to Florence Josephine Wrotnowski, age thirty, and Charles Francis de Ganahl, age thirty-three. He graduated from Harvard in 1925, where he was editor of the *Crimson* newspaper.

In his book *Skyward: Man's Mastery of the Air*, Byrd remembers: "(Joe de Ganahl) said he had to go. I looked him over, sized him up as a good man, and took him. He turned out to be a perfect wonder." In fact, reporting on Byrd's reception in New York City, *The New York Times* noted that de Ganahl received one of the nine medals Byrd awarded, chosen by ballot among the crew. While Mayor James Walker was pinning a medal on de Ganahl's chest, Byrd said, "This boy worked sixteen hours a day, shoveling coal all through the expedition . . ." After leading a blushing de Ganahl to a more conspicuous place on the stage, Mayor Walker told the huge crowd, "And if anything else is necessary to prove the courage of this young man's bravery, let me tell you that he is just getting ready to be married." In fact, he married Josephine M. Coombs (also a signer of the ukulele) on June 30, 1926—just seven days later. Based on his stellar performance in the Arctic, in 1928–1930 he was a member of the first Byrd Antarctic Expedition, and was a member of the Antarctic geological party led by Laurence M. Gould.

Joe de Ganahl. Seaman's Protection Certificate application photo. *Public domain. National Archives and Records Administration; Washington, D. C.*

Felice (Frank) J. De Luca
(January 22, 1894–March 11, 1978)

Frank De Luca was born in Italy. He was first officer aboard the S. S. *Chantier* with his address listed as Brooklyn, New York. In Byrd's book *Skyward: Man's Mastery of the Air*, Byrd describes De Luca as "a great fellow" and tells the following story: "(De Luca) hoisted the body of the *Josephine Ford* from the ship's hold in a swirl of flakes. A change in tide began to close the lane we had opened among the heavy cakes of ice that blocked our course ashore. Yet by tireless work and unswerving determination our men managed to prop the awkward body of the plane on its frail support."

F. De Luca, first officer aboard the *Chantier*. *Photo courtesy of* Expeditions: North Pole Flight, *Admiral Richard E. Byrd Papers, The Ohio State University, Byrd Polar and Climate Research Center Archival Program.*

Epaminodas "Pete" James Demas
(May 31, 1905–November 17, 1979)

E. J. "Pete" Demas was born in Feneo, Corinth, Greece. He emigrated to the United States in 1917 and settled in Washington, D. C., graduating from McKinley Technical High School in 1926. He was working as a bellhop at the Hotel Washington in Washington, D. C., where

E. J. Demas with Byrd's dog, Igloo, in Wellington, New Zealand, 1928. *Photographs of Epaminondas J. Demas, 1926–1979, National Archives.*

R. E. Byrd often dined. Demas's older brother Nick made salads that Byrd loved and subsequently, Byrd became aware of Pete's aspirations to a career in aviation. He signed on as a mess boy aboard the *Chantier*. Demas said of the 1926 Byrd North Pole expedition, "All you needed to take along was your strength. The rest was provided." He later became an expert airplane mechanic, serving on two of Byrd's Antarctic expeditions. Demas was the first person to operate a land vehicle on the Antarctic continent. He also worked on Charles Lindbergh's plane, *The Spirit of St. Louis*. With help from Byrd, he received a scholarship to New York University and graduated. Byrd later named a range of mountains in Antarctica after Demas. He worked as an aeronautical engineer for Lockheed in Burbank, California. He died at seventy-four in Los Angeles, California, in 1979. His signature is located at the lower bout on the left (bass) side.

Robert. E. ("Bob") Donahue
(ca. 1923–date of death unknown)

Robert Donahue was a photo journalist from Pathé Films who accompanied Willard Van der Veer on Byrd's North Pole expedition. Byrd admitted that he simply didn't realize the power of motion pictures and didn't give Van der Veer or Donahue "much time or attention." He later regretted this and referred to the pair as "two good men." Konter was most likely paying Donahue a compliment by including him with the rest of the *Chantier* crew on the left (bass) side of the ukulele.

Winston Wilder Ehrgott
(November 7, 1901–May 8, 1980)

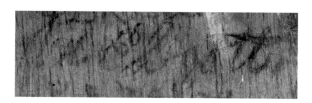

Together with West Point classmate Paul Todaro, Winston Ehrgott showed up at the last minute prior to the *Chantier*'s departure from New York City. They were looking over likely places to stow away when their chance came. Byrd saw them, sized both of them up, and decided to take them. In *Skyward: Man's Mastery of the Air*, Byrd recalls a funny incident: "In the interests of truth, I must record that Ehrgott

Winston Ehrgott. *Byrd Polar and Climate Research Center Archival Program, The Ohio State University.*

was put to work at washing dishes. But when he broke twenty dishes in the first five minutes, I had to shift him to a detail that could better withstand his energy." Ehrgott was born in Pueblo, Colorado, and rose to the rank of lieutenant colonel in the U. S. Army, serving in both World War II and in Korea. He is buried in Fort Snelling National Cemetery, Minneapolis, Minnesota. His faint but identifiable signature appears a few inches below the waist on the left (bass) side.

James A. Feury (December 7, 1899–December 1977)

James A. Feury of Paterson, New Jersey, was born in Manhattan, New York City, one of six children. According to the 1920 Federal Census, he was working in Paterson as a driver for an ice cream company after graduating high school. He was hired on as a coal passer aboard the *Chantier*. He was probably a friend of fellow coal passer John Sutton, also of Paterson. The newspapers often misspelled his last name. He also signed onto Byrd's Antarctic expedition as a fireman. He became a chief yeoman in the Navy and was listed by the time of the 1940 Federal Census as living in Newark, New Jersey. His signature is seen at the lower bout of the left (bass) side.

Frank W. Fritzson (September 11, 1883–March 16, 1966)

A son of Swedish immigrants and hailing from New Britain, Connecticut, Frank Fritzson worked in various factories around New Britain, including the Stanley Rule & Level Co. He enlisted on March 7, 1904, and spent eighteen years in the Navy. He was a chief electrician by the time of the Arctic expedition. He accompanied Byrd on the *Chantier* as an able seaman.

Later, on Byrd's first Antarctic expedition, Fritzson was a crew member of the S. S. *Eleanor Bolling*, as documented by Byrd in *Little America: Aerial Exploration in the Antarctic, the Flight to the South Pole*. His signature appears on the upper-left shoulder of the ukulele, overlapping slightly with Malcolm P. Hanson's.

Frank Fritzon standing between Roald Amundsen (left) and Richard Konter (right) in front of the *Josephine Ford*. *Courtesy of Jean Neptune.*

Alexander E. Geisler (July 20, 1897–February 25, 1987)

A. E. Geisler was listed on the *Chantier* crew list as an ordinary seaman from Bristol, Rhode Island. The term "ordinary seaman" (the lowest rank of merchant seaman) refers to a seaman or deckhand with between one and two years' experience at sea, who showed enough seamanship to be so rated by their captain. Geisler was a bodybuilder who met Byrd at a local Washington, D. C. gym that both men frequented (Bart 2013). In his book *Skyward: Man's Mastery of the Air*, Byrd explains: "It was Geisler who took an oath not to shave until we had flown across the North Pole. He grew a huge bush during the weeks of preparation. When the time came for his great shave he found himself in the hands of the whole crew who took delight in doing the job for him." This hilarious shaving scene can be viewed online in the documentary *Josephine Ford Byrd Arctic Expedition 1926* or *Hollow Earth: 1926 Flight Over North Pole*. Konter furiously accompanies the riotous fiasco on the ukulele, freshly retrieved from the *Josephine Ford*. Geisler died in Collier, Florida, at the age of eighty-nine.

(Left to right) Bennett, Oertel, and Geisler at Kings Bay. *Cropped image courtesy of* Expeditions: North Pole Flight, *Admiral Richard E. Byrd Papers, The Ohio State University, Byrd Polar and Climate Research Center Archival Program, The Ohio State University Libraries.*

Albert E. Gething
(June 11, 1896–date of death unknown)

Welsh-born A. E. Gething came to the United States on March 12, 1920, on the S. S. *Adriatic* on his way to Falls River, Massachusetts. He was assistant cook and baker aboard the *Chantier*, assisting head cook George Tennant.

His signature is perpendicular to the rest of the crew signatures on the left (bass) side, suggesting that he was perhaps one of the last to sign.

Charles F. "Chips" Gould (June 1896–October 21, 1957)

C. F. "Chips" Gould. *Photo courtesy of* Expeditions: North Pole Flight, *Admiral Richard E. Byrd Papers, The Ohio State University, Byrd Polar and Climate Research Center Archival Program.*

Charles F. "Chips" Gould of Fort Myers, Florida, was the ship's carpenter aboard the S. S. *Chantier.* On page 339 of Sheldon Bart's book *Race to the Top of the World,* "Chips" Gould is described as "a tall, lanky ship's carpenter who would winter over in Antarctica with Byrd." Gould served with distinction on the North Pole expedition. Byrd also recruited Gould for the South Pole expedition. Gould Peak (78° 07' 00" S, 155° 15' 00" W) in the southern group of Rockefeller Mountains is named for him. C. F. Gould's somewhat faded signature appears on the left (bass) side, about an inch below the waist.

Walter T. Gray (July 21, 1893–May 24, 1933)

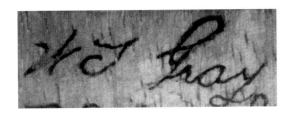

G, stands for Gray, no he's not a waiter, he's always at work on the water circulator.

—From *The Chantier Shovelful*

Walter Gray, certificate photo, 1919.

W. T. Gray of Washington, D. C., was the third assistant on the S. S. *Chantier*. He worked in the engine department of the ship and would typically have been responsible for "electrical, sewage treatment, lube oil, bilge, and oily water separation systems." It was common for the third assistant to carry the nickname "Third Turd" due to his sewage responsibilities. Tragically, he passed away at the young age of thirty-nine from a brain tumor. His clearly legible signature appears on the left (bass) side, right at the waist bend.

Lloyd Kellogg Grenlie
(November 10, 1902–June 7, 1970)

Lloyd K. Grenlie of Chicago, Illinois, was the senior radio operator aboard the S. S. *Chantier*. Like his assistant G. H. James, Grenlie was an ex-Marine who had just resigned from military service. In his diary, *To the Pole 1925–1927*, edited by Raimond E. Goerler, Byrd made the following entry on April 16, 1926, concerning the challenges that his radio operators were facing (page 68): "In spite of the almost superhuman effort of (Malcolm P.) Hanson, (L. K.) Grenlie and (G. H.) James the noises about the ship prevent proper reception. I don't see how Hanson stands the loss of sleep as he does."

Grenlie's signature appears perpendicular to the other signatures, along the back binding of the left (bass) side, just below the waist.

Lloyd Grenlie (left) with G. H. James (*right*) at the radio of the *Chantier*. *Public domain.* From "Wireless with the Byrd Arctic Expedition." *Wireless World*, June 9, 1926.

The commercial 1 kW. Marconi quenched-spark set of the ^ Chantier."

William Cassius Haines (February 1, 1887–April 7, 1956)

H, is our weather man, his name is Haines,
when he predicts good weather, that's when it rains.

   —From *The Chantier Shovelful*

William C. Haines was the meteorologist on Byrd's 1926 expedition to the North Pole, as well as on the 1928 and 1933 Byrd expeditions to the South Pole, serving as third-in-command on the latter. Hailing from Ohio, Haines was recruited by Byrd from the St. Louis Weather Bureau. His meteorological expertise was instrumental to the success of the mission because his forecasts ensured the safety of the polar researchers. Haines was typically a slow and methodical man, but he apparently "moved fast" in a particular emergency, for which the crew gave him the humorous nickname "Cyclone." He earned Byrd's respect and became third-in-command on the second Antarctic expedition. The ice-capped Haines Mountains and Haines Glacier in Antarctica are named for him. His 1956 obituary notes that his prized possession was a wristwatch presented to him by Byrd with the inscription: "To my close friend Bill Haines whose brilliant forecast enabled us to conquer by air the North and South Poles. Dick Byrd, Dec. 25, 1930." He is buried in Arlington National Cemetery. Though his abbreviated first name (Wm.) is abraded, the rest of his signature is clear and appears on the left (bass) side just below the waist.

William C. "Cyclone" Haines, March 25, 1926. Underwood & Underwood Photograph. *C. F. Martin Archives.*

Johan Hangaas (ca. 1906–date of death unknown)

Hangaas was a Norwegian-born sailor who signed on with the Byrd's North Pole expedition with fellow Norwegians Rodman Arnesen and Jalmar Celius. He was listed as having replaced James Joyce (who didn't go) as a fireman in New York City and shared lodging at a boarding house at 111 Pioneer Street, New York City, with Arnesen and Celius. He signed the ukulele directly below A. H. Anderson on the lower bout of the left (bass) side.

Malcolm Hanson (October 19, 1894–August 8, 1942)

Born in Berlin, Germany, Malcolm Hanson emigrated to the Unites States with his family in 1911. Early in his career, he served as a radio engineer on the U. S. S. B.'s S. S. *Brompton*. At the time of the expedition he was a civilian employee of the Naval Research Laboratory in Washington, D. C. Hanson had designed the *Chantier*'s radio transmitter, but the radio was not fully functional upon leaving New York Harbor. Hanson decided to stow away and keep working to fix the problem. He was discovered by Byrd, who had little choice but to let him continue his work. He was successful, but only after the ship was well under way. With the help of senior radio operator Lloyd K. Grenlie and junior radio operator George H. James, Hanson finally figured out

Malcolm P. Hanson, 1919.
Washington, D.C.; National Archives and Records Administration; Application for Seaman's Protection Certificates. Public Domain.

what was causing radio interference. By moving the radio shed away from the ship's equipment room to a position on the stern deck of the *Chantier*, interference was minimized. Hanson was lucky that Byrd interceded on his behalf with the Navy. On April 9, 1926, they received word that Hanson wouldn't disciplined for his actions, but he was required to leave the ship at its next anchorage. Thus, he never made it to Spitsbergen. He bid the expedition farewell in Trondheim, Norway, where the *Chantier* anchored briefly to take on three new expedition members and additional supplies.

Because Hanson's dedication to the radio paid off, Byrd was grateful for his tenacity and engaged Hanson again in 1928 to run the radio communications for the expedition to the South Pole. The Engineering and Technology Wiki says, "During his year at the 'Little America' base camp, Hanson sent the longest-distanced radio signals ever attempted. He also monitored Byrd's eighteen hour and fifty-five minute plane flight to the South Pole. Using code to short wave messages, Byrd's expedition was able to stay in contact with American scientists and commercial radio stations."

Hanson rose to the rank of commander in the Navy and was a pioneer in radar. Byrd named a mountain in Antarctica after him. In August 1942, he died in an airplane crash in Alaska while testing new equipment. He is buried in Arlington National Cemetery. His signature appears with the rest of the *Chantier* crew members' on the upper shoulder of the left (bass) side.

Thomas A. Hewson (ca. 1877–date of death unknown)

Thos A. Hewson (as he signed) of Washington, D. C., was the ship's steward aboard the *Chantier*. The steward's job was to serve meals and take care of provisions and luggage. His faded signature was difficult to decipher until we saw a comparative original at the OSU Byrd Polar Archives. Hewson signed on the upper shoulder of the left (bass) side.

George H. James (April 3, 1903–May 31, 1980)

George H. James of Manchester-by-the-Sea, Massachusetts, was junior radio operator aboard the *Chantier*. He assisted senior operator Lloyd K. Grenlie and stowaway Malcolm Hanson with communications aboard the ship. Like Grenlie, James was an ex-Marine who had just resigned from military service. As noted in Grenlie's entry, the constant noise aboard the ship interfered with proper reception of messages. Byrd's supplemental crew list in the OSU Byrd Polar Archives gives his age as twenty-four at the time of the voyage. Later in life he served as a police officer in Manchester, Massachusetts. He is buried in Pleasant Grove Cemetery in Manchester. His signature appears on the left (bass) side above Noville's on the upper bout.

Martin P. Kaszolka (November 12, 1890–died after 1942)

Martin Kaszolka was a native of Milwaukee, Wisconsin. In 1910, Kaszolka served in the U. S. Navy aboard the U. S. S. *Dixie* as an ordinary seaman. He held the position of oiler aboard the *Chantier*. The oiler maintains and operates the propulsion system, as well as facilities such as sewage, lighting, air-conditioning, fuel, and water. Kaszolka led a peripatetic seaman's life. We last hear of him (from his draft card) in 1942. He was living next to the docks at 107-1/2 West 6th Street, San Pedro (Los Angeles), California. He was fifty-two and unemployed. His abraded and faded signature is barely legible but identifiable, appearing on the left (bass) side at the widest part of the lower bout.

Martin Kaszolka, 1926. Application for Seaman's Protection Certificates.

Thomas Harold Kinkade
(August 23, 1892–February 13, 1963)

K, stands for Kinkead (sic), we know he don't cheat,
but we're very glad to see him back on his feet.
—From *The Chantier Shovelful*

Thomas Harold "Doc" Kinkade was born in Richmond, Quebec, Canada. His family later moved to Bayonne, New Jersey, where he began his aeronautical career in 1911. He was recruited by Admiral Byrd for his great knowledge of engines. A 2009 feature on Kinkade reads, "Great aviation pioneers Charles

Lindbergh, Admiral Richard Byrd and Amelia Earhart all have one Williamsport (Pennsylvania) connection in common—Thomas 'Doc' Kinkade, whose work tuning each of their engines and helped each complete successful milestone flights." Considered an indispensable member of the crew, Kinkade was in charge of the mechanics and supervised the final tests for Byrd's flight over the North Pole. Byrd penned a 1927 article in *American Magazine*, titled "Doc Kinkade: The Man Who Put Us Across." Kinkade oversaw work on Charles Lindbergh's *Spirit of St. Louis* a year after Byrd's North Pole expedition. Both Byrd and Lindbergh considered Kinkade to be the best aircraft engine expert in the business. In fact, Byrd thought of Kinkade as a "doctor of engines" and gave him the nickname "Doc." Kinkade came to Williamsport, Pennsylvania, in 1927 to work for Lycoming Motors. Kinkade also was the engineer for Charles Levine's Columbia and oversaw Levine and Chamberlin's 1927 flight to Germany in the Bellanca airplane. Later in his career, he was chief engineer for Kendall Oil Company in Bradford, Pennsylvania.

Thomas "Doc" Kinkade. *Cropped photo courtesy of* Expeditions: North Pole Flight, *Admiral Richard E. Byrd Papers, The Ohio State University, Byrd Polar and Climate Research Center Archival Program, The Ohio State University Libraries.*

He died in Williamsport, Pennsylvania, in 1963, at the age of sixty-eight. Kinkade's signature appears on the left (bass) side of the ukulele, just below the waist.

Karl Lundstrom (ca. 1901–date of death unknown)

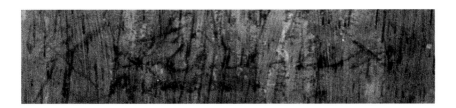

Karl Lundstrom was born in Missouri. His 1926 residence is recorded as New York City on the S. S. *Chantier*'s crew list. He was a merchant seaman who served the Byrd Arctic Expedition as a fireman. Before and after the expedition he was employed as crew on the S. S. *Leviathan* and by 1936 on the S. S. *President Harding*. His presence on many crew lists shows him to be a peripatetic Atlantic sailor. In the 1940 census he was living in New York City. His faint but identifiable signature appears on the left (bass) side, below the lower bout.

James V. Madison (1884–1943)

James V. Madison of Danvers, Massachusetts, was an old Navy shipmate of Byrd's on the U. S. S. *Dolphin* and was the *Chantier's* boatswain. The boatswain (or "bos'un") takes care of the main body or hull of the ship and is responsible for all the ship's equipment. Prior to signing on with the expedition, Madison had extensive experience as a "bluejacket" (enlisted sailor), deep-sea diver, and chief petty officer whose travels took him to virtually every port worldwide. He is credited with making substantial improvements to the deep-sea diving bell of his day, and he received a personal commendation for bravery from President Theodore Roosevelt. Following his pension with the Navy, he was a star tumbler with the Ringling Brothers / Barnum & Bailey circus. His signature with abbreviated first name (Jas.) appears approximately one inch below the waist on the left (bass) side of the ukulele.

James V. Madison.
Cropped photo courtesy of Expeditions: North Pole Flight, *Admiral Richard E. Byrd Papers, The Ohio State University, Byrd Polar and Climate Research Center Archival Program.*

Corporal Robert Harold J. McKay
(October 7, 1901–May 20, 1983)

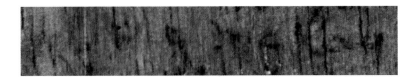

Robert H. J. McKay of Massena, near the St. Lawrence River in the north country of New York state, enlisted in the Marine Corps on July 25, 1918, and was stationed at Paris Island, South Carolina. He served with the 4th Regiment, Santo Domingo, the 10th Regiment at Quantico, and with the Marine Corps Expeditionary Forces, Culebras, Pureto Rico. He was serving in the Marine Corps and stationed in Arlington, Virginia, when he had the "good fortune" (as reported in his local Lake Placid newspaper) to be assigned the position of mess boy aboard the *Chantier.* McKay is present in one of Konter's most treasured possessions—the photograph of Konter arm-in-arm with Roald Amundsen in front of the *Josephine Ford.* McKay was also a special favorite of Byrd's fox terrier, Igloo, during the expedition.

Robert H . J. McKay (*right*) with Richard Konter (*left*). *Courtesy of Jean Neptune.*

His signature, first name slightly faded, appears on the left (bass) side of the ukulele, a few inches below the waist. He served in CWO4 of the Marines in World War II. He is buried in Arlington National Cemetery.

Thomas Bernard Mulroy
(October 10, 1895–June 18, 1962)

M, stands for Mulroy, our chief engineer,
he has to drink coffee, but would rather have beer.
—From *The Chantier Shovelful*

Thomas B. Mulroy was born in St. Louis, one of four children of Irish immigrants. He served Byrd as chief engineer of the S. S. *Chantier*. Later, he served Byrd as fuel engineer on the first Antarctic expedition. He worked as an acoustical engineer in the oil industry in 1930. Sheldon Bart, author of *Race to the Top of the World*, describes Mulroy as "a large, pink-faced man, dark, jowly, beetle-browed, and indefatigable." Mulroy kept an extensive diary of the expedition that was sold in Heritage Auction #629 in 2006. The diary is signed by Byrd and Bennett and contains many fascinating entries, such as this note from April 12, 1926: ". . . just past mid-night we passed near the spot where the *Titanic* went down in 1912 . . ." Mulroy's roommate onboard the *Chantier* was Alton Parker.

Mulroy died in New Orleans in 1962 and is buried in Metairie Cemetery. His signature appears on the left (bass) side of the ukulele, just above the waist.

"Byrd's Arctic Expedition Starts from Brooklyn. The Shipping Board Steamer, —*Chantier*, which is to carry Commander Byrd and his party of arctic explorers as far as King's Bay, Spitsbergen in Norway, sailed from Brooklyn, N.Y. on April 5th. This photo shows L. to R: Capt. M. J. Brennan, Mrs. T. B. Mulroy, and the Chief Engineer-Mulroy on the deck of the Chantier, before she sailed." Original press photo from Pacific & Atlantic Photos. *C. F. Martin Archives.*

Edward J. Nolan (July 15, 1890–September 24, 1977)

A blue-eyed Boston boy, E. J. Nolan from Cambridge, Massachusetts was the third officer aboard the S. S. *Chantier*. He served in World War I as a U. S. Army private, and later as navigator on the S. S. *Chantier*. He was commended by Byrd for his service in a letter to Mr. Kermit Roosevelt on November 22, 1926. In 1940, Nolan and his wife, Alice, and six children lived in Easton, Massachusetts. There, is his listed in the U. S. Federal Census as a laborer. He is buried in Mattapan, Massachusetts.

George Otto Noville (April 24, 1890–January 3, 1963)

N, stands for Noville, a devil with women,
he's going to Paris, but not to go swimin.
—From *The Chantier Shovelful*

G. O. "Rex" Noville, born in Cleveland, Ohio, was a pioneering transatlantic and polar aviator. Noville was an expert in aircraft engines and lubrication. Byrd appointed him third-in-command on the 1926 Byrd Arctic Expedition. Noville was responsible for the crucial task of supervising the restoration of the old United States Shipping Board's mothballed steamer, the S. S. *Chantier*, to seaworthiness. Noville also played a significant role in Byrd's Second Antarctic Exploration (1933–1935) and was the flight engineer on *America*, the second plane to fly nonstop across the Atlantic. Noville was quite handsome and a bit of a playboy. Upon their departure for Spitsbergen, he apparently had to say good-bye to half a dozen different women, each unaware of the others.

Lt. George Otto Noville, third-in-command. *Public domain. George Grantham Bain Collection, Library of Congress, Prints & Photographs Division.*

Dr. Daniel P. O'Brien
(February 25, 1894–August 16, 1958)

he brought golf clubs along, hasn't played at the game.
—From *The Chantier Shovelful*

Dr. Daniel P. O'Brien was invited by Byrd to serve as the Byrd Arctic Expedition's physician. He was born in Torrington, Connecticut, and graduated from Yale in 1915. He received his M. D. from the Johns Hopkins School of Medicine in Baltimore, Maryland, in 1920. At the time of the voyage he was on loan from the Biology Department at Johns Hopkins University Hospital. He was well versed in neurology. Upon reaching Kings

Bay, O'Brien was one of the first people to come ashore with Byrd, along with Kinkade, Bennett, and Leo Peterson. Byrd called upon Johns Hopkins Medical School again with the invitation of Dr. Francis D. Coman, a surgeon, to serve as medical examiner for the 1928 South Pole expedition.

After the 1926 expedition to the North Pole, O'Brien was an assistant director, Division of Medical Education, at the Rockefeller Foundation from 1926 to 1928, and from 1929 to 1948 he served them as assistant director of medical sciences, assigned to Europe and headquartered in Paris. In 1940 he was a member of the Rockefeller Foundation Health Commission in occupied France. After a distinguished international career, he retired

Portrait of Daniel Patrick O'Brien. *Copyright by and courtesy of Rockefeller Archive Center.*

for medical reasons. He died in Acapulco, Mexico, following a diabetic shock. Upon learning of O'Brien's death, his colleague Warren Weaver wrote in an appreciation, "We admired O'B, even when we could by no means understand him. I guess it is fair to say that we loved this big, this handsome, this wild Irishman. We can only hope that he has been released into a happy peace, and that the twinkle has come back into his eyes. If St. Peter still has a few bottles of 1923 Romanée Conti, and perhaps even a jeroboam of 1876 Armagnac, he will find that they are now truly and properly appreciated."

O'Brien's signature appears clearly on the left (bass) side of the ukulele, just above the waist.

Lieutenant Robb Church Oertel
(March 31, 1897–May 17, 1975)

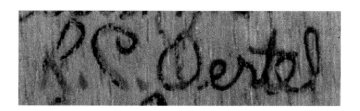

Robb C. Oertel, fourth-in-command on the Arctic expedition, assisted Byrd and Bennett in recruiting the crew from their Navy Building office in Washington, D. C. In his book *Race to the Top of the World*, Sheldon Bart describes Oertel as "a tall, twenty-nine year old aviator from Augusta, Georgia." Bart goes on to explain Oertel's "theory of probability" about the existence of land at the North Pole: "The high latitudes, he reasoned, were dotted with islands. In fact, there wasn't 200,000 square miles of the known Arctic that was entirely devoid of solid ground." Given that the unknown region was five times that large, the odds were heavily in favor of finding land. Oertel replied directly to Konter's letter of March 16, 1926, concerning Konter's assignment to recruitment duty that might have made it impossible for him to join the expedition. Oertel suggested that Byrd might be able to cancel those orders until after the conclusion of the expedition. Oertel's signature appears clearly on the upper-left (bass) bout of the ukulele, directly under Alton N. Parker's. Oertel joined Esso in 1929 and worked there in aviation sales until September 1959. He died in Charleston, South Carolina, and is buried in Arlington National Cemetery.

Robb C. Oertel (left) and Willard Vander Veer (right), 1926. *Photo courtesy of* Expeditions: North Pole Flight, *Admiral Richard E. Byrd Papers, The Ohio State University, Byrd Polar and Climate Research Center Archival Program.*

Alton N. Parker (July 12, 1895–November 30, 1942)

P, is for Parker, always ready for a lark,
but don't trust your daughter with him in the park.

    —From *The Chantier Shovelful*

Alton N. Parker was born in Hazlehurst, Mississippi and was raised by his grandparents. He graduated from Mississippi Agricultural and Mechanical College (now Mississippi State University) and joined the United States Navy during World War I. After the war, he attended naval aviation school in Pensacola, Florida, where he met and befriended R. E. Byrd. As an ensign, he was designated Naval Aviator #2132 in 1919. He accompanied Byrd on his North Pole expedition as a reserve pilot. He subsequently served the first South Pole expedition and was given the honor of being the first American to set foot on the continent of Antarctica. Returning in 1930, Parker joined Western Air Express. That company would eventually become TWA. He was co-pilot on the first airmail flight to Los Angeles and was the recipient of the Distinguished Flying Cross for his service with the Byrd expedition. September 5, 1930 is designated as Alton N. Parker Day in the state of Mississippi, and Parker Peak in Antarctica is also named after him.

Parker is buried in Forest Hill Cemetery in Kansas City, Missouri. His signature is with the rest of the *Chantier*'s crew's on the upper bout of the left (bass) side of the ukulele.

Alton J. Parker in Arctic clothing. *Photo courtesy of Expeditions: North Pole Flight, Admiral Richard E. Byrd Papers, The Ohio State University, Byrd Polar and Climate Research Center Archival Program.*

Alan D. Porter (ca. 1900–date of death unknown)

Alan Porter of Washington, D. C. joined the North Pole expedition as an oiler aboard the *Chantier*. The main duty of an oiler is maintaining, cleaning and, at times, operating ship engine parts, including blowers, compressors, motors, gears, ejectors, and other equipment. They are responsible for operating the lubricant filtering and purifying equipment and keeping logs of the oiling. Prior to the expedition, Porter was enlisted in the Navy from 1917 to 1919, attaining the rank of Quartermaster 2nd Class. His signature appears at the bottom of the left (bass) side.

Jonathan Duff Reed (August 28, 1893–July 11, 1966)

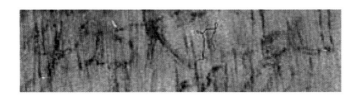

R, is a helmsman, his name is Reed,
Captian says his steering has slackened our speed.

　　—From *The Chantier Shovelful*

"Duff" Reed was born in Louisville, Kentucky. As an officer in France with the U. S. infantry during World War I, he was awarded five battle stars and the Purple Heart with Oak Leaf Cluster. He was a broker (a broker in burlap, that is—somewhat disorienting to a modern reader), one of two brokers on the crew of the *Chantier*. He was a lieutenant in the Army Reserve when he served Byrd as an ordinary seaman and helmsman despite having no

Jonathan Duff Reed. Photo was taken after his marriage to Alice Williams in New York, August 21, 1926. *From the collection of Susan Ellison Reed McQueen.*

maritime experience. Byrd wrote in *Skyward* that Reed and Roy Bryant, "Utterly without sea experience, they knuckled down and stood hardship and toil like old mariners." (Byrd 1928) Sheldon Bart noted that Reed "was in the burlap business and hoped to avoid, he later wrote, 'another sweltering New York summer,' which often arrives at the end of May. The day he left to board the *Chantier*, he hung a sign on his office door: 'Out to lunch.'" According to Gloria Holmes-McQueen (personal communication), Reed, in another act of bravery, saved Igloo, Byrd's dog, when the animal fell over board. Reed was rewarded with a case of Byrd's finest liquor. Byrd later invited Reed to accompany him to Antarctica, but the imminent arrival of Reed's daughter, Susan, in May 1933, made that impossible. Reed and Byrd remained lifelong friends. Reed was an honorary pallbearer at Byrd's funeral. Reed is buried on Heroes and Explorers Hill at Arlington National Cemetery with his wife and son. His partially faded signature is located on the left (bass) side about two inches below the waist.

James Andrew Slaughter Jr.
(October 21, 1897–July 2, 1988)

S, is the second mate, his name is Slaughter,
we suspect he'll be looking for an Eskimo's daughter.
—From *The Chantier Shovelful*

James A. Slaughter Jr. of Centreville, Maryland, was second officer of the S. S. *Chantier.* Slaughter served on the U. S. S. *Nebraska* before he was twenty-one. His name appears in the June 24, 1926 *New York Times* "Official List of Men of Polar Expedition" and on the official crew list at the Byrd Polar Archives at OSU. He also served as navigator on Byrd's Antarctic expedition. His signature clearly appears just below the waist on the left (bass) side of the ukulele.

His photo is from his Application for Seaman's Protection Certificate, August 13, 1919. These were issued beginning in the early 1800s as an attempt to protect U. S. sailors from being pressed into service on British ships. Later they served as an acknowledgment of American citizenship and that the sailor was under the protection of the United States. They were discontinued with the advent of other forms of identification in the 1940s.

James A. Slaughter Jr. From Application for Seaman's Certificate of American citizenship. Washington, D. C. *National Archives and Records Administration; Application for Seaman's Protection Certifcates.*

John Sutton (ca. 1900–date of death unknown)

John L. Sutton of Paterson, New Jersey, was a coal passer aboard the *Chantier.* His signature is seen at the lower bout of the left (bass) side.

John S. Szentpetery
(February 17, 1900–date of death unknown)

John Szentpetery (last name translates to "Saint Peter" in Hungarian) was born in Trenton, New Jersey. He attended two years of high school in Troy, Pennsylvania, but enlisted on March 25, 1918, in the Navy for the duration of the First World War. He received instruction in the Allied Secret Code and served on the U. S. S. *Robin*, 2nd Squadron, Mine Sweeping Division. After being discharged on January 7, 1919, he enlisted in the U. S. Marines on April 25, 1919, and spent much of his remaining life as a Marine. He was qualified as a seaman-signalman, and is listed as an ordinary seaman aboard the *Chantier*. An ordinary seaman, or deckhand, is responsible for performing lookout duty and can often found on a ship's bridge after working hours, taking a turn at the ship's wheel or learning the bridge's equipment. The official crew list notes that Szentpetery has "no address," but his next of kin were listed as being in in Washington, D. C. His faint signature is deciphered at the lower bout on the left (treble) side.

Paul Todaro (ca. 1902–date of death unknown)

The April 6, 1926 edition of the *Iowa City Press-Citizen* newspaper, and others, ran an Associated Press wire story that Paul Todaro and his fellow West Point (class of 1927) classmate Winston Ehrgott were the last two additions to the expedition: "They were looking over likely places to stow away when their chance came." In a July 28, 1928 interview, the Harrisburg, Pennsylvania *Evening News* quoted Byrd as saying: "Winston Ehrgott and Paul Todaro also came aboard with baggage on the last day and announced that they had to go. Mind

Paul Todaro. *Photo courtesy of Expeditions: North Pole Flight, Admiral Richard E. Byrd Papers, The Ohio State University, Byrd Polar and Climate Research Center Archival Program.*

you, I had never even heard of them before. They were former West Pointers. I had a hunch and took them. They, too, lived up to expectations." Byrd's supplemental crew list in the OSU Byrd Polar Archives gives Todaro's age as twenty-four in 1926, so we have estimated his birth year as 1902. We don't believe he graduated from the U. S. Military Academy, and we have been unable to locate additional biographical details.

His signature appears below the waist bend of the left (bass) side.

Alcide A. Touchette
(December 15, 1898–February 26, 1976)

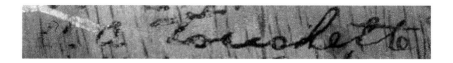

T, the utility man's name is Touchette,
at last information, he'd not found the fish net.
—From *The Chantier Shovelful*

Alcide (Archie) A. Touchette was born in Concord, New Hampshire. He held the title of supercargo aboard the *Chantier*. He was responsible for overseeing the ship's cargo, including the all-important Fokker plane, the *Josephine Ford*. Despite his relatively young age (twenty-seven), he clearly possessed a thorough mechanical knowledge of the plane's assembly. He was also consulted about the choice of runway locations in Spitsbergen. There is an entry on page 63 of Richard Byrd's *Diary 1925–1927* that gives a small insight into Touchette's role: "We have stored our great 63-foot wing in the forward hold and have exercised exquisite care to prevent any thing from falling on it. One's sensations are not the pleasantest when tons of weight are hanging over that wing. Touchette was lowering a big pyrene today into the hold. The line got away from him and ran through his fingers so fast it burnt his hand. But he clamped down on it and stopped it, taking the skin off his finger rather than let the wing be injured."

Alcide A. Touchette. *Photo courtesy of E*xpeditions: North Pole Flight, *Admiral Richard E. Byrd Papers, The Ohio State University, Byrd Polar and Climate Research Center Archival Program.*

Touchette married Edna Smith on November 17, 1934, while a soldier at Fort Knox, Kentucky. He died in Boston, Massachusetts, in 1976. His signature appears on the left (bass) side just below the waist.

Willard Van der Veer (August 23, 1894–June 16, 1963)

V, stands for Van der Veer, never lets you intrude,
when he's photographing beautiful girls in the nude.
    —From *The Chantier Shovelful*

Born in Brooklyn, Academy Award winner Willard Van der Veer started his stage career at the age of ten in *Polly of the Circus* and Sir Arthur Conan Doyle's *The Sign of the Four*. In 1914, he lived at 385 Central Park West in Manhattan. He was an Army Signal Corps photographer during World War I. He was a newsreel cameraman and photographer on both of Byrd's polar expeditions, making him the first person to photograph both North and South Pole expeditions. He filmed more than one hundred thousand feet of film under what Byrd described as impossible (60 degrees below zero) conditions. At these temperatures, both the film and the equipment would freeze. Though his footage from the North Pole expedition was groundbreaking, it was his 1930 film *With Byrd at the South Pole*, filmed in partnership with Paramount cameraman Joseph T. Rucker, that won Van der Veer the 1930 Academy Award for Best

Willard Van der Veer with camera aboard the *Chantier. Photo courtesy of* Expeditions: North Pole Flight, *Admiral Richard E. Byrd Papers, The Ohio State University, Byrd Polar and Climate Research Center Archival Program, The Ohio State University Libraries.*

Cinematography. After the Antarctic expedition, Van der Veer returned to Paramount. He died in Encino, California, and is buried in Forest Lawn Memorial Park in Glendale, California.

His legible signature appears on the left (bass) side, close to the neck joint.

Josephine M. Coombs
(November 24, 1902–August 5, 1993)

Josephine Coombs born in Brooklyn and grew up in Scarsdale, New York. She attended college at Bryn Mawr and spent two years at the Julliard School (which at the time was known as the School of Musical Art). She married Joseph de Ganahl, a member of the Byrd Arctic Expedition, on June 30, 1926, just days after the return of the *Chantier* to New York. Her husband taught her to fly, and she was one of the first female pilots who flew for pleasure. She died of heart failure in 1993 at her home in McLean, Virginia, and was buried in Arlington National Cemetery. Her signature appears with the crew of the *Chantier* on the upper-left shoulder of the ukulele, close to the neck joint.

Confidence = Probable:

Rodmar Arnesen (1892–date of death unknown)

Norwegian R. Arnesen signed on as a seaman with the *Chantier*. He took the place of J. Meade, who for some reason couldn't go. We see a variety of different spellings for Arnesen, but this correct spelling is taken from his own signature on the official crew list. His signature appears below Alan Porter's at the bottom of the left (treble) side of the ukulele.

Charles Leroy Kessler
(January 29, 1903–January 3, 1976)

Charles Kessler was a coal passer aboard the *Chantier*. This strenuous job involved bringing coal from the ship's hold to the furnaces and removing the ashes. He was a private in the Marine Corps when he was given leave to accompany Byrd. He also served with Byrd as a member of the 1928–1930 ship's party in the first Byrd Antarctic Expedition. Kessler Peak (83°37 S 167°50 E), "a conspicuous cone-shaped peak (2,180 m / 7,152 ft) in the Queen Alexandra Range," is named for him. He revisited the continent in 1962 and

Corporal Charles L. Kessler, U. S. M. C., March 8, 1926. *Public domain. National Photo Company glass negative.*

1965. Kessler would eventually earn the rank of captain in the Navy and become the director of Selective Service System for Virginia. He lived his later years in Richmond, Virginia, and is buried in Arlington National Cemetery.

We believe we have located his very faded signature at the bottom of the left (bass) side with the rest of the *Chantier* crew, below Fred Coliver's. Kessler is identified by Konter as one of four men in the photograph of Konter receiving the ukulele back from Floyd Bennett after the polar flight.

Oliver Wolcott Gibbs
(March 15, 1902–August 16, 1958)

Wolcott Gibbs (he hated his first name, Oliver), was the editor of *The New Yorker* magazine from 1927 until his death in 1958. He was also a humorist, playwright, critic, and author. Although his precise relationship to Byrd and his expeditions is unknown, in 1931 Gibbs authored a satirical book entitled *Bird Life at the Pole* that lambastes the expeditions and all of those involved. Given his prominent editorial role in New York City, and his clear familiarity with Byrd's endeavors, it is plausible that his signature would appear, though due to the faded first name, we must categorize this signature as "Probable" instead of "Certain." Regardless, the signature is located adjacent to the neck on the left treble side.

Author and playwright Wolcott Gibbs. *Public domain.*

Confidence = Possible:
Wieno Johannes "John" Lauren
(March 13, 1905–February 12, 1977)

Lauren was born in Åbo, Finland, and immigrated to the U. S. in 1923. He had a New York City address at 15 West 126th Street on the original *Chantier* crew list. He replaced J. Hannigan of New York, who was slated to be a fireman. Lauren served in the Army in World War II. His signature appears on the lower area of the left (bass) side below Johan Hangaas's and above Leo Peterson's.

13

Signers on the Back

THE BACK OF THE UKULELE was signed by at least fifty-nine individuals. They are listed below, first by confidence category, then alphabetically by signer category.

Confidence = Certain:

Gertrude Caroline Ederle	Athletes
Amelia Gade-Corson	Athletes
Rev. Big Chief White Horse Eagle	Celebrities
Anna Alexander	Dick's Ukulele Club
Ethel Anderson	Dick's Ukulele Club
Clifford F. Bradney	Dick's Ukulele Club
Thea G. Carpenter	Dick's Ukulele Club
Johanna Cohen	Dick's Ukulele Club
Cynthia Corti	Dick's Ukulele Club
Hector Corti	Dick's Ukulele Club
Marian Mildred De Graff	Dick's Ukulele Club
Charles Patrick Gray	Dick's Ukulele Club
Adelaide M. Kaiser	Dick's Ukulele Club
Dorothy Kaiser	Dick's Ukulele Club
Betty G. Moore	Dick's Ukulele Club
Lillian Reis	Dick's Ukulele Club

Clara Sauerman	Dick's Ukulele Club
Violet E. Thoma	Dick's Ukulele Club
Robert H. Thoma	Dick's Ukulele Club
Elizabeth K. Werfelman	Dick's Ukulele Club
Lillian Willing	Dick's Ukulele Club
Captain Robert Abram Bartlett	Explorers & Aviators
Frederick Trubee Davison	Explorers & Aviators
James Fitzmaurice	Explorers & Aviators
Clarence Alvin "Duke" Schiller	Explorers & Aviators
Henry W. Armstrong	Musicians
Mother Rachel Frohman Davison	Musicians
Daniel Frohman	Musicians
William Green Pool	Musicians
William Aloysius Rider	Musicians
Edward Chandler Swayne	Musicians
Theodore Roosevelt	Politicians & Military
Kay Golding	Signature Unidentified
Joseph G. Hüngady	Signature Unidentified
Lil Richmond	Signature Unidentified

Confidence = Probable:

Dorothy Clark	Dick's Ukulele Club
Margaret M. Fabrizio	Dick's Ukulele Club
Helen Mack	Dick's Ukulele Club
Dora Maniscalco	Dick's Ukulele Club
Sylvia Miller	Dick's Ukulele Club
Harold Denny Campbell	Explorers & Aviators
Ronald Thomas Shepherd	Explorers & Aviators
Edward le Roy Rice	Musicians
E. Etsie	Signature Unidentified
Flora Ettlinger Whiting	Sponsors

Confidence = Possible:

Greta	Dick's Ukulele Club
Kathleen	Dick's Ukulele Club
Judy Davison	Dick's Ukulele Club
Harry Hudler	Dick's Ukulele Club
Helen M. Sterba	Dick's Ukulele Club
Mabel I. Thoma	Dick's Ukulele Club
Clara Grabau Adams	Explorers & Aviators
Sir Douglas Mawson	Explorers & Aviators
James Roosevelt II	Politicians & Military
Loleta G. Borak	Signature Unidentified
Nathalea Halgesen	Signature Unidentified
Steven D. Lester	Signature Unidentified
John McLeRoy	Signature Unidentified
Scratched Out Signature (Whitaker?)	Signature Unidentified

Confidence = Certain:

Gertrude Caroline Ederle
(October 23, 1905–November 20, 2003)

"Queen of the Waves" Gertrude Caroline Ederle was one of two women to have both swum the English Channel and signed the back of Konter's ukulele. She was the first woman to have accomplished the channel swim, on August 6, 1926. Upon her return home to New York City, she was congratulated at City Hall by another signer of the ukulele, Mayor Jimmy "Beau James" Walker. She was also feted at the White House by President Coolidge, who called her "America's Best Girl." She played herself in the movie *Swim Girl, Swim*, and toured the vaudeville circuit, appearing in Billy Rose's Aquacade. Her subsequent career was marred by two unfortunate events. First, her incompetent manager

Gertrude Ederle. *Public domain. George Grantham Bain collection at the Library of Congress, Washington, D. C.*

241

mishandled her show business career, which never really took off. Second, in 1933, she fell down the steps of her apartment building, leaving her bedridden for several years. By 1939, she had recovered enough to appear at the New York World's Fair. Gertrude Ederle was the recipient of both a song and a dance step named in her honor, and was inducted into the International Professional Swimmers Association as an associate member for life. The IPSA organized on September 21, 1927, at the Hotel McAlpin in Manhattan, also the headquarters of Byrd's expedition. Her partially faded signature appears on the lower half of the back, two signatures below and just to the right of Theodore Roosevelt Jr.'s.

Millie Gade-Corson (February 11, 1897–May 1, 1982)

The second of two female swimmers to sign the back of the ukulele, Amelia "Millie" Gade-Corson was a naturalized American, born in Denmark. She was the seventh person, the third American, and the second woman to successfully swim across the English Channel. She accomplished the feat in fifteen hours, twenty-nine minutes on August 27, 1926. Before her channel

Amelia "Millie" Gade-Corson. *Public domain. Biblioteque Nationale de France. Date d'édition: 1921*

swim, Gade-Corson had completed the forty-two-mile swim around Manhattan, as well as swimming the Hudson River from Albany to New York City. After her channel swim, she returned to New York City on the RMS *Aquitania* and was welcomed with a ticker-tape parade up Broadway to City Hall where, never one to miss out on a good thing, Mayor Jimmy Walker welcomed her. Like her colleague Ederle, Gade-Corson was voted in as an associate member for life of the International Professional Swimmers Association, headquartered at the McAlpin Hotel.

Her light signature appears on the lower-left side of the back, two down from Theodore Roosevelt, Jr.'s.

Big Chief White Horse Eagle (aka, Ko-Sa-Mia) (ca. 1822–1937)

Big Chief White Horse Eagle was a colorful Osage "Indian chief," movie star, lecturer, teller of tall tales, and man about town. His wife was "Queen Wa-Te-Na." He starred in the classic films *The Covered Wagon* and *The Iron Horse*. A glimpse of this talented bullshitter is offered by a feature writer for *The Brooklyn Daily Eagle*, Cyrilla P. Lindner:

"Big Chief claims a knowledge of every root, bark and herb in existence, and its use; the weather signs and their portent, the location of all minerals, gold, silver, and oil, and much more pertaining to natural history. His eldest sister, 114 years old, and his youngest, 64 years of age, share his knowledge, as do all the other brothers and sisters, but he exceeds their training in having had a special education in Indian lore, on which he now lectures. He also claims to be the only authentic reader of the paintings on the rocks, done by the American Indians, and, too, of the Egyptian hieroglyphics."

Big Chief White Horse Eagle at Myron Herrick's funeral, Paris, 1929. Herrick was serving as United States ambassador to France at the time of his death on March 31, 1929. *Public domain. Press photo by Agence Meurisse. Obsèques de Myron Herrick : White Horse Eagle : [photographie de presse] / Agence Meurisse.*

His 1931 autobiography, *We Indians: The Passing of a Great Race*, has been called "one of the more bizarre Indian biographies of its era." *We Indians* "was elicited by Edgar von Schmidt-Pauli, a German academic whose chief scholarly interest lay in demonstrating the inevitability of the rise of the German race in general and of Adolf Hitler in particular" (Browder, 123-124). There is ambiguity about the chief's accurate date of birth, since one of his online biographies states that he was 111 years old at the time of his passing.

Big Chief White Horse Eagle's connection with Konter and the ukulele is unknown. However, the chief was in New York on several occasions, as reported in the contemporary press. Native Americans had been at the Hotel McAlpin as early as 1915. The Hotel McAlpin served as the headquarters of Byrd's expedition, as well as for other organizations whose members signed the ukulele (see Gade-Corson and Ederle entries). The Hotel McAlpin was the site of the June 24, 1926 reception for Byrd and his men after Byrd's Carnegie Hall lecture. Several other signers of the ukulele attended this reception in the Winter Garden on the twenty-fourth floor of the hotel, including Admiral Robert E. Peary's daughter Marie—by that time, Mrs. Edward Stafford. It may have been at this reception that White Horse Eagle autographed the ukulele. The chief is buried at Valhalla Cemetery in North Hollywood. His signature is seen faintly at the lower-left bout of the back.

Anna Alexander (1909–date of death unknown)

Anna Alexander was a member of Dick's Ukulele Chorus and a familiar name to Jean Neptune, daughter of Johanna Pool Konter. She appears as "Baby Anna Alexander" in a list of the Ukulele Club members published in *The Brooklyn Daily Eagle* of Saturday, June 28, 1924. Her signature is on the left side of the back, just above the waist.

Ethel Anderson (dates of birth and death unknown)

Based on the location of her autograph, Ethel Anderson was likely a member of Dick's Children's Ukulele Chorus, but we have no direct evidence of this. Her signature appears at the near the left side waist of the back, just below Cynthia Corti's.

Cliff Bradney (1911–date of death unknown)

Cliff Bradney was a member of Dick's Children's Ukulele Chorus. His signature appears on the upper section of the back below Betty Moore's.

Thea G. Carpenter (dates of birth and death unknown)

Thea Carpenter was a member of Dick's Ukulele Chorus. Her signature is on the right side of the back, below the boldly inked signature of Kay Golding.

Johanna Cohen (Pool) Konter
(January 20, 1907–May 9, 1982)

The daughter of Arthur and Rickie Cohen, Johanna was the love of Konter's life. Arthur was an English immigrant and butcher. We don't know a lot about Johanna's early life or when Dick Konter may have met her for the first time. At the age of seventeen, she is listed as a member of Dick's Ukulele Club in the Saturday, June 28, 1924 *Brooklyn Daily Eagle*. In the New York State Census of 1925, Johanna was listed as an "Office Assistant." There is a radio programming listing in *The Brooklyn Daily Eagle* of Monday, March 22, 1926, for a radio performance at 9:05 p.m. by "Konter and Cohen, ukulele and guitar duets" on WCCP AM 1190 in Manhattan. Although we cannot be 100 percent certain, it seems likely that Konter was playing the guitar and the ukulele player was the nineteen-year-old Johanna.

Johanna Cohen aboard the *Macom* as it is tied up to the *City of New York*. *Courtesy of Jean Neptune.*

Konter proposed marriage to Johanna just prior to his departure on the Byrd expedition, but family lore has it that Johanna's father did not allow it, due to the significant twenty-five-year age difference. Johanna married William Pool on June 16, 1930. She was "Josie" to Bill Pool. The date of their marriage was two days after the first Byrd Antarctic Expedition returned to New York City. Pool died in September 1953. In June 1961, at the age of fifty-four, Johanna married Dick Konter, who at that time was eighty. They remained a devoted couple until Konter's death at age ninety-seven. Johanna's signature appears with those of members of Dick's Ukulele Club on the upper area of the back.

Cynthia Corti (ca. 1917–date of death unknown)

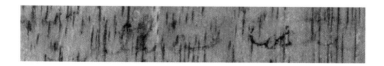

Cynthia Corti was one of the younger members of Dick's Children's Ukulele Chorus. She was from the Bronx. Her faded but still legible signature appears on the upper section of the back, about one inch below and to the left of

Violet Thoma's. Another partially faded signature appears to be that of "Hector Corti," who was Cynthia's older brother.

Hector Corti (October 14, 1909–July 1976)

Hector Corti was the older brother of Cynthia Corti. Like his sister, he may have also been a member of Dick's Ukulele Chorus, though only his sister is formally mentioned in newspaper accounts like that in *The Brooklyn Daily Eagle*. His signature appears on the left side of back near the waist above Lil Richmond's.

Marian De Graff (October 31, 1915–February 16, 1995)

We have located a number of documentary sources about Marian De Graff. There is an entry for four-year-old Marian De Graff in the 1920 United States Federal Census. She is living with her grandmother on Bedford Avenue in Brooklyn, New York. A "Marion DeKnight" is listed in a 1924 issue of *The Brooklyn Daily Eagle* as a member of Dick's Ukulele Club. Despite the rather large error in names, perhaps this was typo, and it is, in fact, referring to Marian M. De Graff. In the 1925 New York State Census, nine-year-old Marian M. is listed as living with her grandmother on Bedford Avenue in Brooklyn. Additionally, the November 20, 1931 issue of *The Brooklyn Daily Eagle*, lists "Marian DeGraff" as a member of the Central Presbyterian Church Choir at their autumn dance.

Perhaps most significantly, an article in *The Brooklyn Daily Eagle* of January 7, 1932, features a story on a planned yearlong, round-the-world "university cruise" on the liner S. S. *Resolute* by Mrs. Marian T. De Graff and her granddaughter, Marian M. De Graff, sixteen years old and a third-year student at Erasmus Hall High School in Flatbush, Brooklyn. Mrs. De Graff lived in the Hotel Granada in Brooklyn, built in 1927, and one of the finer hotels in Brooklyn. Mrs. De Graff was a woman of means.

Marian M. DeGraff with her grandmother, Marian T. DeGraff. From *The Brooklyn Daily Eagle*, January 7, 1932.

Young Marian M. was a member of the basketball, baseball, swimming, tennis, hockey, and significantly, cantata clubs at Erasmus Hall. According to *The Brooklyn Daily Eagle* article, the cruise represented the second semester of the sixth annual Floating University cruise. Both Mrs. De Graff and Marian were busy on board. The elder lady, whose first year of high school was her highest grade completed, was writing a book but intended to "drop in at various classes in which she is interested, as members not working for academic credit are permitted to do. Marian, who has inherited her grandmother's literary gifts and a distinct artistic talent will study art, modern civilization, French, drama, and dancing. She will keep up her sports, since the ship provides facilities for every popular diversion of the kind and she expects to keep a diary, to paint her impressions of various countries, *and to make a collection of odd musical instruments* from many lands." (Emphasis added.)

Luckily, we have located two direct connections between Marian M. De Graff and Richard Konter, and, as one might expect from Marian M.'s interests, they are musical. First, and although here she is not identified by name as a member of his ukulele club, Marian M. performed on the same radio broadcast on WHN (Manhattan, 360) as Richard Konter and various other members. The longwave broadcast took place on Saturday, December 15, 1923, between 3:45 and 5:30 p.m. Interestingly, the club itself is not credited in the program notes, but some of its individual performers are, including various combinations of duos, and trios (such as "Johanna Cohen and Elizabeth Werfelman, singing 'Annabelle' and 'No, No, Nora'"). Marian's performance is listed as "Talk by Marion (sic) De Graff." She was eight years old at the time of her "talk." It is likely that her artistic and musical interests (and later, her peripatetic nature) would have strongly appealed to the sailor/musician Richard Konter.

Second, an article in *The Brooklyn Daily Eagle* from Saturday, June 28, 1924, describes "A unique program of songs, dances and selections on the ukulele" presented the evening before at Kenilworth Baptist Church by Dick's Ukulele Club, and organization made of Flatbush children." She is named first: "Among those on the program were Marion Degraf . . ." Although Marian M. was one of its younger members, she was not its youngest, as "Baby Lily Willing" and "Baby Anna Alexander" also are named.

Marian M. is listed in the 1940 United States Federal Census as being twenty-four years of age and living on Laurelton Road in New Castle, Westchester, New York, with her grandmother, eighty years old. Marian M. is recorded as working seventy-hour weeks, fifty-two weeks per year as a secretary, we suppose to her grandmother. Sometime after the death of her grandmother (date unknown to us), Marian M. took a husband.

In 1992 she lived in Madison, Wisconsin, on Sheboygan Avenue. Her married name was Swain. She died in Madison in 1995. Her signature is clearly incised in pencil near the lower-left bout beneath the autograph of Big Chief White Horse Eagle.

Charles Gray (1913–date of death unknown)

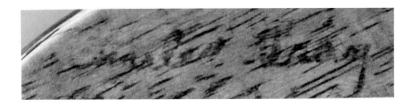

Charles Gray was a member of Dick's Children's Ukulele Chorus. His signature appears at the uppermost left shoulder of the back.

Adelaide Kaiser (1912–March 27, 1943)

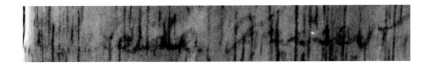

The children of Arthur and Catherine Kaiser of Queens, New York, Adelaide Kaiser and her sister Dorothy were members of Dick's Children's Ukulele Chorus. Adelaide's mother, Mrs. A(rthur) Kaiser, is listed as the chaperone and pianist of Dick's Ukulele Club in at least one radio program notice in *The Brooklyn Daily Eagle*. Adelaide was born in Brooklyn and, after graduating from Newtown High School, she attended the American Arts Academy. She was an all-round entertainer, an instrumentalist, singer, dancer, and actor. The May 24, 1925 issue of *The Brooklyn Daily Eagle* tells us that Adelaide was a drama student of Miss Adelaide I. Buck. Adelaide later performed in the ensemble cast of the two-act musical comedy *Great Day* at the Cosmopolitan Theater, 5 Columbus Circle, Manhattan, for thirty-six performances between October 17 and November 16, 1929. In the 1940 U. S. Census, she is listed as a singer.

Adelaide died in a 1943 plane crash with two other U. S. O. entertainers near Vancouver, British Columbia. They were returning from a performance at an outpost camp in Alaska. Johanna Pool Konter's daughter, Jean Neptune, recalls that the Kaiser family name was often mentioned by her mother and stepfather. Her slightly faded signature appears on the left side of the back, right at the waist.

Based on her age and physical similarity to her sister we know also to be in the Ukulele Club, we feel it is likely that in the photo on page 35 the girl seated on the ground in between the boy in the plaid jacket and another seated girl is Adelaide. We also believe that this photo shows her sister Dorothy standing behind her, second from the right in the row in front of the tent.

Dorothy Kaiser (1911–June 25, 1943)

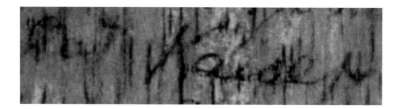

Dorothy Kaiser was Adelaide Kaiser's older sister and also a member of Dick's Children's Ukulele Chorus. Their father Arthur was a fireman with the FDNY and their mother (Catherine, or Mrs. A[rthur] Kaiser), is listed as the chaperone and pianist of Dick's Ukulele Club in at least one radio program notice in *The Brooklyn Daily Eagle*. "Dot" was born in Brooklyn and graduated from Newtown High School. She and her Adelaide were recognized entertainers around New York City, appearing at benefits, radio programs, and veteran's hospitals, including Walter Reed Hospital in Washington, D. C. As an adult, she studied and taught at the Imperial School of Ballet in London and operated dance schools in New York, including the Dorothy Kaiser School of Dance. She was a member of the New York Society of Teachers of Dancing, the Dancing Masters of America, and the Imperial Society of Teachers of Dancing, London.

Dorothy was engaged in January 1942, but she died of a long illness on June 25, 1943, the same year her sister Adelaide was killed in a plane crash. Her fiancé was Mr. Richard Horrigan of Brooklyn, a former assistant attorney general, at the time of her death. *The Brooklyn Daily Eagle* of June 26, 1943, on page 5 said that she "suffered a setback and never rallied upon learning that her sister had been killed." Dorothy is buried in St. John's cemetery in Brooklyn. Her faint signature, with first name abbreviated to simply "Dot," appears on the upper-right side of the back, adjacent to Betty Moore's.

Betty Moore (November 25, 1912–July 1989)

Betty Moore was listed in *The Brooklyn Daily Eagle* as a member of Dick's Children's Ukulele Chorus. Her signature appears clearly on the upper section of the back, directly under Johanna Cohen's. Johanna's daughter, Jean Neptune, told us that Betty Moore was a good friend of her mother's, who mentioned her often. Among the various images of the ukulele club we have obtained, Johanna Cohen is pictured in several among the same group of girls from the club. It is likely that Betty is among them. She married sometime after 1940 and took the married name Whitcomb.

Lillian Reis (dates of birth and death unknown)

We do not know who Lillian Reis may have been. There was a member of Dick's Children's Ukulele Chorus (*Brooklyn Daily Eagle* of December 21, 1924) named Lillian Gerken, who was born in 1909 and listed living in Brooklyn in the 1920 U. S. Census. It is possible that Lillian Gerken married and became Lillian Reis by the time she autographed the ukulele. (Several of the chorus members were in their late teens in 1924 and would have been of marriageable age by 1926.) However, we have found no record of such a marriage. Although the autograph is located in the area on the back that Konter reserved for members, below and to the right of Cliff Bradney's, it is oriented at a roughly forty-five-degree angle to most of the other horizontally oriented club member signatures, perhaps indicative of a later signing by someone unaffiliated with the club. There appears to be another faint signature above it, oriented similarly, but it is too faint to read.

Clara Sauerman
(ca. 1910–date of death unknown)

Clara Sauerman is listed as a member of Dick's Children's Ukulele Chorus in the December 21, 1924 issue of *The Brooklyn Daily Eagle*. She was born in about 1910, for she is listed in the 1915 New York State Census as age five. At that time, she was living on Montauk Avenue in Brooklyn with her parents, Robert and Ida, and her brother Robert Jr. Her father was a butcher. She was attending high school in 1927–1928 at Hempstead High School in Hempstead, Nassau, New York. Between 1927 and 1928 she was a member of the French, Spanish, history, and literary clubs at school, from which she graduated in 1928. In the 1930 U. S. Census, Clara was still living with her family and a new younger brother, Walter, seven years her junior. In 1930, she was working as a stenographer in the real estate industry. By the time of the 1940 U. S. Census she was living in Queens, New York, with only her mother.

Clara Sauerman. Photo from 1928 Hempstead High School yearbook, Hempstead, Nassau, New York.

Though it is quite faint, we are confident that her signature appears at the waist of the back. It does seem odd that in front of "Clara" there seems to be the name "Kathleen." We speculate that one of the ukulele club members may have signed there with her first name only.

Her photo is from the 1928 Hempstead High School yearbook.

Violet Thoma (ca. 1913–date of death unknown)

Violet Thoma was a member of Dick's Children's Ukulele Chorus. She was Mabel Thoma's younger sister (by three years). Her partially faded but identifiable signature appears on the upper section of the back below Cliff Bradney's.

Robert H. Thoma (dates of birth and death unknown)

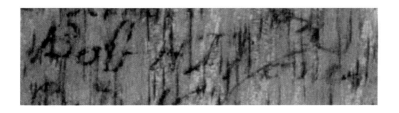

Bob Thoma is listed as a member of Dick's Children's Ukulele Chorus on page 10 of the December 26, 1924 *Brooklyn Daily Eagle*.

Though we are uncertain of the exact relationship, it is likely he was a cousin or more distant relative, but not a brother, of Violet and Mabel Thoma. This is because the 1920 U. S. Census records Violet and Mabel Thoma, along with only two brothers, Carl F. Thoma or Walter F. Thoma. Thus, neither of the boys is named "Bob" or "Robert." It is unlikely that one of these two brothers was nicknamed "Bob." Also, if at the time of the census Bob had not yet been born, he would have had to have been under four years of age by the time of the newspaper article. This, however, is unlikely, because in a different *Brooklyn Daily Eagle* story, of June 28, 1924 (page 7), "Baby" precedes the names of some of the children (Lily Willing and Anna Alexander, for example). Thus, we conclude he was a member of the club, but not a brother of Violet and Mabel.

We have found a record in the 1920 U. S. Census of a Robert Thoma, born about 1910. That is the same year Mabel Thoma was born. The census record indicates that Robert lived with his parents, Herman and Lydia, and his sister Ethel and brother Edward. No mention of Violet or Mabel is made. The New York State Census of 1915 lists the same family and includes Robert H. F. Thoma, age five.

His signature appears on the upper section of the back, directly to the right of Johanna Cohen's.

Elizabeth Werfelman (March 3, 1911–June 27, 1994)

The daughter of German immigrants, Elizabeth (Betty?) Werfelman is identified as a member of Dick's Children's Ukulele Chorus in the December 21, 1924 issue of *The Brooklyn Daily Eagle*. She is listed in *The Philadelphia Inquirer* of December 15, 1923 as playing in New York on the "out-of-town station WHN (360 meters) in a duet with Johanna Cohen at 9:10

PM, immediately following a talk by Little Miss Marion De Graff about the children's ukulele club." In 1910, Elizabeth lived in Queens, New York, and in 1926 she was living in Brooklyn, Ward 29, with her parents. Ancestry.com records her marriage to Edward Armand Guilbert, and the 1928 birth of a daughter, Annette. Her signature includes her nickname (Betty) and, more faintly, her last name. Her autograph is found on the back near the upper-right bout, just below Lillian Reis's.

Lillian Willing (1915–date of death unknown)

Lillian Willing was one of the youngest members of Dick's Ukulele Club. She appears as "Baby Lily Willing" in *The Brooklyn Daily Eagle* of Saturday, June 28, 1924. Her signature appears on the left side of the back below Adelaide Kaiser's.

Robert "Bob" Abram Bartlett
(August 15, 1875–April 26, 1946)

Born in Newfoundland, Bob Bartlett grew up as a sealer and became a competent mariner at an early age. "Captain Bob" was an Arctic seafarer and explorer, well known before any of Byrd's expeditions. Thoroughly knowledgeable about all aspects of ships, he spent his entire life charting Arctic waters and led more than forty expeditions in the northern region. In 1908-1909, he captained Commander Robert Peary's ship, the S. S. *Roosevelt*, for Peary's early attempt(s) to reach the North Pole. Peary's achievements would not have been possible without Bartlett's navigational and sledging contributions.

He is probably best known as the captain and savior of the ill-fated *Karluk*, one of three ships of the Norse-Canadian expedition, led by Vilhjalmur Stefannson in 1913. Their goal was to find new lands north of Alaska. Bartlett had been hired to captain the flagship *Karluk*, a rickety old wooden vessel ill-suited for Arctic maritime use. A series of disasters ensued. Stefansson abandoned his ship, deserting the expedition with five others.

Robert Edwin Peary (*left*) with a young Captain Bob Bartlett (*right*), Battle Harbour, Labrador. 1909. *Public domain. George Grantham Bain Collection, Library of Congress.*

The *Karluk* drifted and was eventually crushed by the ice and sunk. Bartlett saved all aboard by with his foresighted rescue of the ships provisions, and kept the survivors alive over a winter, until he could lead them safely to the uninhabited Wrangell Island. He then traveled two hundred miles on foot over the ice to get help in Siberia. All were rescued.

Bartlett holds the distinction of being the first to sail north of 88° north longitude. The National Geographic Society presented him with its Hubbard Medal in recognition of coming within one hundred fifty miles of the North Pole. He also was awarded the Charles P. Daly Medal and the Peary Polar Expedition Medal.

Bartlett's signature is considerably darker than the others on the lower-left area of the back. This may indicate that his autograph was added later than many of the others. In any case, a different ink was used. There also seems to be additional surface preparation around his signature

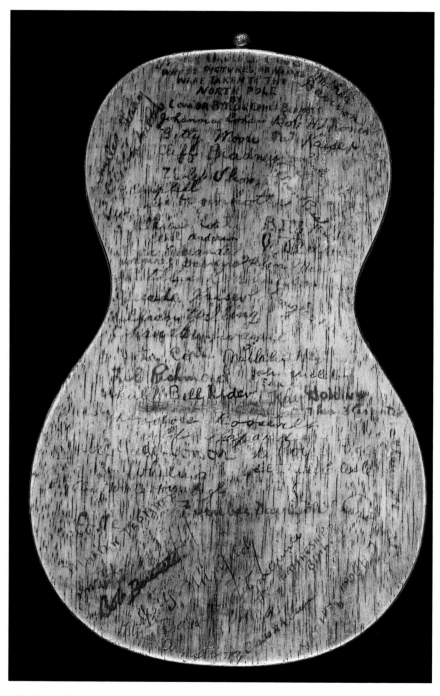

The Back. *Photograph by E. Keats Webb, Museum Conservation Institute, Smithsonian Institution.*

Frederick Trubee Davison
(February 7, 1896–November 14, 1974)

F. Trubee Davison was an early American aviator who formed the Yale Naval Aviation Unit. In 1917, while attempting to become a Navy pilot, Davison fainted prior to taking his flying test. He nevertheless pressed on, and during the flight he lost control of his seaplane and crashed into the sea. The plane was split in two, and Davison suffered a broken back and a serious spinal cord injury. His convalescence was long, so Davison never saw World War I combat. However, he remained extremely active during the war. For his dedicated non-combat work, he was awarded the Navy Cross. Davison's father died in 1922, leaving him $4.5 million. After World War I, he returned to Yale, then went on to Columbia University Law School, where he earned a degree. Davison is pictured on the cover of the August 1925 issue of *Time* magazine. He served as Assistant Secretary of War for Air from July 1926 to March 1933. During World War II, Davison was an important military figure and eventually rose to the rank of brigadier

Frederick Trubee Davison (1896–1976) as Assistant Secretary of War at Bolling Field, 1926. *Public domain. National Photo Company collection at the Library of Congress, Washington, D. C.*

general. In 1951, he became a trustee of his alma mater, Yale. He served later as the first personnel director of the newly formed Central Intelligence Agency, and as the president of the American Museum of Natural History. His boldly inked autograph is centered on the back of the ukulele about two inches up from the bottom.

James Michael Christopher Fitzmaurice
(January 6,1898 – September 22, 1965)

Fitzmaurice is Ireland's best-known aviation pioneer. Born in Dublin, he enlisted in the British Army's 17th Lancers Calvary unit in 1915. Fitzmaurice was wounded in France and served at the Battle of the Somme in July 1916.

Fitzmaurice made his first attempt to cross the Atlantic by air in 1927 in the *Princess Xenia* (a Fokker aircraft), co-piloted by Maurice Piercey and Robert Henry MacIntosh. They were forced to return due to extreme headwinds after a five-and-a-half-hour flight that took them only three hundred miles off the Irish coast. Undeterred by this setback, Fitzmaurice is today best known as navigator, co-pilot, and liaison officer on the first successful east-to-west transatlantic aircraft flight with pilot Hermann Köhl on April 12–13, 1928, on the *Bremen* (now owned by the Henry Ford Museum in Dearborn, Michigan, and on display in Bremen, Germany), which took off from Ireland. The crew landed the *Bremen* successfully on a shallow ice-covered lagoon on Canada's Greenly Island. However, as the plane came to a stop, it broke through the ice, with the plane's tail sticking up in the air. Despite this final bit of bad luck, all were safe—if a bit soggy. On May 2, 1928, President Calvin Coolidge bestowed the Distinguished Flying Cross on the *Bremen* crew (including "Duke" Schiller, below).

Fitzmaurice's signature appears adjacent to "Battleship Bill" Pool's on the lower part of the back.

James Fitzmaurice, Ireland's foremost aviation pioneer. *Public domain.*

Clarence Alvin "Duke" Schiller
(June 18, 1900–March 13, 1943)

"Duke" Schiller was colorful and gregarious Canadian bush pilot who earned a reputation as that country's best aviator. He was discharged from the Canadian Army after it was discovered he was only fourteen years old. He attained fame as a combat pilot during World War I. His monoplane was called *The Royal Windsor*, and he attempted (unsuccessfully) to complete a 1927 flight from Windsor, Ontario, to Windsor, England. Schiller piloted the first plane to reach German aviators of the *Bremen* who had been stranded on Greenly Island, Quebec, after their successful first east-to-west crossing of the Atlantic Ocean between April 12 and 13, 1928. The island separates Newfoundland from Labrador and Quebec. Schiller served as a flight instructor and pilot in World War II, but tragically, his plane crashed during a 1943 night landing in Bermuda.

Canadian bush pilot Clarence Alvin "Duke" Schiller in front of the Stinson SM-1B Detroiter *Royal Windsor. Public domain. San Diego Air and Space Museum Archive.*

His inverted and angled signature is located on the lower right of the back. Reflectance transformation imaging, using a 660nm bandpass filter, revealed clearly that the last name is "Schiller." With this, we were able to identify his full signature because his name appears in the caption to a photograph with James Fitzmaurice, Floyd Bennett, and Bernt Balchen, all signers of the ukulele.

Henry W. "Harry" Armstrong
(July 22, 1879–February 28, 1951)

Harry Armstrong was a noted Tin Pan Alley composer. He was also a booking agent, producer, pianist, and singer. He was born in Somerville, Massachusetts, and at an early age became a master of the keyboard, with his sights set on a career as an organist. Taking a different path, by the age of seventeen, he had become a well-known amateur welterweight boxer around Boston. At boxing training camps, he often played the piano for the other boys, who enjoyed his improvisations. In 1896, Armstrong was composing for a quartet made up of athletes and came up with the music for a tune that would eventually become a huge vaudeville success.

Henry Armstrong, musician and composer. *Public domain.*

It was originally called "My Old New England Home," but when no local music publisher showed interest, Armstrong packed his bags for New York City. With the help of lyrics by his new friend Dick Gerard, "Sweet Adeline," became a hit when the Quaker City Four sang it at the Victoria Theater in New York City in 1904. Soon, the entire country was singing "Sweet Adeline." The song not only made Armstrong $75,000, but encouraged him to change his name from Henry to Harry. A piece in *The St. Louis Post-Dispatch* from July 18, 1943, quotes Armstrong: "The printer made a mistake on the sheet music and my name appeared as Harry Armstrong. I rushed down to the publisher and he just laughed at me. He said: 'A hundred thousand copies say you're Harry Armstrong, so you'd better be Harry Armstrong from now on.'" "Sweet Adeline" was just one of over three hundred songs written by Armstrong. British music hall singer Gertie Gitana made Armstrong's "Nellie Dean" her signature song, and it went on to become a popular British pub song, as well.

As with Dan Frohman, it is likely that Konter and Armstrong were acquainted though their musical interests. Armstrong's deeply incised signature is below Frohman's at the bottom center of the back.

Sheet music cover to "Sweet Adeline" by Harry Armstrong. Originally published by M. Witmark & Sons. *Public domain.*

Rebecca Frohman Davison (aka "Mother Davison") (1867–September 11, 1937)

Mother Davison, as she was widely known, was born in Sandusky, Ohio, in about 1867. She became the wife of Manhattan physician David H. Davison on May 9, 1883. She was the sister of noted theatrical producer, manager, and early film producer Daniel Frohman (also a signer). Her brother Charles, also a theatrical producer, died in the sinking of the *Lusitania* in 1915. Mother Davison possessed considerable musical talent, often performing privately in

Mother Davison (left) with members of Dick's Ukulele Club. Johanna Cohen and Bill Pool visible at right center. *Courtesy of Jean Neptune.*

261

her home, but it was her son Daniel, upon departing for military service in 1917, who convinced her to entertain for and subsequently correspond with a multitude of servicemen. A October 24, 1924 article in *The Bridgeport Telegram* boasts that "one million soldiers looked unto Mother Davison of New York City as their mother during the world's crisis." She also performed in hospitals with her group Mother Davison's Hospital Entertainers. General John J. Pershing (also a signer) bestowed upon her the title of Official "Mother" of the Army and Navy.

On October 30, 1925, Brooklyn sculptor Pietro Montana paid tribute by unveiling a bust of her at the "Mother Davison Y. M. C. A. Hut" on Governor's Island, where she performed faithfully every Wednesday night for ten years. She was also referred to as "New York State's busiest woman," and a great cook to boot! Apparently, on a visit to New York City, former French premier Georges Clemenceau sampled one of her home-baked cinnamon buns and was so enthralled that he had to request another. Konter and the members of his ukulele club performed often. For example, *The Brooklyn Daily Eagle* lists a WHN (Manhattan) radio performance from 4:15 to 5 p.m. on Saturday afternoon, September 29, 1923, by Dick Konter's Kiddie Ukulele Club together with Mother Davison's Hospital Entertainers, in which they performed "Humming," "Dearest," "Rose of the Rio Grande," and "O Sole Mio," among other numbers.

Her fairly clear signature appears at the upper-right shoulder of the back.

Daniel Frohman (August 22, 1853–December 26, 1940)

Dan Frohman was born in Sandusky, Ohio, and became a theatrical producer, manager, and an early film producer. Frohman started in the movies as a partner and producer with Adolph Zukor in the Famous Players Film Company. He worked out of offices on West 26th Street in New York City, and between 1913 and 1917, he was part of the production of more than seventy films, including *Cinderella*, *Tess of the Storm Country*, and *Snow White*.

Daniel Frohman, American theatrical producer and early film producer. *Public domain. Bain News Service, George Grantham Bain collection at the Library of Congress, Washington, D. C.*

Frohman is buried in the Union Field Cemetery in Ridgewood, New York, near his brother Charles, who had died in 1915 in the sinking of the RMS *Lusitania*. As fellow musicians in New York City, Konter and Frohman were certainly acquainted through Frohman's sister—another prominent signer and affiliate of Dick's Ukulele Chorus—Mother Davison. His signature appears near the bottom of the back, just above fellow musician Harry Armstrong's.

William Green Pool (June 23, 1891–August 26, 1953)

When Richard Konter's marriage proposal to Johanna Cohen was nixed by her father, "Battleship Bill" Pool (not to be confused with "Ukulele Bill" Rider, who also signed the instrument) proposed. He married her just two days before Richard Konter returned from the Byrd Antarctic Expedition of 1928. Bill is known to us from *The Brooklyn Daily Eagle* of Friday, November 10, 1933. The article mentions the pair at a 1933 performance for a Brooklyn social club, the Three Score and Ten Club of Brooklyn. This article specifically mentions "Dick Konter and Battleship Bill, retired sailors, who gave ukulele selections." Bill's signature appears near the bottom on the back of the instrument at a roughly forty-five-degree angle, in an area of the ukulele replete with other right-handed signatures. Bill Pool knew Dick Konter from his days in the Navy between 1897 and September 1927, when Konter received his honorable discharge, as confirmed by Bill's daughter, Jean

William G. "Battleship Bill" Pool. *Courtesy of Jean Neptune.*

Neptune of Springfield, Illinois. It was originally frustrating to us that this signature had no surname. Once we understood how close the relationship was between Pool and Konter, it became clear that a last name was completely unnecessary.

William A. "Ukulele Bill" Rider
(June 21, 1897–January 1966)

"Ukulele Bill" Rider was born in Williamsport, Pennsylvania. He became as the manager of the musical merchandise department of Frederick Loeser & Co., a well-known Brooklyn department store located at 484 Fulton Street, near the entrance to the Brooklyn Bridge. Loeser & Co. provided the china for the immigration station at Ellis Island. The company closed in bankruptcy in February 1952. Rider was a talented player, performing often in the store to drum up business. He also performed frequently on WLTH Radio, Brooklyn. He gigged with his trio in Brooklyn and Long Island. No doubt he crossed paths often with Konter in Brooklyn, when they performed on the same radio stations. He died in Brooklyn in 1966. His signature appears to the left of Kay Golding's on the lower half of the back.

Theodore Roosevelt III
(September 13, 1887–July 12, 1944)

Theodore "Ted" Roosevelt III (generally known as Theodore Jr.) was an American political, business, and military leader, a veteran of World Wars I and II. He was the eldest son of President Theodore Roosevelt and Edith Roosevelt. He graduated from Harvard. He was instrumental in the founding of the organization in 1919 that was to become the American Legion, following his valiant service in the United States Army during World War I. He volunteered to be one of the first Americans to go to France after the United States declared war on Germany. Notably, he purchased combat boots for all the men in his battalion with his own funds. Roosevelt was wounded and gassed at Soissons (July 18–22, 1918), the same battle where Adolph Hitler won the Iron Cross (First Class). There were a total of 275,000 French, German, and American casualties.

Between 1921 and 1924, he served as assistant secretary of the Navy. In 1924, he ran for governor of the State of New York, but lost to incumbent Al Smith. He was at political odds with both Franklin and Eleanor Roosevelt,

Theodore Roosevelt III with Calvin Coolidge at the White House, 1924.
Harris & Ewing Collection, Library of Congress, Washington, D. C.

but stayed active in politics, serving as governor of Puerto Rico, governor-general of the Philippines, chairman of the board of American Express Company, and vice president of Doubleday Books. He returned to the Army in 1940. Roosevelt was awarded the Congressional Medal of Honor for directing troops during Operation Overlord at Utah Beach, Normandy, on D-Day (June 6, 1944) in World War II. He died in France thirty-six days later, holding the rank of brigadier general.

His signature appears below and to the left of Kay Golding's in the lower center of the back.

Kay Golding (dates of birth and death unknown)

It is ironic that one of the boldest and most prominent signatures on the ukulele is that of a person who remains unknown to us, but such is the case with Kay Golding. The location of her signature suggests that she may have been a member of Dick's Ukulele Chorus, but like several others in this section, she is not listed on any of the rosters researched for this book.

J. G. Hüngady (perhaps Hängady)
(ca. 1898–date of death unknown)

This signature is too distinct to ignore, and it has a prominent position and size on the back. There is a single record for a male person of this name in New York City in the 1940 census. He is listed as an electrician in the census record. He may have known Konter professionally.

Lillian? "Lil" Richmond
(ca. 1909–date of death unknown)

Lillian Richmond was born around 1909 and lived in Brooklyn, the locale of Dick's Ukulele Chorus. There are no other Brooklyn residents of this name born around this time, so we conclude this is likely to be her. The positioning of her signature on the ukulele suggests that Lil was a member of Konter's ukulele club, but like several other "non-dignitaries" who signed in this area, she is not listed on any of the club's membership lists discovered in our research for this book.

Edward Chandler Swayne
(January 14, 1910–date of death unknown)

This autograph, located on the left side of the back near the waist directly under Lillian Willing's, may read "Chandler Swayne." In the 1925 New York Census, a fifteen-year-old boy with the name Chandler Swayne, born around 1910, was living in the Bronx with his parents and sister.

We have located a connection between Mr. Swayne and Dick's Ukulele Club. An article in the May 16, 1925 issue of *The Brooklyn Daily Eagle* lists a performance for the Masonic Order of the Amaranth at the new meeting room of the Queen Esther Court, No. 7, in the Brooklyn Masonic Temple at Clermont and Lafayette avenues. "Music was provided by Dick's Ukulele Club, led by R. W. Konter. Also, there were solos by Edward Swayne, boy soprano; Clif. Bradney, Marion De Nice and Miss Marguerite Ackerman." It is likely that "Edward Swayne" is, in fact, the signer. We have located the draft registration card for an Edward Chandler Swayne of New York with a birth date that is perfectly in line with a young man of this age.

Confidence = Probable:

Dorothy Clark (dates of birth and death unknown)

Dorothy Clark was listed as a member of Dick's Children's Ukulele Chorus in the December 21, 1924 issue of *The Brooklyn Daily Eagle*. Without additional information about her, it will be difficult to identify her confidently. The 1920 U. S. Census lists seven separate "Dorothy Clark" entries in Brooklyn, each one living in a different Brooklyn assembly district, and all born between 1911 and 1914. Thus, each of them is roughly the correct age to be a member of the ukulele club. In searching the back for her signature, this faint one would appear to be the sole possibility, located by the lower-right bout next to F. Trubee Davison's.

Margaret Fabrizio (December 18, 1901–October 3, 2000)

We originally believed that Margaret Fabrizio was likely to have been a member of Dick's Ukulele Club, because she signed on the back of the ukulele in an area Konter seems to have reserved for their signatures. She was not listed on any of the club's rosters researched for this book. However, a listing in *The Brooklyn Daily Eagle* for a radio broadcast on December 17, 1926, under the direction of "Ukelele (sic) Bill Rider" shows that he was "assisted by" Anna and Margaret Fabrizio.

The 1920 U. S. Census enumerates a Margerete (Margaret) Fabrizio, born in New Jersey "about 1902" to Italian immigrant parents, Frank and Rose. The family was living in Brooklyn by the time Margaret was eight. Among their other children was her younger sister, Anna Fabrizio. Additional information from the Social Security Administration gave us her actual birth and death dates.

In 1954, Margaret married Dominic Villani in Brooklyn. She died in 2000 in Vero Beach, Florida. Her signature is located on the left side of the back, below Anna Alexander's.

Helen Mack (November 13, 1913–August 13, 1986)

We believe this to be the signature of American actress Helen Mack, who was born Helen McDougal in Rock Island, Illinois. She started her acting career as a child, educated at the Professional Children's School of New York City between 1921 and 1929. She became an actress in silent films, moving on to Broadway plays and touring the vaudeville circuit. Her greater success as an actress was as a leading lady in the 1930s. Eventually Mack transitioned into performing on radio, and then into writing, directing, and producing some of the best-known radio shows during the golden age of radio. Later in life, Mack billed herself as a professional writer, writing for Broadway, stage, and television. Her career spanned the infancy of the motion picture industry, the beginnings of Broadway, the final days of vaudeville, the transition to "talking pictures," the golden

Helen Mack, American actress. Radio Pictures publicity photo. *Photo by Robert Coburn. Public domain.*

age of radio, and the rise of television. She played leading roles opposite well-known actors including Lee Tracy, George Raft, and Harold Lloyd, as well as lesser roles, like that of Mollie Malloy in *His Girl Friday*, starring Cary Grant.

It is possible that she was a member of Dick's Ukulele Chorus based on her presence in New York in the 1920s, her age, and the location of her signature by the other members', as well as the fact that she is seen with a ukulele in a still from the movie *Son of Kong*, in which she played Hilda Petersen. This signature appears above that of Clara Sauerman near the right-side waist of the back.

However, this may be the signature of an entirely different person, Helen Marx. In the 1920 U. S. Census there is a girl of that name, born about 1911, living in Brooklyn Assembly District 3 with her parents and two brothers. However, we have no listing of anyone of that name in the Ukulele Club, nor any other reliable information.

Dora Maniscalco (June 24,1912–date of death unknown)

Dora Maniscalco was listed (as "Dora Manescala") as a member of Dick's Children's Ukulele Chorus in the December 21, 1924 issue of *The Brooklyn Daily Eagle*. She appears in the 1930 U. S. Census as the only child of Italian immigrant parents, her father a druggist. She was born in Brooklyn. At first glance, there appears to be the last name "Manescaleo" signed directly beneath Betty Wertelman near the right waist of the back. Upon very close inspection, it seems that the large loop of the "M" is formed into a "D" for Dora, and the combination forms a heart shape. This type of cute cleverness is often seen in teenage handwriting.

Sylvia Miller (September 14, 1909–June 9, 2001)

Sylvia Miller's name is familiar to Johanna Cohen's daughter, Jean Neptune. She is mentioned as a member of Dick's Ukulele Club in *The Brooklyn Daily Eagle* of June 28, 1924, in a performance the night before at Kenilworth Baptist Church in Flatbush, Brooklyn. We know that Sylvia and Johanna Cohen appeared together in performance on radio station WGCP (Manhattan, 252) on December 5, 1925. Johanna played the ukulele, while Sylvia, a soprano, gave a vocal performance. This radio listing allowed us to identify her as the same Sylvia Miller who had, while a student at Girls Commercial High School, won the first gold medal of the citywide music contest for junior sopranos that same year. She sang "Cherry Ripe" and the "The Little Shepherd" (her picture is from that article in *The Brooklyn Daily Eagle*). Her vocal abilities must have been impressive, for winning this award was no small feat—among the judges in the Music Week competition was Sergei Rachmaninoff. Indeed, she is identified as the gold medal winner in another radio listing for May 21, 1925, when she performed at 3:45 p.m. on WNYC, Manhattan. Immediately preceding her in the broadcast was Fiorello H. La Guardia, speaking on "The Port Authority." By February 3, 1929, she was performing at the Capitol Theater at Broadway and 51st Street as part of the Capitol Grand Orchestra ,as a featured soloist performing between films such as MGM's *The Trail of '98* and *Show People*.

Harold Denny Campbell
(March 30, 1895–December 29, 1955)

Harold Denny "Soup" Campbell (aka "Devil Dog" Campbell) was born in Waterbury, Vermont. He was an American Marine aviator. He received his B. S. from Norwich University in 1917 and was commissioned that same year, becoming part of the "Pancho Villa Expedition." He served in World War I in France during 1917–1919. Campbell was designated Naval Aviator #2988 in 1921. He was later touted as the "world's safest flyer," and in 1926, President Calvin Coolidge presented Campbell with the Schiff Trophy for nearly nine hundred hours of flight time without an accident. During World War II, he reached the rank of major general in the United States Marine Corps. Campbell's decorations included the Legion of Merit and the Purple Heart. He was buried in Arlington National Cemetery. Located on the upper-left area of the back, the letters of the last name are clearer than the extremely faded first name, so we categorize this signature as probable.

Harold Denny Campbell. *Public domain. Courtesy of Norwich University Archives.*

Ronald Thomas Shepherd (1896–1955)

Ronald Shepherd was a British aviator and test pilot for Rolls-Royce. He was the first person to fly an aircraft fitted with a Rolls-Royce Merlin engine. He was born in Kensington, London, in 1896. At first, he was employed by Vickers-Armstrong in the manufacturer of guns, but on the outbreak of World War I, he joined the Honourable Artillery Company. He joined the Royal Flying Corps in 1916, left the RFC in 1918, and rejoined in 1921, serving in England and Egypt until 1929. After a few years as a civil flying instructor, he joined Rolls-Royce in 1931. In 1935, he was appointed chief test pilot. Shepherd was responsible for the first flight of many of the company piston and jet engines.

Because Shepherd was a prominent aviator, the presence of his signature on the ukulele is plausible, but the signature is unclear and we know of no connection between him and Konter. Moreover, the disparity in spelling (possibly the result of incorrect re-inking by Konter) raises some question. The question of where Shepherd might have encountered Konter, plus the faded nature of the actual signature itself force us to judge it as "Probable." The signature is located directly below Theodore Roosevelt Jr.'s.

Edward LeRoy Rice (August 24, 1871–December 1, 1938) or LeRoy C. Tyack (1904–1994)

We are confident that this signature belongs to one of these two men; we simply cannot say with certainty which. We are, for now, giving the nod to Edward LeRoy Rice.

LeRoy Rice produced minstrel shows and was the leading authority on their history. He was born in Manhattan, New York City. He had minstrelsy in his blood, the second son of William Henry Rice (1844–1907), a minstrel performer. He first performed onstage in Morristown, New Jersey, on July 18, 1890. Starting in 1907 he wrote a column called "Man in the Bleachers," which ran in the New York *Evening World*. He authored of the definitive history of minstrelsy at the time, *Monarchs of Minstrelsy*, published in 1911, and wrote a syndicated column, "Anecdotes of Old-Time Actors." He died on December 1, 1938, in Manhattan. Rice was buried at Calvary Cemetery in Woodside, New York. His archive is housed at Princeton University.

Edward Le Roy Rice in 1911. *Public domain.*

LeRoy Tyack was a lifelong amateur radio enthusiast and electrical engineer. In 1928, while living in Tulsa, Oklahoma, he was scanning the continent for conversation when he suddenly made radio contact with Antarctica. A radio operator (possibly Malcolm Hanson) with Admiral Richard E. Byrd's polar expedition locked on to LeRoy's signal, W5BAT, anxious for news from his Norman, Oklahoma, family. Roy brought the crew member's parents to his home for a chat with a son they hadn't heard from in months. We don't know exactly how or when Konter might have encountered Tyack to get his signature, but the appearance of the middle initial "C" provides evidence that this may be Tyack's autograph rather than Edward LeRoy Rice. Konter's involvement in radio over the years (including his receipt of the Edgar F. Johnson Pioneer Citation of the Radio Club of America) suggests the two men could have had a connection.

The signature appears near the right-hand waist of the back, above Gertrude Ederle's.

E. Etsie (or Etsle) (dates of birth and death unknown)

This fairly clear signature on the lower-left area of the back remains unidentified.

Flora Ettlinger Whiting (1876–1971) or Emily Lilian Whiting (1859–1942)

Although the last name Whiting" is distinct, the first and middle names are extremely faint. There seem to be two possibilities for the owner of this autograph, both women.

Flora Ettlinger Whiting was a philanthropist and supporter of the arts in New York City. She was married to industrialist Giles Whiting. As a benefactor and socialite, it is possible she would have encountered other sponsors of the expedition, or at least had the opportunity to attend one of the celebratory events.

Emily Lillian Whiting was the daughter of Illinois State Senator Lorenzo D. Whiting. She was literary editor of *The Boston Traveler* and editor of *The Boston Budget*, and afterward spent much of her time in Europe. The two obvious connections are her history in the Boston area, where both R. E. Byrd and Amelia Earhart had residences, and the fact that she makes mention of Alaska and the North Pole in her book *The Golden Road*. She died in 1942.

The signature in question is located under Millie Gade-Corson's at the left waist of the back.

Confidence = Possible:

Greta (dates of birth and death unknown)

This small signature near the upper-right bout of the back appears to be simply the first name "Greta," presumably a yet-to-be-identified child member of Dick's Ukulele Club.

Kathleen (dates of birth and death unknown)

This faint signature, which may read "Kathleen," may simply be a single name if some of the children in Dick's Ukulele Club signed using just their first names (e.g., "Greta"). Or perhaps, because of its proximity and general alignment and spacing, it could be the first part of (Kathleen) Clara Sauerman's signature. The autograph is on the left side of the back near the waist, directly above Adelaide Kaiser's. We have no evidence, however, that Clara Sauerman had another given name, so this remains a mystery.

Judy Davison (dates of birth and death unknown)

This signature may read "Judy Davison." Another signer of that name, Mother Davison, had four children, but none was named Judy.

Harry Hudler (dates of birth and death unknown)

Harry Hudler was listed as a member of Dick's Children's Ukulele Chorus in the December 21, 1924 issue of *The Brooklyn Daily Eagle*. A very faint and tiny signature with a stacked "H" common to both the first and last name is possibly deciphered on the back to the right of Lillian Reis's.

Helen Sterba (July 21, 1912–February 26, 1984)

Helen Sterba was listed as a member of Dick's Children's Ukulele Chorus in the December 21, 1924 issue of *The Brooklyn Daily Eagle*. In the 1920 U. S. Census she and her twin sister, Florence, are listed at both aged seven years, and again in the 1930 census as aged sixteen years. There is the ghost of a very small, modest, and faint signature on the back, partially obscured by Kay Golding's bold lettering. It is possible that this is Helen's signature.

Mabel Thoma (ca. 1910–date of death unknown)

Mabel Thoma is listed in *The Brooklyn Daily Eagle* of December 21, 1924, as a member of Dick's Children's Ukulele Chorus. Johanna Pool Konter's daughter, Jean Neptune, confirms that the Thoma family was familiar to her mother and stepfather. We believe that Mabel's nearly completely faded signature may exist on the upper section of the back (where it would seem to belong), below and to the left of her sister Violet's.

Clara Grabau Adams
(December 3, 1884–February 1971)

Clara G. Adams was known as a "first flighter" and the "maiden of maiden flights." Although she was not a pilot, she was the first passenger on round-trip commercial flights across the Pacific, between New York and Bermuda, and between San Francisco and New Zealand. She is remembered primarily as the first woman to fly across the Atlantic as a ticketed passenger aboard the Graf Zeppelin on its return flight from New York in October 1928, but she also set a world record as the first woman passenger to complete an around-the-world air journey. She certainly helped to popularize air travel and promote flight safety with the American public. After her death at age eighty-seven, her ashes were scattered from a plane. Her resting place is listed as "the ocean." Aware of the historical significance of what she was doing, she had the foresight to autograph almost anything she could get her hands on, including, perhaps, this ukulele.

However, another Clara Adams may have been the signer. As mentioned above, one of Konter's "Jolly Troupers" novelty orchestra was a lady of the same name: "Clara Adams sits at a piano, backwards, and plays real tunes on it . . ." However, we do not know if he knew this Ms. Adams before he traded the ukulele (1952), nor do we know her middle initial, which, on the signature, appears to be a "G."

The signature appears near the lower-right binding of the back.

Sir Douglas Mawson (May 5, 1882–October 14, 1958)

This signature is located on the back at the right side near the waist, to the right of Adelaide Kaiser's. Given the faded nature of the tailing letters of the last name, we must categorize this signature as "possible."

Douglas Mawson was an Australian. His background in geology, like Laurence Gould's, led him to explore the continent as an expedition leader during the early years of Antarctic exploration. Based on 1903 fieldwork, he published *The Geology of the New Hebrides*, one of the first major contributions to the geology of Melanesia. Mawson led the 1911–1914 Australasian Antarctic Expedition. His 1929–1930 and 1930–1931 British, Australian and New Zealand Antarctic Research Expeditions (BANZARE) on the ship *Discovery* did not use land bases. Mawson's team was the first to map much of the coast, and this provided firm foundation for establishing the Australian Antarctic Territory.

Portrait of Douglas Mawson. *Public Domain.*

Significantly, Mawson was among the first to propose using an aircraft for Antarctic exploration. However, he abandoned the idea after a test flight in Adelaide, Australia, crashed, nearly killing the pilot (Byrd 1930:13).

Mawson was in Wellington on business in November 1929, as Byrd had just arrived at the beginning of the Antarctic expedition. Byrd met Mawson, whom he considered to be "the greatest Antarctic authority then living" (Rodgers 1990:51). The two men spent an afternoon and evening together. Although we have no direct evidence that Konter was at that meeting, he was in Wellington with Byrd and may have been able to obtain Mawson's signature.

James "Jimmy" Roosevelt II
(December 23, 1907–August 13, 1991)

James Roosevelt was just nineteen years old in 1926, when Byrd and Bennett undertook their North Pole expedition. The oldest son of Franklin D. Roosevelt and a politically motivated Harvard student between 1926 and 1930, he campaigned fervently in 1928 for Democratic presidential nominee

Al Smith. The very faint hint of a first name "James" paired with the an even more faint hint of a "Roos___," stacked directly below and immediately adjacent to the clearer signature of his more distant relative Theodore Roosevelt Jr., has led us to allow for the possibility that this could be his signature. It certainly remains in the category of improbable conjecture, though James would have traveled extensively in elite circles between Boston, New York, and Washington and could easily have attended celebratory events involving Byrd and hence Konter.

(Left to right) Vice President Jack Garner, President Roosevelt, James Roosevelt II, and James Farley. *Photo by Harris & Ewing. Library of Congress, Washington, D. C.*

Loleta G. Borak (dates of birth and death unknown)

Extremely faint, illegible. Our best guess is that this signature could be that of Leo A. Borah, a guest at the National Geographic Luncheon held in Washington, D. C. on June 20, 1930, to honor the members of the first Byrd Antarctic Expedition. Konter also attended. Borah was a member of the editorial staff of *National Geographic* magazine.

Nathalea Halgesen (dates of birth and death unknown)

The location of this faint signature suggests that this unidentified person may have been a member of Dick's Ukulele Club, but like several other "non-dignitaries" in this section, the name (at least as we perceive it) is not listed on any of the rosters researched for this book.

Steven D. Lester (dates of birth and death unknown)

The letters of this signature are blurry but somewhat discernible, yet we have no suggestion as to who this unknown person might be.

John McLeRoy (dates of birth and death unknown)

Looks like John MLeRoy or McLehoy, definitely John Mc____. Last letters are there.

Scratched-out signature

Upon the use of imagery from the Smithsonian Institution's Museum Conservation Institute, this signature starts to emerge from behind an obvious attempt (most likely by Konter) to scratch it out. The surname may be "Whitaker," but we don't know what the first name might be. It seems that it may begin with "El . . ." The reason Konter defaced the signature is unknown.

14

Signers on the Headstock and in the Sound Hole

THE HEAD PLATE OF THE instrument (the front of the headstock) was signed by a single individual, the queen of Romania.

Marie Alexandra Victoria   Dignitaries

Confidence = Certain:
Queen Marie Alexandra Victoria of Romania (October 29, 1875–July 18, 1938)

Konter allocated the most prominent position on the ukulele, the front of the headstock, for the signature of Her Majesty Queen Marie of Roumania (Romania). Marie was the last queen consort of Roumania, the wife of King Ferdinand I, and the granddaughter of both England's Queen Victoria and Tsar Nicholas II of Russia. Her father was Queen Victoria's second son, Alfred. In 1882, Queen Victoria commissioned the famous pre-Raphaelite artist John Everett Millais to paint Marie's portrait while she was Princess Marie of Edinburgh.

Marie, Queen of Roumania. *The George Grantham Bain Collection, Library of Congress, Washington, D. C.*

Queen Marie was internationally popular during the 1920s. She visited the United States in 1926 with two of her children on a diplomatic tour, arriving from France in New York City aboard the S. S. *Leviathan* on October 18, 1926. She was welcomed, much like Byrd and his crew earlier that year, with a ticker-tape parade attended by thousands. The same day she went by train to Washington, D. C., and that evening attended a formal dinner.

The web site historylink.org reports in an article headlined "Queen Marie of Romania visits Seattle on November 4, 1926" that "The Queen arrived in the United States October 18, 1926. After a visit to President Calvin Coolidge in Washington, D. C., and several days in New York, she traveled on her special train across the continent. The Queen visited towns and cities along her route and many minute details of her activities were reported widely by the press contingent traveling with her."

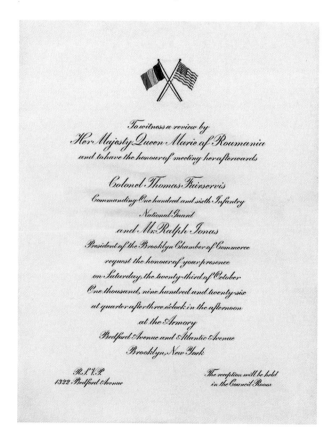

Invitation to attend the review by Queen Marie of Roumania, at the Brooklyn Armory, October 23, 1926, 3:15 p.m. *Public domain.*

Queen Marie visited Brooklyn on Saturday, October 23, 1926. She reviewed the 106th Infantry at the Armory at 1322 Bedford Avenue at 3:15 p.m. that day and attended a reception in her honor following her review. The event was sponsored by the National Guard and the Brooklyn Chamber of Commerce. We are nearly certain that Konter attended this event held on his home turf. Although no photograph documents the event, it was almost certainly where he requested Marie sign the headstock of the ukulele. Further, we can infer she autographed the ukulele within a four-hour time window. She signed sometime between 3:15 and 7:30 p.m., because Byrd and his wife were invited by Marie to attend a dinner that same evening at the Biltmore Hotel at 7:30. It is extremely unlikely that Konter was invited to that dinner.

Marie's remarkable story is captured in her autobiography, *The Story of My Life*, published in 1934–1935.

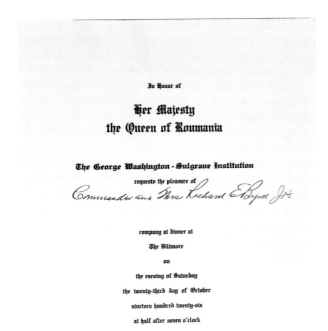

In Honor of

Her Majesty the Queen of Roumania

The George Washington - Sulgrave Institution

requests the pleasure of

Commander and Mrs. Richard E. Byrd Jr's

company at dinner at

The Biltmore

on

the evening of Saturday

the twenty-third day of October

nineteen hundred twenty-six

at half after seven o'clock

IN RESPONDING
KINDLY USE THE ATTACHED APPLICATION FORM
AND SEND TO JOHN A. STEWART, EXECUTIVE CHAIRMAN,
THE GEORGE WASHINGTON-SULGRAVE INSTITUTION
TWO THIRTY-THREE BROADWAY
NEW YORK

Invitation to Commander and Mrs. Richard E. Byrd Jr., to attend a dinner in honor of Marie, Queen of Roumania, October 23, 1926, 7:30 p.m. *Courtesy of* Expeditions: North Pole Flight, *Admiral Richard E. Byrd Papers, The Ohio State University, Byrd Polar and Climate Research Center Archival Program.*

As mentioned above, inside the sound hole, three things are visible. First is the C. F. Martin & Co. manufacturer's stamp. Second is an inked ownership by Konter. Finally, a label is present in that position that has been there since before July 1, 1926. It is from the Clarence Williams Music Publishing Co.

Although the label is not a signature, Clarence Williams deserves consideration because of his role in the development of American music and his connection to Konter.

Confidence = Certain

Clarence Williams
(October 8, 1893? 1898?–November 6, 1965)

Clarence Williams was a titanic figure in American music. He was an African-American jazz musician, music publisher, producer, and entrepreneur. He was born in either 1893 or 1898 in Plaquemine, Louisiana, to a musical family with Choctaw and Creole roots. The energetic Williams was a gifted pianist and composer who cut his teeth as a singer in Billy Kersands's minstrel show. He started a suit cleaning business, managed his own cabaret, and began writing songs that led to the establishment of Williams & Piron Music Publishers music publishing company in 1915 in New Orleans. With the help of W. C. Handy, Williams and his violinist Armand John Piron "stole the show" at an important Atlanta concert performed for a both white and black audience.

Clarence Williams.
Public Domain.

Williams claimed to be the first songwriter to use the word "jazz" on sheet music. His business card proclaimed him to be "The Originator of Jazz and Boogie Woogie." Williams produced or performed in early recordings by Louis Armstrong, Sidney Bechet, and Bessie Smith. He moved to Chicago in 1920, where he eventually owned two lucrative music stores. His business skills were perfectly suited to promote the increasingly popular recordings of black female blues singers; in fact, in 1921 he married Eva Taylor, one of the first female singers heard on the radio. He managed Bessie Smith and accompanied her on piano for most of her early recordings, many of which he personally wrote, produced, and published.

Williams moved to New York City after selling his Chicago stores. Duke Ellington's mentor, the stride piano master Willie "The Lion" Smith, stated that Williams was the first New Orleans musician to influence jazz in New York. The Lion thanked Williams for helping other African-American songwriters like himself, James P. Johnson, and Fats Waller. Williams and

Konter were music publishing colleagues. We know, for example, that Konter arranged "You for Me, Me for You From Now On," by Cecil Mack and James P. Johnson, for Clarence Williams Music Publishing Co. (see illustration of this music that includes the identical logo found on the ukulele label). The address listed on the ukulele label, 1547 Broadway, corresponds to an address in the Gaiety Theater Building in Manhattan known to be used by Williams from 1921 until at least 1926 (Lord 1976). Williams moved to Brooklyn in the early 1950s. His diabetic condition kept him sidelined for the last decade of his life.

Konter wrote at least two ukulele arrangements for Clarence Williams Music Publishing. Two tunes by Clarence Williams and (none other than) Thomas "Fats" Waller—"The Heart That Once Belonged to Me" (with a copyright date of July 7, 1925) and "Squeeze Me" (with a copyright date of July 31, 1925)—both credit "Dick Konter" with the ukulele arrangement (Copyright Office, Library of Congress, Catalog of Copyright Entries, 1952, Third Series, Volume 6, Part 5B, Number 1).

The definitive work on the music of Clarence Williams is Tom Lord's 1976 book *Clarence Williams*, Storyville Publications and Co., Ltd.

BIBLIOGRAPHY

Amundsen, Roald and Lincoln Ellsworth. *First Crossing of the Polar Sea*. George H. Doran Company, New York, 1927.

Bailey, David and David Halsted. *Pluralism and Unity*, vol. 2017. Michigan State University, 1998.

Bart, Sheldon. *Race to the Top of the World: Richard Byrd and the First Flight to the North Pole*. Regnery History, Washington, D. C., 2013.

Bartlett, B. *The log of Bob Bartlett; the true story of forty years of seafaring and exploration*. New York, London, G. P. Putnam's Sons.

Bartlett, B. and R. T. Hale. *Northward ho! the last voyage of the Karluk*. Boston, Small, Maynard.

Bown, Stephen R. *The Last Viking: The Extraordinary Life of Roald Amundsen*. Aurum, London, 2012.

Brannan, Captain Michael J., Arma Virumque Cano. *The Rudder Club News* 1(8):1, 7, 1945.

Browder, Laura. *Slippery Characters: Ethnic Impersonators and American Identities*. 2000

Byrd, Richard Evelyn. *Skyward: Man's Mystery of the Air As Shown by the Brilliant Flights of America's Leading Air Explorer*. G. P. Putnams Sons, New York, London, 1928.

Byrd, Richard Evelyn and Raimund E. Goerler. *To the Pole: The Diary and Notebook of Richard E. Byrd, 1925-1927*. The Ohio State University Press, Columbus, 1998.

Byrd, Richard Evelyn and Laurence McKinley Gould. *Little America: Aerial Exploration in the Antarctic, the Flight to the South Pole*. G. P. Putnam's Sons, New York, London, 1930.

Corn, Joseph J. *The Winged Gospel: America's Romance with Aviation, 1900-1950*. Oxford University Press, New York, 1983.

Cudahy, Brian J. *Around Manhattan Island and Other Maritime Tales of New York*. Fordham University Press, New York, 1997.

Cross, Wilbur. *Disaster at the Pole: the tragedy of the airship Italia and the 1928 Nobile Expedition to the North Pole*. Lyons Press, New York, 2000.

Freed, Stanley A. *Anthropology Unmasked: Museums, Science, and Politics in New York City*. Orange Frazer Press, Wilmington, Ohio, 2012.

Gabbacia, D. R. *We Are What We Eat: Ethnic Food and the Making of Americans.* Harvard University Press, 1998.

Gould, Laurence McKinley. *Cold: The Record of an Antarctic Sledge Journey.* Brewer, Warren & Putnam, New York, 1931.

Greenburg, Michael M. *Peaches & Daddy: A Story of the Roaring Twenties, the Birth of Tabloid Media, and the Courtship That Captured the Heart and Imagination of the American Public.* First ed. Overlook Press, Woodstock, NY ; New York, NY, 2008.

Harris, Luther S. *Around Washington Square: An Illustrated History of Greenwich Village.* Johns Hopkins University Press, Baltimore, 2003.

Jasen, David A. *Tin Pan Alley: The Composers, the Songs, the Performers, and Their Times: The Golden Age of American Popular Music from 1886 to 1956.* Donald I. Fine, New York, 1988.

———. *Tin Pan Alley: An Encyclopedia of the Golden Age of American Song.* Routledge, New York, 2003.

John, P. A. S. *USS Essex CV/CVA/CVS-9.* Turner Publishing Company, 1999.

Keegan, John. *The First World War.* First American ed. A. Knopf ; Distributed by Random House, New York, 1999.

Konter, Eibertus. "Improvement in Cigar-Perforators," edited by U. S. P. Office, pp. 2. vol. 133864. Eibertus A. Konter, United States, 1872.

Konter, Richard Wesley. 1920 Title., in press.

———. *Dick's Ukulele Method Showing How to Apply Chords on the Ukulele, Ukalua, Ukulele-Banjo, Taro Patch and Tenor Banjo.* First ed. Richard W. Konter. Edward B. Marks Music Co., Sole Selling Agents, New York, NY, 1923.

"Man Overboard!" In *Vacation Fun*, pp. 2. Scholastic Magazines, Inc., Dayton, Ohio, 1967.

Konter, R. W. 1920. "Wreck of the U. S. S. Charleston, Camiguin Island, Nov. 2nd, '99." Manuscript on File, Library of Congress, Naval Historical Foundation collection. 14 pages.

Konter, R. W. Adventure Ahoy! Part I, Konter Files, National Archives and Records Administration, College Park, Maryland.

Konter, R. W. Adventure Ahoy! Part II, Konter Files, National Archives and Records Administration, College Park, Maryland.

Konter, R. W. Adventure Ahoy! Part III, Konter Files, National Archives and Records Administration, College Park, Maryland.

MacMillan, Donald Baxter and W. Elmer Ekblaw. *Four Years in the White North*. Harper & Brothers, New York, London, 1918.

Niven, J. *The Ice Master [the doomed 1913 voyage of the Karluk]*. St. Paul, Minn., HighBridge Co.

Onkst , David H., "Barnstormers," U. S. Centennial of Flight Commission, http://www.centennialofflight.gov/essay/ Explorers_Record_Setters_and_ Daredevils/barnstormers/EX12.htm [accessed March 18, 2004].

Parry, Albert, Harry T. Moore, Albert Parry and Paul Avrich Collection (Library of Congress). *Garrets and Pretenders: A History of Bohemianism in America*. Rev. ed. Dover Publications, New York, 1960.

Rodgers, Eugene. *Beyond the Barrier: The Story of Byrd's First Expedition to Antarctica*. Naval Institute Press, Annapolis, Md, 1990.

Rose, Lisle A. *Explorer: The life of Richard E. Byrd*. University of Missouri Press, Columbia, 2008.

Seiple, Samantha. *Byrd & Igloo: A Polar Edventure*. Scholastic Press, New York, 2013.

Solomon, Susan. *The Coldest March: Scott's Fatal Antarctic Expedition*. Yale University Press, New Haven [Conn.], 2001.

Soren, Noelle. Fox Theater. National Register of Historic Places Inventory, Nomination Form, edited by N. P. S. U. S. Department of the Interior, 1975.

Tranquada, Jim and John King. *The 'Ukulele: A History*. University of Hawai'i Press, Honolulu, 2012.

Walden, Jane Brevoort. *Igloo*. G. P. Putnam's Sons, New York, London, 1931.

Walsh, Tom and John King. *The Martin Ukulele: The Little Instrument That Helped Create a Guitar Giant*. Hal Leonard Books, Milwaukee, WI., 2013.

Webb, Keats, Emma Tucker and Alicia Hoffman. *Imaging to Enhance Vestigial Signatures on the Konter Ukulele From the 1926 Byrd North Pole Expedition*. Smithsonian Museum Conservation Institute, 2014.

Whitaker, Jan. *Restauranting Through History*. 2009.

INDEX